The Person in Personalisation

The Person in
Personalisation

The Story of How Marketing's Most Treasured
Possession Became Anything but Personal

David Mannheim

BROWN
DOG
BOOKS

ISBN printed book: 978-1-83952-679-4
ISBN e-book: 978-1-83952-680-0

Cover design by The Loft Agency
Internal design by Mac Style
Edited by Malcolm Croft

Printed and bound in the UK

This book is printed on FSC® certified paper

Contents

About the Author   x

Foreword   xi

Preface   xiii

Let's Get Personal   xv

Part I: The Ordinary World   1

Chapter 1   Hype Versus Reality   3

Chapter 2   Awesome Versus Shit   5

Chapter 3   Good Versus Evil   8

Chapter 4   Definition Versus Definition   11

Part II: The Call to Adventure   13

Chapter 5   Rubbish Recommendations   15

Chapter 6   Diverse Definitions   22

Chapter 7   Pecking-Order of Personalisation   25

Chapter 8   Insisting On Individualism   30

Chapter 9   Connection & Conversation   34

Part III: Paradise Lost   39

Chapter 10   Don't Believe the Hype   41

Chapter 11   Origin Story: The History of Personalisation   45

Chapter 12   The Years of Personalisation   49

Chapter 13   Vendor-Tinted Glasses   57

Chapter 14   The Fear Factor   62

Part IV: The Three Dragons   71

Chapter 15   Know Thy Enemy: The Golden Dragon   73

Chapter 16   Amazon Versus The Golden Dragon   75

Chapter 17   Victoria's Real Secret   79

Chapter 18   Sexy Sparks & Spencer   83

Chapter 19   Defeating the Golden Dragon   87

Chapter 20   Money Makes Personalisation Go Round   97

Part V: The Stubborn Dragon   101

Chapter 21   Know Thy Enemy: The Stubborn Dragon   103

Chapter 22   Data, Data, Data: The Mouse House's MagicBands   105

Chapter 23   Too Much Trouble: AI Engines   112

Chapter 24   Slaying the Stubborn Dragon   120

Part VI: The Deepfake Dragon   129

Chapter 25   Know Thy Enemy: The Deepfake Dragon   131

Chapter 26   McPersonalisation   133

Chapter 27   Unexpecting the Expected   139

Chapter 28   Vanquishing The Deepfake Dragon   142

Part VII: The Six Spells   147

Chapter 29   The Memory Spell   149

Chapter 30   The Acknowledgement Spell   152

Chapter 31   The Listening Spell   157

Chapter 32   The Observation Spell   163

Chapter 33   The Appropriate Spell   169

Chapter 34   The Care Spell   176

Part VIII: The Great Unknown   187

Chapter 35   Follow the Money: Advertising   189

Chapter 36   Spin Cycle: Everything That Goes Around Comes Back
                Around   192

Chapter 37   Acquisition-Cost-a-lot: Accelerating   196

Chapter 38   Data-Mine-Your-Business: Disciplined   198

Chapter 39   Say Hi to AI: Awesome   201

Chapter 40   2024: The Year of Personalisation   206

Chapter 41   The Final Word   208

Acknowledgements   209
Notes   211

About the Author

David Mannheim has worked in the digital marketing industry for more than 15 years. He founded his first company at the age of 28 – User Conversion – focusing on conversion rate optimisation. As a prolific voice in the experimentation, optimisation and personalisation community, he went on to work alongside several of the UK's biggest retailers. The company was acquired in 2021. In tandem with writing this book and speaking about himself in the third person, David has begun to kickstart his second venture, a software business that helps retailers identify the intent of their audience: Made With Intent. No need to put him on a pedestal just yet.

This is a book about personalisation so it makes sense to be personal. Getting up close with David, outside of the optimisation industry, and in no particular order of preference, he occasionally swears, doesn't drink and exercises rarely because he is busy being a husband, father of two and watching all of the Disney films. He lives in sunny Southport by the beach, a town full of care homes and chippies. This is his first and last book – some would call this an exclusive. His opinions, such as *Hercules* is the best Disney film, period, are nothing but his own reductive, pessimistic, yet equally hilarious thoughts.

Foreword

D o you even believe in Personalisation as a business concept, David? Is personalisation a good thing or a bad thing?

The cynicism and the sarcasm that permeates David's book can certainly make you wonder these questions. After our first few meetings about the topic and how to put it into a book (two books – if you also count my book *Hello $FirstName*), I asked David these questions openly.

This book is indeed a personal story about a complex and paradoxical topic, but after having had several deep conversations with David it was clear to me that the key to his cynicism and sarcasm is not as much directed against the topic as it is against the conflicting nature of it. A subject that leads to countless misunderstandings, frustrations, broken promises and poor customer experiences.

I deeply envy David's amazing sense of humour and the way he constantly keeps the reader engaged and entertained with his brilliant writing skills and the fairy tale metaphor that forms the background of this story. The major challenges have become the dragons that our marketer hero needs to fight using the six spells. As fictitious and peculiar as this sounds, both the dragons and the spells are very real and I'm certain that all marketers will find the book both entertaining and useful.

The first problem with personalised marketing is that it often isn't very personal. Which is why David argues that we need to put the person back into personalisation. Personalised marketing is often too myopically focused on creating short-term revenue and conversions. But take it too far and this creates the second problem, where it can become a bit too personal. It's one thing to get an email from your favourite retailer offering you a discount on your favourite product. It's quite another to get an ad for that same product following you around the internet like a stalker. It's like that one person who keeps sending you texts even though you haven't replied in weeks. David goes deep into both the history of personalisation and what it means, could mean and should mean.

Despite his cynicism, David does believe in personalisation – and that it will ultimately drive not only short-term sales but, indeed, also better customer experiences to drive real emotional customer loyalty and a higher customer lifetime value. He also makes it clear that, as marketers, we need to face the dragons. No dragons, no treasure. And we had better be armed to the teeth with swords, spells and whatnot.

I'm sure you'll enjoy reading this fairy tale as much as I did!

Rasmus Houlind, Author of *Hello $FirstName*, CXO at Agillic

Preface

L et's be honest, most books about marketing, or sales, or business, are boring. There, I said it. They're either overly inspirational, redundant with revelation, or cold and charmless, focusing on dry practicality with arbitrary models that no one can ironically use practically. I've tried to be different. Not for the sake of it but because I believe action comes from irreverent humour, taking things back to basics and critical thinking, not from telling you, the reader, exactly what to do.

In December 2021, the idea to write a book — *the* book — about personalisation came to me in a moment of deep frustration. I am a big Disney fan. I can't help but Marvel at their knack for creating wonder, escapism and nostalgia. It has everything a big kid like me could ask for, especially as a parent to two young boys. However, while waiting in a *long* queue for *Monsters, Inc. Laugh Floor*, at Disney World, Orlando, a "monstrously funny" show deliberately designed to reduce the audience to tears, I found myself in a state of despair. Here I am for the thirty-second time in my life (yes, that's how many times I've been to Disney. I'm a creature of habit) and I'm expected to laugh at Mike, Sully and the crew, but it's the same experience despite the number of times I've been to see the show. Irrespective of the loyalty I've shown to the Mouse, I'm still expecting to queue for six hours. Despite the number of people in the park that day, probably around twenty-thousand guests, I felt like just a number. A number that is being nickel-and-dimed by Big Business, being sold extortionate sodas and hot dogs.

This isn't the world of personalisation that I was promised, I thought. This isn't a place where *I* feel as significant as all their movies tell me I should feel. Where I'm Flynn Rider or Captain John Smith or Prince Eric. In a place built literally as a love letter to brand identity, I didn't feel like I was the prince, but a background character, small and insignificant. This despite all their efforts to make me feel otherwise and personalise the guest experience and spending over $1 billion doing so. I felt they had failed in their quest.

Quite the opposite to their intention, it was all so impersonal. *Why?*

Eighteen months later, as I prepare to publish this book, the irony that its genesis came to me while standing in the *Monsters, Inc. Laugh Floor* queue now tickles me — finally. After returning from my final adventure park for that year, I sought to ask 10 marketing leaders and captains of industry questions about personalisation. I was curious to hear their answers. Soon 10 became 20, 20 became 50, 50 became more than 150. It was then I felt I had stumbled upon the idea to not only write a book about personalisation, but to take it personally too. I didn't want to write about the subject in a way that was stale or theoretical, or too dry and academic. This book is not an ode to marketing. That doesn't interest me.

While this book can (and should) be utilised by brands, marketeers and practitioners practising personalisation — that's a mealy mouthful; get used to them — this book is an extension of myself. It had to be personal. I had to practice what I preach. And what better way to get up close and personal than to tell stories. As you'll come to learn, telling stories — mostly Disney-owned ones — is a representation of who I am, a big kid. And, let's be honest, if you're reading a book about personalisation, you're probably into the same nerdy things I am. So, I'm hoping we can geek out together on some risqué satire and nerdy 90s references.

This book is a personal story about what it means to be personal. As I was writing, it felt incongruent to not inject my somewhat pithy, half-cheeky, half-self-deprecating personality. However, don't be fooled by the colloquialisms and hilarious wit. This is a serious book about alliterations and the tales of three; a subject that requires our attention, regardless of whether you preach, practice or fall prey to personalisation.

I hope you enjoy this book as much as I enjoyed writing it. The majority of it, at least.

Let's Get Personal

The P-word. It can P-off. What is personalisation? When did it start? How does it work? Why does every year feel like *the* Year of Personalisation, yet no year does? How do you personalise at scale when the suggestion of that feels so oxymoronic?

In all my experience in founding, and running, a successful conversion optimisation consultancy, and working with several of the biggest brands in the UK, I felt like I should be able to answer these questions.

So, I wrote this book. However, there's nothing more powerful than community, so to help me on my destiny quest I asked a bunch of standardised questions about personalisation to more than 150 top marketing industry leaders to see if they had the same answer as me on the continuous question mark that suffixes – and suffocates – this subject: *"WHAT THE HELL IS HAPPENING TO PERSONALISATION?"*

The answers are fascinating.

Before I dive into all that though, let me dim the lights and set the scene and tell you why personalisation is important to me.

I love stories. From thrillers to comedy, sci-fi fantasy to erotic fiction (OK, maybe not that last one). The stories I love the most, however, are epic quests of daring adventures and fairy tales. Basically, anything Disney does. Except for *Treasure Planet*. That was awful. My therapist would call my love of these tales "escapism", and she may well be right. Fairy tales are the simplest of stories, universal in their appeal and narratives, that foster a deep, enduring connection between our imaginations and epic storytelling adventures. My earliest memory is probably way back when I was four years old or so and being plonked in front of a *Spiderman* cartoon and just sitting there wide-eyed, buzzing from Spidey webbing his foes, and eating way too many chicken nuggets. If I ever need to feel happy – even today as a grown man, a parent of two children, a husband and a founder of a new thriving software business – I still plonk myself down in front of a U-rated film and eat way too much chicken. It's my safe space.

As a child, my parents encouraged my love of stories and fed my imagination. To live out my own adventures, they would whisk me away to the magic (and queues) of Florida's Disney World where I fell in love with the princesses, heroes, villains and derring-do in worlds far, far away from our own. As I've grown into a bigger kid, that longing for enveloping my imagination in stories, and creating worlds, has stuck with me. In more ways than one, it's come to define who I am – and what I've become. This is personal to me. Watching enthralling and exciting stories unfold in front of my eyes has been, without a doubt, the one constant in my life. Without them, I'd be sad, lonely and working in banking.

As I've matured in my approach to stories, so has my interest in them. I carried it through to when I was a teenager and studied A-level English. Don't let that fool you into a false sense of security regarding my ability to write. My English teacher, Mr Schuan, pulled me into a crisis meeting in his office, four months into studying, to tell me in his near-indecipherable Scottish tone, "Son, you're not even going to get a D at this rate."* His accent didn't help. His lack of confidence in me didn't bother me. I studied English not because I felt I was any good at it – far from it – and it wasn't for the academic technicality of it all either, it was simply because I enjoyed the escapist magic of the stories buried deep within the language and literature. And I still do.

Breakthrough: Perhaps my therapist is right? Shit.

As I grew older, I migrated from the world of Disney's happily-ever-afters™ and the dimly lit office of Mr Schuan telling me off, to late-night, detailed thematic dissections of Pixar characters with friends down the pub. It's absolutely a normal thing for a 30-something heterosexual male to do, don't let my wife tell you otherwise. For example, did you know that there are only seven different types of stories in fiction? That's all, folks. Joseph Campbell's study of "The Hero's Journey" taught me (and a lot of man-boys my age) that and, once I knew it to be true, everything I knew about the world started to make much more sense. From rags to riches, heroes to villains, voyage and return, comedy and tragedy, rebirth and the quest for adventure – every story can be reduced to a nutshell.

Even the story of personalisation. In fact, *especially* personalisation.

Pixar, the iconic and beloved animation studio (owned, of course, by its Mouse Master, Disney), goes one step further. It's a religion that is founded on 22 essential

---

* I got an 'A' by the way. Thanks Mr Schuan!

rules of storytelling. All of them are highlighted in the brilliant 2014 book *Creativity, Inc.* by Ed Catmull, a co-founder of Pixar. My favourite is his eleventh rule:

"Give your characters' opinions. Passive/malleable might seem likeable to you as you write, but it's poison to the audience."[1]

Opinions shape characters, and they shape us, the audience, too. They bring us together and separate us. And that conflict breeds drama. The push/pull tug of war that exists within individual opinions is probably the only thing I remember from Mr Schuan's class — he taught me that was the foundation of good storytelling. Everything else is detail.

As geeky as this might sound, it's that conflict within the concept and execution of personalisation that I find so enthralling, so entertaining — it's drama, laid bare. And conflict is at the heart of personalisation. It has heroes and hyperbole, myth and reality, monsters and magicians, backstory and romance, art and science. It's loaded with a beautiful dichotomy where, on one hand, it has this perpetual hype that doesn't seem to ever wane. And yet, on the other, doesn't ever dare wow us into submission. Personalisation has become the Marvel Cinematic Universe. Where hype and belief remain, despite some of the more recent and subjectively terrible releases of *Thor: Love and Thunder* and *Ant Man: Quantumania*.

Today, research and statistics tell us constantly that personalisation is the greatest thing since *Avengers: Endgame* or sliced bread:

- 7 in 10 retailers who invest in personalising their customer experience enjoy an ROI of at least 4x.[2]
- 40 per cent of people will spend more than planned when the consumer experience is personalised.[3]
- 66 per cent of consumers remain loyal, and frequently purchase, from a brand due to consistent personalised, and relevant, communications.[4]

Those statistics conflict with each other, too, with the ROI of personalisation being purported to be anywhere between 15 per cent[5] to 30 per cent[6] increase, depending on the source. Which is it? In either case, the point remains the same: every year since the millennium has become "*The* Year of Personalisation", without ever actually crowning. We seem to always be at the peak of inflated expectations in the product

xviii   THE PERSON IN PERSONALISATION

hype lifecycle, to the point where personalisation is rebranded, renamed, reinvented. Most recently it became the arbitrarily named "Hyper-personalisation" and rebooted as much as the *Terminator* franchise, without actually delivering the goods. Much like the *Terminator* franchise. Sounds unnecessarily hyperbolic, doesn't it? In a few years, "Hyper-personalisation" will no doubt say "I'll be back" and morph into something else that will only have one thing in common with its predecessor: none of us having a bloody clue about what any of it actually means.

The range of opinions within the industry suggest that personalisation's hype still isn't realised. Its implementation seems still non-existent. It's either poorly implemented, not achieved, incorrectly associated, unattributed, or all four.

Now, this could simply be perception. Gartner states that 80 per cent of marketers will abandon personalisation by 2025.[7] With such a statement, how can we not sit up and take notice, even if it is designed to be a clickbait headline in and of itself. Some go as far as to state that "Personalization has been the most demoed, but least implemented, function of digital experience platforms for over a decade."[8]

Good or bad, this entertaining personalisation paradox – something that's clearly beneficial, if we were to read the vast majority of evidence and the self-serving case studies out there, and the laughable lack of implementation – is convincing and confusing in equal measures. And this conflict creates a drama that has been fascinating to watch, even better to write about, and now, hopefully, hugely entertaining to read.

Actually, the entertainment isn't in the writing but in the critical thinking I hope we can now apply to the subject. That's what this book hopes to achieve. To engage deeply with what personalisation actually is, what it's supposed to be, and what it means in the future for brands, great and small. Maybe even yours.

It's time, I say, to start dismissing the perpetual hype, stop reducing it down to a single tactic or add-on strategy designed purely to make money and instead rebirth personalisation entirely. This makes it sound like I want to start a personalisation cult – I don't – though I'm happy to be the cult leader, if you ask nicely. David Messianic Mannheim has quite the alliterative ring to it. As you'll come to read, much like that egotistical name, the tales of marketing alliteration are rife.

For me, personalisation is full of personality, wonder, drama, heroes and villains, and that all makes for a damn good fairy tale. It's not as though Pixar will make a film on it starring some cute anthropomorphic cowboy (voiced by Tom Hanks, probably, he does everything) searching for the perfect owner (see, it writes itself) – but if they do, I'll be the first one lining up to see it.

No, if the story of personalisation were a film, I feel it would be a quest. One that has power, mystery, history, deception and betrayal, with a splash of comedy, all engulfed in a conflict that, just as Mr Schuan taught me, provides the paradox between what consumers and the industry wants versus what they have to sacrifice or be forced to do in order to achieve it. As with the truly great stories — think *The Empire Strikes Back* — usually there is no winner.

As both practitioners of personalisation and victims of it, it is the person in personalisation that I feel has been lost. Frankenstein's dead, and all that is left is his brainless monster. The titans of the personalisation industry, Amazon and Netflix, commercially defined what personalisation should be for us all without realising what it takes to make a relationship work — a personal touch. And I want to know why. And can it change?

The Person in Personalisation is my personal quest to understand more about the alliterative paradigms at the heart of personalisation and defeat the monsters that seek to devalue it, or deceive it, and stop it from kissing its Prince Charming. It is my belief that, just with writing a story, understanding the motivations, the history and the villains that surround this subject, and using that information to destroy its enemies — á la the Death Star — makes for an even more satisfying happy-ever-after come the final act.

So, let's start where all epic quests must: the beginning...

Part I

The Ordinary World

Today, the state of personalisation is in a right mess. Chock-full of conflict. Built on foundations of disagreement and division. We even disagree on how it's spelled — is it with an "s" or a "z"? Both sides of the pond disagree. At the heart of it all beats a deafening paradox I hope to silence. Or at least reduce to a low mumble.

It's fascinating to me that there's an overwhelming inherent belief in personalisation that never seems to evolve or resolve. Brands want it to do well. They're cheering it on like a proud parent watching their little boy in the egg and spoon race on Sports Day, even after he's dropped the egg repeatedly. Plenty of brands (who shall remain nameless here, you know who they are) are doing personalisation just for the sake of being seen to do personalisation. They want a participation medal but don't care about crossing the finish line. Their desire to personalise is born out of ego, legacy, FOMO, arbitrary advice and, my favourite excuse, "just because".

The desire to personalise is evident in just how big the technology side of the market is. Let me tell you, it's not small. The global personalisation software market is valued at $943 million in 2022.[1] It's not much less than the reported value of its slightly bigger brother — the optimisation software market, which is $1.1 billion.[2] Despite that, the growth rate of the personalisation market is more than double, at 23.5 per cent compared to just 9.6 per cent in optimisation; personalisation is accelerating.

Within my interviews, the naysayers were largely those already practising personalisation. About half of the top-level marketing leaders I interviewed for this book didn't believe in it. Half! Not because they saw it as some dark-art voodoo, but because they saw it had limiting returns. To get a 1 per cent uplift on a website with a single solution when targeting everyone is achievable. To equal that, when limiting the reach of that solution, the uplift has to be disproportionately higher — 10 per cent instead of 1 per cent. Marianne Stjernvall, also known as the Queen of CRO, told me: "From the research that I've done, the more segmented the test does not always mean much bigger results than just targeting everyone."[3] There was also a common belief that personalisation is at the deep end of the maturity scale when, in reality, brands are still treading water at the shallow end.

So, which is it? Do brands want (read: need) personalisation or don't they? Is that the same answer from those preaching personalisation as well as those on the receiving end of it? And, even if everyone wanted it, how would something so personal even work for *everyone*? At its most simple, is definition in personalisation even *truly* possible? Herein lies the conflict.

Chapter 1

Hype Versus Reality

"It's over hyped and under done."

Tim Axon, Founder, Lean Convert[1]

I n *Star Trek*, there's a famous episode called *The Menagerie*, where the former captain of the starship *Enterprise*, Christopher Pike, was abducted by an alien species known as the Talosians, humanoid aliens with the ability to construct their own new planet through mental force (they created illusions that were indistinguishable from reality). This sparked the phrase, now famously used in reference to Steve Jobs, "reality distortion field", where the hype or belief in something is an illusion of its actual state.

As a result of this reality distortion and the allure of more money, more brands want to invest in personalisation. Who wouldn't want to? There are claims that organisations that invest in it exceed customer expectations and grow revenue 1.7 times faster than those that do not. These brands also increase customer lifetime value, the elusive and yet unattainable measurement of true success by, 2.3 times more.[2] Personalisation works, clearly. Tales of eHarmony averaging a jaw-dropping, earth-shattering, believable yet paradoxically unbelievable 220% increase in ROI by personalising creative copy to address individual customer concerns are all too common.[3]

Actually, the standard increase in revenue that brands can usually see is between 6 and 10 per cent according to Boston Consulting Group.[4] Not to mention 44 per cent of brands that implemented personalisation say their organisation's top line has increased over the past two years.[5]

It's crazy how the constant drumbeat of "more personalisation equals more revenue" has created this sense of FOMO within our industry. It's like everyone's hopping on the bandwagon, chasing after the elusive promise of higher profits. Let's be real here, some folks are just blindly following the herd, believing the hype without even questioning it.

Hearing fables of the mythical case studies and seeing those arbitrary research papers that supposedly prove the gospel of personalisation is alluring. But let's not kid ourselves – research or no research, statistic or no statistic – this whole notion that personalisation is the be-all and end-all of marketing principles seems to be etched in stone for some.

Hold on to your overpriced, merchandised Mickey Mouse ears, because while that might be the case in theory, in practice it is much different. Google recently reported that retailers invest just 0.7 per cent of their revenue in it.[6] Whilst they clearly want to use personalisation and see its benefits, brands just don't put their money where their mouth is. Only 44 per cent of retailers personalise more than half of their shopper journey[7] – what's happening to the other half?

Despite being labelled as the quintessential marketing principle, there is a clear inability to implement it successfully. A place where the theory works but the practice does not. A place where, according to Sailthru, the customer engagement platform, 71 per cent of retailers think they excel in personalisation, yet only 34 per cent of consumers agree.[8] A place of ego, perhaps.

Customers don't believe brands do a good job at personalisation. The left hand is disagreeing with the right, right?

Chapter 2

Awesome Versus Shit

"The same people come up as leaders in personalisation all the time. Here's the thing, it's fine for some not for others. One man's treasure is another man's trash."

Ben Malki, Vice President of Customer Success,
Americas, at Dynamic Yield[1]

If there's a methodology to personalisation that is so heavily weighted towards being good for the user, and there is a dearth of evidence to suggest that, and it is employed by all the world's major multinationals, why can no one seemingly do it well?

Seriously? I want to know.

Who does personalisation well?

The Sailthru personalisation index tries to answer this question by analysing over 80 different attributes to rank 500 or so brands.[2] If we need a more objective answer to the question of which brand is good at personalisation, last year that answer would be Thrive Market and Sephora taking the top spots, followed by DSW and Adidas.[3] (Note, no Netflix or Amazon.) Best Buy, too, "has become synonymous with in-store and online personalisation, making the electronics giant one of the best to do it".[4] I bet my bottom dollar that, when reading this, you didn't expect those brands to come up as leaders in personalisation.

It felt, in all my interviews, as though no one admitted to doing personalisation well themselves. "Still in our infancy" was the general response. It lined up with Google's interpretation that 85 per cent[5] of all marketers believe their company is not doing enough within the realm of personalisation. I couldn't quite figure out whether it was humility or a level of imposter syndrome that drove that response. I feel more inclined to suggest the latter, given that a McKinsey survey[6] of senior marketing leaders in 2021 discovered that just 15 per cent of CMOs believe their companies are on track with their personalisation efforts. Everyone is in the same boat; don't worry.

If the interviewees I spoke with were reluctant to point to themselves as being a good example of personalising, despite being well-known and reputable brands, who would they recommend as an example of this? I asked them to name a brand that they believe excels in personalisation. Not one of them could point me in an evidenced direction. Google cropped up (note: not Alphabet). Facebook, too (note: not Meta). However, most defaulted to those brands that have built a narrative around personalisation as the purpose of their business. If it wasn't for Jeff Bezos' public letters citing personalisation as a value, or Netflix's engineering advocacy of recommendations, would we even know they cared about personalisation? We assume these big boys, and others like them, do personalisation well because of how much they talk about it or because it's the basis of their commercial models. As a result, we default to them.

But personal experience dictates your opinion on personalisation, not the wealth of evidence that suggests otherwise.

This was great for me. The critical and subjective opinions about doing something well versus simply doing it poorly are designed to spread conflict and confusion, the two facets of great storytelling. As the infamous professional bowler Pete Weber once famously said, "Hate me or like me, you watched me."[7] Drama needs a fight, and at this rate, my book is going to be a bestseller.

The finger pointing of Amazon, the infamous and often-cited example within my interviews, has its critics. We're talking about the first online company to propagate the desire to personalise as part of its core business strategy back in 1998. Twenty-five years later, the company still thinks that personalisation means recommending a toilet seat to a customer who just bought a toilet seat. I appreciate some people may have two toilets in their house, so they probably need more than one, but that's not the point: the point is believing this is personalisation when in reality it's not.

In one broad swath of my interviews, there were those that applauded Amazon's efforts to personalise. Marcel Rduch, RVP Customer Success at Dynamic Yield said: "They're doing a great job, in terms of answering my needs as an individual, no one does it better."[8] On the flip side of the coin, Tim Stewart, owner of TRS Digital,[9] has clearly been remarketed too many toilet seats when he suggests that "Amazon continually recommends that I buy items I'm just never going to buy".

If the OG* of personalisation is often cited as having poor personalisation experiences, something must be wrong, right? And if two prolific marketing leaders

---

* OG is a colloquialism meaning "original goat", which is a colloquialism for "original greatest of all time".

like Stewart and Rduch have contrary opinions, which side of the coin is right? Heads or tails? And why can't they agree?

The other poster child of personalisation, Netflix, also receives both plaudits and condemnation. In a recent 2021 LinkedIn survey,[10] I asked my network of industry leaders to classify their personalisation efforts into just two buckets: good or bad. The split wasn't directly down the middle, however, only 63 per cent said that Netflix is "good" at personalisation, suggesting some level of disagreement. Given that people spend 1.8 seconds on average[11] considering each title they are given, it's not unreasonable to suggest that people spend an inordinate amount of time choosing what it is they want to watch. The average person spends up to 90 seconds in total browsing for content before they stop looking and do something else.[12] "Netflix and chill" usually. This results in opinionated frustration and perhaps throwing your TV remote at the wall. To put it succinctly, Simon Elsworth, Global Head of Experimentation at Whirlpool explained to me: "Trying to find content on Netflix is fucking impossible."[13]

Whilst that may be subjectively true, the internal statistics at Netflix reveal that, actually, with better personalisation, time to choose is significantly reduced, improving the experience for both consumer and creator. Their data suggests they have been successful, too. Two decades ago, just 2 per cent of everything someone chose to watch on Netflix was driven by a recommendation of some kind. Today, that figure sits at 80 per cent.[14]

It's somewhat moot when no amount of data can help how individuals feel about their experience, especially those as passionate as Elsworth. If the implementation doesn't match the hype, as I discussed in my previous chapter, this is a case of fact versus opinion. And so, while it might actually be getting better, it *feels* as though it isn't. Personalisation or no personalisation, when brands ask us how we feel, 63 per cent said our experiences have stayed the same or gotten worse over the last 12 months. Only 37 per cent of us say our experiences have gotten better.[15] Whether this is a case of expectation or a whiff of ego in the air, it doesn't matter − all the evidence points to the same thing: personalisation is just hot air and opinion.

And brands − I'm sorry − but you can't control opinion. Not yet.

Chapter 3

Good Versus Evil

"Many people are against personalisation when the goal is to persuade. It's a force for evil rather than good. It needs to be reinvented because right now, it's seen as manipulative. If you want to manipulate people, you personalise."

Dr Paul Marsden, Consumer Psychologist, Syzygy[1]

To control opinion, that's exactly what those *in power* want to use personalisation for. By "in power" I don't mean God or Darth Vader. No, I mostly mean Mark Zuckerberg.

A world where content is personalised for us, the consumers, sounds amazing. In theory. Personalisation helps us see the products, or experiences, that are most relevant for us in a sea of choice and sameness. The Internet has no shortage of content or products. And it wants us to consume and buy. Without our attention or wallets, the Internet is dead; we might as well go for a walk like a Neanderthal. The challenge for brands is to find content that fits the user like a glove (and retain their attention), not a one-size-fits-all approach as it currently exists (and lose that attention to a competitor). Personalisation is symbiosis. And, if done well, it should be beneficial collectively, for consumer and brand.

Yet with great power comes great responsibility, our friendly neighbourhood Spiderman taught us that. Giving the power of personalisation to the dark side — those who wish to control — means that its use cases are largely self-serving. In today's online age, I would relate that to the need for more money and more power. Greed both controls and separates our species.

Our tendencies as humans are to protect our pre-existing attitudes. Largely because it's much easier to accept them than to change our beliefs. We have de facto selection biases. This means that our circle of friends is predominantly similar to us in that our belief systems, values and outlook are all aligned. Thus, according to studies, we find information that agrees with our prior-held beliefs more credible, often dismissing incongruent ideas.[2] That encourages likes, comments, emoji responses, shares and continued engagement within social media platforms, which is, coincidentally, fully aligned with the commercial goals of the very same platform. And guess what? Popularity begets popularity. It will come as no surprise, therefore, that the top 50 videos that YouTube recommended most often had been viewed an average of 456 million times. Each.[3]

How those in power use personalisation to control content has created echo chambers, sometimes known as "Filter Bubbles".[4] The content you see is the content they want you to see because it keeps you engaged with the platform and doesn't waiver outside of your preconditioned biases and thoughts. You like to listen to Moana? We'll show you Moana, and only Moana. Famed documentaries like *The Social Dilemma*,[5] and best-selling books, such as *The Black Box Society* (2016),[6] both highlight the invisible algorithmic editing of the web for personal control; "evil personalisation".

> "This moves us very quickly towards a world in which the Internet shows us what it thinks we want to see, but not necessarily what we need to see."
>
> Eli Pariser, Author[7]

Eli Pariser, a renowned believer that "Technology and media should serve democracy," said that sentence over a decade ago, in 2011. His quote above stems back to the idea of relevancy, where Mr Zuckerberg once said, "A squirrel dying in front of your house may be more relevant to your interests right now than people dying in Africa."[8] It's not being more relevant that's the question, but the purpose of that relevancy.

From a commercial standpoint, there is an acceptance that greater relevance is best for both the customer and the brand. A win-win. When researched, customers suggest that they are more than twice as likely to add items to their basket and 40 per cent more likely to spend more than planned when experiences are relevant and personalised to them.[9]

Yet, from an economic and ethical perspective, I question whether the squirrel actually pushes people apart.

There is no longer a Top 40 to which we all belong, there is just *your* Top 40. There is no longer news that is ranked on its importance to society anymore, just news that is ranked on your interests as an individual. It doesn't matter who Adriana Grande is dating or how a Georgian black bear died after an overdose of cocaine; all that matters is what interests *you* the most. As this has become possible and scalable across commercial and media platforms, it has now created separation where there was once none. Tribalism is human nature[10] and that feeling of collectiveness is vital to our survival. In Andy Crouch's *The Life We're Looking For: Reclaiming Relationship in a Technological World* he suggests that "this has created a cycle of dependence on the personalised, when what we, as humans, are dying for is the personal". Where, because of this separatism, we became the most powerful and affluent people in history, but at the same time the most lonely and depressed. All thanks to personalisation, the thing that promotes and invites isolation.

It's my feeling that personalisation *had* good intentions. Past tense. But as it has become scalable and commercial, wielded by those with power, I ask, has the current incarnation of personalisation created a collective sense of impersonalness? Or impersonalisation?

Whether you're part of the Rebellion or the Dark Side, there's something so primal about good vs evil. When George Lucas created *Star Wars* with *Episode IV: A New Hope* in 1977, the themes of conflict, battle and purity were central to his vision. (As well as shooting lasers at each other and – forty-year-old spoiler warning – disobedient children.) It should therefore come as no surprise, that the battle of good vs evil, simplistically reduced down to purpose and intent, is central to this conflict within personalisation.

Chapter 4

Definition Versus Definition

"It's used in so many meetings that you're a part of without everyone having a shared understanding of what personalisation actually is."

David Keown, Digital Product Owner, Screwfix[1]

In all the interviews with experts I conducted while researching personalisation, I received no more difference in opinion than on the actual definition of personalisation. That's because, again, personalisation's core is rooted in conflict.

The opinions I received provided me with an exhilarating boxing match full of give and take. In the red corner, Ryan Jordan, Strategy Director at Brainlabs, told me personalisation is about emotional connection and tailoring needs and journeys.[2] In the blue corner, Peep Laja, CEO of Wynter, valued personalisation as simple as segmenting audiences and communicating with those segments.[3]

They're still duking it out.

If I asked 100 people for their definition of personalisation, I would get 100 different answers. That's often the cited claim, anyway. It's my opinion that the answers would be different, sure, but the sentiment behind them wouldn't. I'm sure they'd all contain some form of phraseology such as "right people", "right message" or "right time". And that's largely a problem with any global definition that tries to squeeze a complex issue down into an accessible generalisation. Ironic, don't you think, given that personalisation is intended to be the exact opposite of that.

The varying differences in responses I received to a very simple question — "What is personalisation?" — not only highlighted that the vast majority didn't know, but that their answers seemed to stem from nothing more than pre-conceptions and bias.

To some, the definition of personalisation means one-to-one; individual messaging. Where every single user receives a different experience, variable, or thing, making their time more personalised. This is quite a common response, probably in relation to the examples set by its aforementioned leading co-stars, Amazon and Netflix. They kickstarted the origin story of what personalisation is, but then promptly led it down a dark alley. Everyone else just followed blindly, assuming Amazon would figure a way out. The dark alley of one-to-one personalisation – where Bezos believed that "if we have 4.5 million customers, we shouldn't have one store, we should have 4.5 million stores".[4]

To others, personalisation doesn't need to be that complex, and so treat it with another pre-conception. One where the dark alley of one-to-one turned into the cul-de-sac of recommendations; another definitional conflict. Because Amazon and Netflix show personalisation as recommendations, there's a definitional preconception that recommendations are just personalisation and vice-versa. A concept of pure relevancy, matching products or services to individuals only because, well, what else is there? A lot, as we'll come to find out, falls within the fallacy of that definition.

The truth is, that definition is based on the application, the implementation and the purpose. The fact that personalisation means something different for TikTok than for The New York Times is less a question of definition, and more an appreciation that they serve two different purposes. Just as email marketing personalisation has a different utility than that of personalisation within web design. Or personalisation for shoe design is different from personalisation within web experiences. The context in which it is held is the defining factor in how to define it.

Either way, it is these contrasting opinions and definitions – whether you're in the blue corner or the red corner – that made this subject start to feel like the classic hero's quest. Or, as I named it, my call to adventure.

Part II

The Call to Adventure

There are plenty of definitions that exist for personalisation. And I'm going to try and see if one fits, much like Cinderella's glass slipper, but far less dainty. Currently, the lack of an agreed definition is the critical factor holding back personalisation from achieving its potential. Without an aligned definition, there can be no real progression.

> "Someone somewhere needs to put a definition on personalisation."
>
> **Shiva Manjunath, Experimentation Manager at Solo Brands**[1]

When I interviewed Shiva, he gave me a look that implied that "someone somewhere" should be me. This was to be my calling, then. Shiva wanted me to define personalisation. If no one could define it succinctly, and seemingly that is the one thing holding back the reality from the hype, surely this was my superhero origin story. This was the thing that would give me the answer to why I was in so much generic despair waiting in an endless line at *Monsters, Inc. Laugh Floor.*

The problem is, however, that I don't agree with the narrative that the lack of definition is the thing that is holding back the progression of personalisation. We, the consumer, and the industry, don't need another definition of something to add to the millions already out there. The definitions out there are ... fine. We all know that personalisation somehow relates to a more tailored consumer experience being served to a subset of people. Dictionaries such as Gartner, Collins, Wikipedia – inform us that these definitions all hold the same virtue. We don't need another definition in our lives, redefined or called "new" for the sake of personal or commercial glory.

We also don't need more models that interpret these definitions. They usually involve some trio of unnecessary alliteration, as Sunikka and Bragge, 2012,[2] defined it: "Offering the right product and service to the right customer at the right time and the right place." OK that was four things, not three. As an homage, this chapter will capture the true essence of the industry's incessant need to provide practitioners with unnecessary alliterations. While being flippant, I'll also seek to pin a definition on the personalisation donkey.

Before embarking on our pithy alliterative journey of what personalisation is, it feels right to first acknowledge what it isn't. And the answer to that one is easy.

Chapter 5

Rubbish Recommendations

"Personalisation is not only about recommendations. Recommendations are such a small part of what I'd say personalisation is."

Ryan Jordan, Director of Strategy, Brainlabs[1]

There is a rumour being whispered through the air of the marketing community that personalisation is simply "just" about making recommendations to consumers. So much so that this is more than just a rumour – *it has become the defining definition in and of itself.* The idea that personalisation is purely recommendation is ludicrous – it's merely the most popular. And, because of the conflict, confusion and complexities of the personalisation concept, we default to the belief that what is collectively most popular is best for me. There's some irony for you.

The association between recommendations and personalisation is so strong that the concept of personalisation doesn't exist anymore, it's just about recommendations.

And boy, are recommendations everywhere.

Our Instagram, Twitter, Spotify and TikTok experiences are all built on nothing but recommendations. It's central to our interaction with the digital world in everything that we do. The University of Minnesota now offers a course on "Master Recommendation Systems". There is an annual conference on Recommender Systems, called RecSys; it's been around since the early 90s. The Amazon researchers, Linden and Smith, concluded their paper "Two Decades of Recommender Systems at Amazon.com" with: "Every interaction should be a recommendation."[2] If you thought the future was concentrated on creating hoverboards and betting on sports games, think again. It's about recommendations, apparently.

There are four reasons for why "Recommendations is personalisation" – not three, unfortunately.

1) Recommendations Are Seen As Easy

Retailers nowadays can pick a recommendation vendor off the shelf for peanuts. That being said, it's completely dependent on the approach that brands take; off the shelf or custom built. These range on a scale from the simple to the uber complex, but not all brands need an AI system based on a three-part ranking funnel that harvests 65 billion features and produces 90 million model predictions per second, even if Instagram does.[3] As with anything that can be commercialised and commoditised, companies have jumped on the personalisation equals recommendations bandwagon and this can now be bought from one of the thousands of vendors selling this as a product.

2) Recommendations Are Attributable

Brands struggle to attribute personalisation. How do you attribute emotional connection, relevance and resonance? When I am more personable with my friend Ryan, at the pub, as opposed to being a less personable arsehole not remembering it was his birthday, or his son's name, how can I attribute that variable to how much he likes me?

Luckily, in a more retail and commercial setting, because recommendations require a direct click and purchase – unlike the slightly fluffier niceties of being personable – they are seen as having a direct impact on the return on investment. And so, recommendations bubble to the top.

3) Recommendations Are Extremely Visible

One of the difficulties in answering "Who does personalisation well?" is that good personalisation is often deemed invisible. It's tailored to us as individuals, so no one else can see it. It harkens back to Jeff Bezos's quote about there being 4.5 million different and individual Amazon stores. Recommendations are something that we can usually see as a module or component right before our very eyes. This is highlighted even further by the fact that it's framed with a giant title above it that says "We Recommend". Personalisation, on the other hand, seems more ethereal than that; it is intangible in nature and difficult to do.

4) The Role Models Of eCommerce Are Shouting About It

My favourite – and I think most impactful.

Spotify talks about how they are "evaluating fairness and bias with their recommendation algorithm" on their blog.[4] Zalando shouts about using their

"Algorithmic Fashion Companion (AFC)" at events and in news.[5] In a world of transparency and seemingly wanting to help, sometimes cynically seen as a method to get the best talent, the so-called "best" shout about how they are personalising the user experience: through making recommendations. If two of the most popular sites in the world, Amazon and Netflix, rave about recommendations as one of their core commercial principles, it says something. And if they do it, well, that's the precedent that's been set. Let's all follow Jeff and Reed.

So, therefore, it's pertinent to ask:

> "What's the difference between personalisation and recommendations? Netflix don't actually do personalisation, they only do recommendations."
>
> **Bhavik Patel, CEO of Causl[6]**

Patel makes a good point. Why do Netflix and Amazon call it personalisation ... if they only do recommendations? That is their definition of personalisation, surely.

Our global definition of personalisation impacts the definitions of those around us. A view shared by Manjunath, who told me that, "People define things the way they want to define them, and as a result, they box people into their narrow definitions without thinking maybe their definitions aren't correct."[7]

Take the example of the last manager you had. Remember them? Of course you do. They either have had a profound impact on you or a negative one. Mine was a [insert generic farmyard animal here]. Not literally, she was just a really mean person. Their way of thinking and beliefs will have unintentionally impacted your own. If your interpretation of, say, email marketing is weekly marketing newsletters, it's likely you'll hire others who have a similar view rather than hiring those with a definition of email marketing as relationship building, for example. The echo chamber of hiring. Because of confirmation bias, we keep thinking that email marketing only means this one thing, especially in that company.

To define something is to put it in a box, consciously or not. Personalisation is in the recommendations box. Amazon's Jeff Bezos and Netflix's Reed Hastings have unknowingly been our managers with inherent confirmation bias shouting at us, "Personalisation is *just* recommendations."

Nonsense.

It is so much more.

In 1898, E St Elmo Lewis[8] devised a hierarchical four-tier triangle to better understand how advertising works. (Why are models always pyramid shaped?) This was the AIDA model: Awareness, Interest, Desire and Action. A model that suggests that when consumers decide what to buy, they go through these steps. Lewis suggested:

> "The mission of an advertisement is to attract a reader, so that he will look at the advertisement and start to read it; then to interest him, so that he will continue to read it; then to convince him, so that when he has read it, he will believe it. If an advertisement contains these three qualities of success, it is a successful advertisement."[9]

If Lewis knew that he created a model for selling, yet brands only focus on one of the four parts, he would be turning in his grave (he definitely passed away in 1948; I double checked before making that statement, it's possible to be 125 years old.). Recommendations are designed for product discovery, helping people find a product that suits their needs; awareness. That's only one quarter of the battle, according to Lewis. The Interest, Desire, and Action in the AIDA model are then neglected, jettisoned. Offers, content, messaging and journeys are nascent. When brands ask, "How do we personalise?" and often fail to come up with an answer, they lean back on the de facto answer; recommendations. Why?

> "There's more to personalisation than just recommender systems. What's the purpose and job to be done by personalisation technology? It's to save people time and effort."
>
> **Dr Paul Marsden, Consumer Psychologist, Syzygy**[10]

Personalisation, in Marsden's sense, is largely misrepresented because societal implementation leads us down a road of pure content or product discovery, pigeon-holing the concept of personalisation into the executional sense of recommendations. Partially preconditioned by our hypothetical managers and the showpieces of Netflix and Amazon, but most likely done on purpose by SaaS vendors. Who wouldn't want to commercialise this opportunity by making a complex concept seem simple and accessible? I'm not emotionally ready to go down that rabbit hole just yet; I need a coffee. And a sedative.

The first step in personalisation therapy is to acknowledge that personalisation is so much more than just recommendations. There are three other parts to the model of personal selling that Lewis would want us to value — Interest, Desire and Action.

This brings us back to an appreciation of what the benefits of personalisation actually are. They are not for the brand, but for the customer. When you phrase it like that, these benefits are so much more than just discovering products or services. What exactly are they?

Luckily for us, Google and Ipsos[11] already did this research. They agree with Marsden. They found the answer to why we, as consumers, like personalisation so much falls into three (of course it's three) categories:

1) Saves Time
2) Offers Discounts
3) Displays the Right Products

Really, it's two. The third category seems to be the cause of the first, where you display the right products in order to save time.

Really, it's one. The anomaly within these three is the point of offering discounts. It feels overly specific and biased because who doesn't want to save money? According to the same survey,[12] the answer to that is 13 per cent. Yes, 13 per cent of global shoppers say getting a good deal is unimportant to them when deciding which retailer to buy from. It must be the bourgeoisie.

So, personalisation's all about saving time, then?

Timo Boldt and James Carter founded the meal kit retailer Gousto in 2012. Boldt had the "light bulb moment" for the brand when he was 26 and working at a Goldman Sachs-spinoff hedge firm. A time-poor culture known for workaholism. Gousto provides customers with boxes of food that contain easy-to-follow recipes and pre-measured fresh ingredients. They cater to busy, time-poor families such as what Boldt experienced within his work, as well as those who still appreciate home-prepared food. It is literally a business built for customers for the primary, although not exclusive, reason of saving time — a business made for personalisation (if you are to believe those three reasons above).

As the business has grown, so too have their recipe options. They feature as many as 75 recipe changes every week. Given Boldt's now-famous quote, "We are a data company that loves food," and the original purpose of setting the company up, it shouldn't be a surprise that they have a top-notch system for making recommendations: the *Rouxcommender*, named after legendary French chef Michel Roux.

The *Rouxcommender* was initially run as an experiment where only a certain number of users would see the recommendations system, shown to users under the option "Chosen for You". Gousto found a positive uplift, as you have now come to expect from many case studies of recommendation systems. Research from Salesforce shows that shoppers who clicked on recommendations are 4.5x more likely to add these items to their cart and 4.5x more likely to complete the purchase.[13]

Imagine the surprise when, against all the research purporting that recommendations increase revenue, usually said by vendors self-servingly selling the same thing, at Gousto, they didn't work for everyone. They found that the only positive influence seen was among users of a certain profile: those who chose quickly and had a desire to save time.

There are largely two types of browsing patterns among users within Gousto: those who choose quickly and those who explore. Such is the nature of a typical restaurant experience, you're either the type to know what you want on a menu because of pre-conditioned tastes (like me – always chicken nuggets), or you're slightly more adventurous and like to discover new, exciting options (like my wife who takes ten hours to make a decision when sat at the McDonald's drive-thru).

Which profile the user is within – choosing quickly or exploring – is generally inferred from temporal behaviours: choosing recipes within one minute suggests that you might be less adventurous with eating, whereas if you take your time, that might suggest you're more of an explorer.

It can be related to the specific requirement of the user, too – are they looking for something that others will enjoy within their family or do they need permission from their better half? Not to mention their personality profile of risk, discovery and openness, which determines how likely it is that they will discover a new meal and try it out.

To suggest that every person wants a recommendation is impersonal in and of itself. It's disrespectful because it's ignorant of a large percentage of every brand's composition of audience.

Gousto acknowledged this. The *Rouxcommender* recommendation engine was found to only affect those with "Quick Chooser" profiles. This hangs the hat on the hat rack of saving time. In a single experiment of showing recommendations vs no recommendations, Gousto found that it took users 4 per cent less time to choose a recipe. The primary, and seemingly only, benefit of this experiment was that recommendations reduced the amount of time it took users to complete a specific action. Period. Valuable, but specific.

Dr Paul Marsden, a chartered psychologist specialising in consumer behaviour, calls personalisation "convenience technology" for this very reason. Or, should he say, recommendations? "Most of the time, our behaviour is habitual or automatic," he told me. "We have other things to do. If I don't have to search, I have defaults related to my preferences that will save me time and effort. Given our busy lives, technology can save us time. This is all about relevancy and the proliferation of choice."[14]

Take, for example, Google Drive, which claims that personalisation saves users thousands of hours each week.[15] Convenience technology? Given that there are over one billion users of Google Drive, their attribution is equal to that of a 20-year career's worth of work saved every day. Clearly, Google Drive is a business that makes money — $2.6 billion a quarter,[16] to be exact. The two motivations aren't mutually exclusive. But, improving the user experience by saving time is a proxy metric for the platform, and people will pay for that.

So, is personalisation about saving time? The answer comes down to the diverse definitions already in play within personalisation ...

Chapter 6

Diverse Definitions

With the challenge from Manjunath to personally devise an aligned definition of personalisation, it was time to get to work. My first step was to do what every wannabe author does to find answers. I Googled it. However, the more I looked, the more definitions of definitions I found:

> "The lack of common terminology still represents one of the obstacles to fully understanding the concept and all its facets. [Personalisation is] A dynamic process in which an object is changed for an individual in order to provide added value for the individual herself/himself."
>
> **An Exploration of Personalization in Digital Communication,**
> **Nobile & Kalbaska (2020)[1]**

What does that even mean?

Googling "personalisation" became exhausting. Someone somewhere must have already been on this quest that I could plagiarise?

In 2022, a group of adventurous researchers[2] set out on their own journey to bridge the academic personalisation market, which they called "fragmented". That's being kind, in my opinion. They undertook what's known as a "bibliographic study", which is a systematic literature review. Essentially collating and synthesising a tonne of research already in existence – 383 publications, to be precise. Our hero's goal was to arrive at a single, aligned definition. This was just what I was after and would help me pass off their work to Manjunath as my own. I'd probably give it a new definition, like so many before me, to try and make it sound new and clever. Here you go, Manjunath, I present to you "fragmented personalisation".

The group of researchers – Shobhana Chandra, Sanjeev Verma, Weng Marc Lim, Satish Kumar and Naveen Donthu – took great effort and care to publish their findings. And after reaching the top of the mountain and acknowledging the different definitions that others have given, guess what?

They were unable to give their own consolidated and aligned definition.

The reason why is because they came across so much contention, much like my own adventure to date.

The meaning of personalisation, they agreed, was so broad that it spanned across multiple categories and, in doing so, did not settle within any of its own.

One of the core challenges in defining it is not the definition, but the variety in the application. Those different applications were recognised as acquisition, its use in CRM and web experiences. The power of three.

Not just that, but they found variety in the implementation itself: strategy, layout, content and learning. With three different applications and four different implementations, it's no wonder defining personalisation has given all of us a headache. Where to start?

It's my belief that the research-driven definition reduces the term to nothing but a sequence of words and thus removes meaning. It dissolves the ambiguity. There are varying types of definitions available to us. Dictionary, nominal, stipulative, descriptive, explicative, ostensive. Yet, the dictionary definition is what people want, which is, by its very nature, overly generic — the arch-nemesis of personalisation. It consists of a bunch of words that are strung together. Usually with additional verbs thrown in to cover all bases. *Forrester's Glossary*, for example, defines personalisation thusly:

"An experience that uses customer data and understanding to frame, guide, extend and enhance interactions based on that person's history, preferences, context and intent."[3]

You can imagine the team at Forrester spending weeks to craft the perfect definition of personalisation here. Sending emails back and forth to cover all different avenues. It feels as though each adjective or verb was added by an individual who fought for that word personally. In doing so, creating this Frankenstein's monster of a definition designed to cover all bases and, in doing so, did not get close to any. While it can be interpreted, in reality, it feels as though it means almost nothing.

I argue that personalisation doesn't need a new definition. It is more of a construct like leadership or entrepreneurship. Try defining creativity and you'll probably run into exactly the same problems. One could think of the difference between asking "what is a tiger?" and "what a tiger is". Bear* with me on this. It's not about a tiger, it is the

---

* Grammar police do not come after me. I spelt *bear* like this on purpose as it is word play, being so similar to that of a tiger. I appreciate it's not terribly funny, but as a dad I gave it a little chuckle.

difference between meaning and interpretation. There is a real definition of what a tiger is, which really should constitute a zoologist's definition of a tiger as the real definition. But this may fail to provide the insensible parts. The more philosophical fact is that we are all tigers living in a caged zoo, with Mark Zuckerberg as our zookeeper. It feels that, given the three different applications and four different implementations, it's less a question of *what* is personalisation, but more *why* personalise?

No, it's not personalisation's definition that needs remoulding, but the contextual understanding relevant to your business.

I learned in my quest that personalisation is more conceptual than oriented around a single discipline. And so, personalisation doesn't need a definition, and certainly not a new definition like Manjunath was looking at me to try and do all the hard work for. Redefining it wasn't going to help. Fragmented Personalisation. Super Personalisation. Persona-lisation. Such new or slightly altered definitions are not going to change the stigmas that are associated with the word. It will just create new problems of redefinition, which personalisation once held.

In fact, giving personalisation a definition places a binary label on it. That is, when we put it into practice, you can say that you're either doing it or not. By asking what the definition is, we are asking to place a complex concept into a box. Personalisation is not only a construct, it also holds contextual and individual stigmas and experiences with it. Difficulty is bound to arise. Everyone thinks it means something and, in doing so, tries to assign a singular value to it. Like life, it's not that simple. In my discussions with digital marketing leaders, I learned that personalisation is much more abstract.

And so, personalisation should be more of a series of belief systems rather than a singular entity. I see it being more aligned with something conceptual, such as creativity. Rather than, say, marketing, which is more of a discipline. I can hear marketers sharpening their pitchforks! To be successful, the belief systems held within the application must be both aligned and purposeful. That is of much more value than a series of words strung together to form an arbitrary sentence.

Chapter 7

Pecking-Order of Personalisation

ersonalisation isn't a scale of one to two; are brands personalising or not. It's a scale of one to ten; how much are brands personalising. There are milestones that help brands understand where they sit. These milestones represent something not unlike a quest, vanquishing dragons and slaying boardroom members.

Those milestones are famously called, from the left to the right: one-to-all, one-to-many, one-to-few and one-to-one. There's nothing quite like a quirky, alliterative, overly generic model to get the marketing blood pumping. Only a shoe-horned four-letter acronym can really beat it. That is, when brands create experiences, these alliterative phrases describe for whom they are designing the experiences. One-to-all suggests the experience is designed for everyone. One-to-one is designed for the opposite purpose. Where does personalisation sit on this scale?

One-to-all: Response variables
At its most basic, personalisation can be defined as a response variable.

This was a common reply I got when asking others to define personalisation. It felt like the lowest common denominator on the far left of a maturity scale. Like an if/else statement,* where a user sees something that is specific to them based on a variable change. If you log in to an account online, the top right might say "Hi David", given that you are now a logged-in user. This is a variable change responding to the fact that your name is David and, therefore, could be classified as personalisation.

It's a place where the user might be in a specific state, and therefore a variable requires changing to acknowledge that state. This is a dangerous rabbit hole of possibilities. "If someone is on a mobile device and we show them a mobile version of our website, does that count as personalisation? What about if they come from a specific traffic source, like Facebook, and we show them something related to where they came from?"

---

* In programming, an if/else statement is a conditional statement that executes a distinct series of statements based on whether an expression is true or false.

Where do you end? How specific should you go? If this is not personalisation, what is it?

In that example, there is an input — the user is on a mobile device. There is also an output, which is that the mobile version of the website is shown. It can't just be that simple, can it? Simply responding to a variable?

Steven Shyne, Co-Founder and COO, CXperts, says no: "Your account message isn't personalisation. It's system feedback. That state has changed. The user has changed their state, and it is a case of making the state more relevant for them." But isn't relevancy the nucleus of personalisation, Steven?

Spotify illustrates Shyne's point nicely when you play a *Star Wars* theme and it replaces the track progression bar with a lightsaber. But can we call that personalisation? (I don't care personally, it's so frickin' cool.)

If I'm put on the spot, I side with Shyne and I also don't believe it is. I believe this is just a response variable — "system feedback" — not personalisation. That being said, we're talking about the delivery mechanism, not the intent. Changing a track bar to be a lightsabre isn't personalisation, but saying "Hi David" is absolutely intended to be a form of being more personable, is it not? An appreciation of who you are as an individual. An attempt to be more familiar. That's personalisation to me — being more personable.

State changes like this would, of course, create an infinite number of use cases. Logging into an account is just a simple recognition that a user, indeed, does have an account. It excludes a tonne of other inputs such as location, type of account, what was previously purchased, how much and how many were purchased, and what device was used. I could go on. It's devoid of context. It's most likely a reason why personalisation platforms exist, they're effectively very good pseudo-content management systems. Much like a front-end layer that sits on the site, when a variable is triggered, a response is given. Placing those variables into the code of a website would surely become unmanageable and likely annoy those who are trying to keep any codebase as clean as humanly possible. Or, as Marianne Stjernvall, Queen of CRO, flippantly said: "Personalisation is anything that our development teams do not want to put in the source code."[1]

She's not wrong.

One-to-many: Optimisation

As we move further up the maturity scale, we find that there were those in my research who believed that personalisation was just optimisation; only a more focused version of it. After all, what is the difference between personalisation and optimisation? The end goal remains the same.

Let's work through one example ...

Say a brand is working really hard just to improve a single part of their user's journey — the famous product detail page. Is that not personalisation? In this case, we have a specific variable of the "product detail page" that is being improved. That is the only thing that is being improved. The variable is being isolated and amended, but other variables — a checkout, a listing page, a homepage — remain the same. Emma Travis, Director of Research, Speero, told me, "Just running a test for desktop users is a form of personalisation, or returning users. It's the same. We're all personalising, right?"[2]

Is personalisation therefore much more than specific optimisation? On the scale of "we're going to make stuff better", when does something turn from "we're optimising something" into "we're optimising something specific"?

Does it really matter?

If the purpose is the same, how brands undertake that purpose does need to be defined. I think when you look at it through this lens, it's all optimisation; personalisation can be seen as just a more specific form of it. The trouble comes that, because this is a mythical scale and not a binary series of milestones, knowing when optimisation turns into personalisation is difficult, a near-impossible task, and I'm sure there's an arbitrary Venn diagram in existence just waiting for such a debate. It means that those who practice this witchcraft can't turn around and simply say, "We're doing personalisation now," which is one of the reasons why defining it is so difficult — there's no cut off point. Again, I question whether this actually matters.

Let's assume it does for the sake of ... uh ... ego?

In a world where, on the far left of this well-known personalisation maturity model, we optimise something for everyone, and on the far right, we optimise something for fewer people, what sits between them? These two poles, one-to-many and one-to-few, are nothing but definitions of segmenting the audience. A means to an end. Everything that sits between the two poles is segmentation. The question should then be more about where these delineations lie and how brands delineate?

One-to-Few: Segmentation

"What's the difference between segmentation and personalisation? To me, it's all segmentation, where some segments end up with only having one user in that segment."

Ton Wesseling, Conversion Optimisation
and Experimentation Consultant[3]

So, to Travis's point, is personalisation just a more focused form of optimisation? Or is it actually just a form of segmentation? At what point does one morph into the other, and is that even important? Am I asking too many questions?

Let's break it down, again.

When practitioners are optimising, think of segmenting between desktop users and mobile users. Then desktop users who come in from a paid media source, such as Google Ads. Then desktop users who come in from a paid media source, such as Google Ads, who are logged in to their account. Where do brands stop? It's not uncommon to blindly stumble into a grey area between what is segmentation and what is personalisation, all classified on a single scale of achieving the same goal: optimisation. That overlap is 50 shades of grey.

While I argue whether it matters or not because the end result is all the same – a better customer experience – I do think there is a difference.

Actually, it's not just me. A recent survey by Sailthru[4] agreed. They found that 75 per cent of marketers believe that segmenting an audience fulfils just the bare minimum requirements for personalisation, there is so much more.

The majority of respondents – 64 per cent – believed that brands needed to use customer behavioural data and preferences to dynamically provide unique content to be classified as such. Thirty-three per cent agreed that the bare minimum to classify it is predicting the next set of actions a customer is likely to take and tailoring those experiences to that customer.

Thoughtworks, a global tech consultancy, believes that there is, indeed, this delineation between segmentation and personalisation, where that distinction is context-dependent.[5] If you're looking for microwaves and are also served microwave-safe serving dishes as a recommendation, it's not paying attention to customer needs. Instead, it's solely focused on product-related associations. Personalisation is therefore all about being customer-first, a phrase I'm sick of hearing and not seeing enough of. Customers have nuances and context that are often ignored because brands don't listen enough, foreshadowing my adventure to follow.

This quandary that's been created is a hat tip to the way personalisation is currently implemented by brands, where the current belief is that personalisation is purely a segmentation play.[6] This narrative is crafted by the brands that implement personalisation, when really it's just segmenting audiences – to Thoughtworks' explanation, because its devoid of context. Again, the fallacies being told and believed from the gods, Jeff and Reed, above us. I'm creating a new term right now for commercial gain as so many have done before me – "contextualised segmentation".

This needs a shift. In their research for a definition within personalisation, Chandra *et al.* suggested redeeming its true purpose to point towards the individuals within segment, not the segment itself.

"More often than not, personalisation is treated as a subset of segmentation, where the segment is taken as a whole, which does not embody the true meaning of personalisation. The comprehensive review herein makes clear that personalisation considers the aspects of purpose and context in its conceptualisation, and the drivers, parties involved, and context in its operationalisation, thereby making personalisation unique to the individual customer rather than to the entire customer segment."

Chandra et al., 2022[7]

Individualism it is, then.

Chapter 8

Insisting On Individualism

"The biggest opportunity is in reframing personalisation to be more user-centric."
Chris Gibbins, Chief Experience Officer, Creative CX[1]

O K, so personalisation is more than segmentation. We know that now. Chandra *et al.* (2022)[2] believe the pot of gold at the end of the rainbow is engraved with "one-to-one", and that's certainly what most believe too.

If personalisation, according to Sailthru, is therefore only classifiable as using customer behavioural data and preferences, as well as being able to predict the next set of actions a customer will likely take, then surely the only possibility is to classify it at a one-to-one level? By speaking to customers at this specific and individual level, the far right of this mythical maturity model, would this finally warrant the title of personalisation?

"It feels as though the definition and narrative have been crafted to talk about one-to-one personalisation and if we're not doing one-to-one, we're not doing personalisation. This is a scale, and that scale has been so warped by the preconditioned narrative that we feel, in order to deem that we are doing personalisation, we have to go really specific to be classed within that bucket."
Paul Randall, Senior Experimentation Strategist, Speero[3]

Randall's point above is something that's repeated a lot within personalisation watercooler conversations. Most likely because it's heralded as the ultimate place to be – the Olympic gold medal of marketing. Peppers & Rogers spoke about it in their 1993 book, *The One to One Future*,[4] the concepts of which were predicated on the age-old consumer sales model of walking into your local store, the salesperson recognising you, acknowledging you and personally helping you physically or with guidance based on prior knowledge of your purchases. Basically, the equivalent of walking into a pub and the bartender saying "the usual?" and pouring the beer a customer always has.

This is the utopia and has been crafted over years of redefinition and reinvention to talk about one-to-one personalisation being the *only* form of personalisation – almost as if everything else isn't worthy of such a title. If brands aren't doing one-to-one, they're not personalising. It explains why just changing a mobile experience for some customers isn't considered as personalisation. It's just not sexy enough.

Few things are. Except David Beckham.

Think of experiences that are hyper-personalised, like the bill you get from your Sky account, the popular UK broadband and media provider, demanding more money every month. "Every interaction and everything Sky knows about us as a customer is on the bill; it's literally one-to-one personalisation, but no one will ever say that's a great use of personalisation, even though you can't get more personalised than that," argues Simon Elsworth, Global Head of Experimentation, Whirlpool.[5]

OK. Technically speaking, the Sky account bill example is perfect personalisation. But in reality, it is just a series of a lot of response variables that are formulaic in nature. We learned about those recently.

There's something here about the level of investment in the personalised experience versus the granularity of the personalisation itself. Sky isn't redesigning the entire bill for customers, are they? They've invested in a structure, a format – a template – and they're populating that with basic, but still personalised, information. Yes, it's one-to-one, but there's a transactional nature to that kind of personalisation that loses its soul.

"What is personalisation?" is the question being asked in this slightly rhetorical and unnecessary conceptual thought. The answer to which we are narrowing down away from response variables, away from specific optimisation, past segmentation, and redefining what it means to be an individual; a soul. In this instance, it just feels too scientific.

Despite being one-to-one, the science of recognition trumps the purpose of the art. This is why it's cast to one side for not being sexy enough to actually represent personalisation properly. It speaks to us, but in a way that's soulless. It's relevant, yet it doesn't resonate. I think it's important to recognise that there is a difference between the two.

The fact of the matter is that in marketing, "one-to-one" is a term that's overused, overvalued and overwrought. Technically and philosophically, the concept of one-to-one can be achieved. However, practically, it's so rarely achieved that examples that do so are either dismissed for not being sexy enough, or they focus so much on the scale of reaching millions of people that, in doing so they lose their souls, where the personalised becomes paradoxically impersonal. There's also something to be said for consumers who have such distressingly high expectations of personalisation that, unless it's considered as talking to them individually, they ignore it. Not to mention the money, only the elite can splash the case to achieve one-to-one; unless you're Netflix and generate $31.47 billion[6] in revenue (in 2022), of course.

That doesn't stop the dreamers, though.

> "I do see adding your name to an experience as personalisation, you're giving a different variable for every single person. We hype it up to be something so incredible, and it has to be that every different person sees a different landing page, but these small little moments of me using your name, or just asking, 'Hi there, how's everything going?' is me personalising the content slightly. Me mentioning one of your pain points, is already personalising. It speaks to me and adds value."
>
> **Daphne Tideman, Growth Advisor & Consultant[7]**

"It speaks to *me*."

Speaking to people feels so barbaric in today's day and age. The idea of picking up a phone and talking fills everyone beyond a Millennial with dread. Yet, this is the most obvious way to define the term personalisation – and ironically, the most overlooked: the necessary presence of a person. Remember them?

"The lack of person in personalisation is a bad case of mislabelling," according to Andrew Frank of Gartner.[8] What is currently claimed as personal isn't personalised at all. Instead, it's an audience segment that doesn't always – rarely, in fact – use personal data. Where Thoughtworks once suggested that personalisation isn't personalisation because it lacks context, Frank suggests that it, in fact, lacks information about the person.

When a website audience is anonymous, rather than an individual, how can brands personalise toward them? Instead of giving a new user such as "David" an offer, brands might choose to give new users in general an offer. This lack of information about the individual is segmentation, not personalisation, because it omits information about the individual, according to Frank.

The prerequisite for personalisation is therefore is the use of personal data. Hereto we enter another debate — "What is classified as personal data?" Conflict still exists, with some claiming that even the inclusion of personal data isn't a good enough delineation — such as Matt Scaysbrook, Founder, WeTeachCRO.[9] "Is this personalisation? Do I consider the page that they went to as a personal attribute? Probably not."

There's no probably about it.

To delineate between data that is used for personal purposes and data that isn't, Gartner coined the term "Personification". It still has the word "person" in it after all, but it tries to focus on the impersonal word "persona" rather than "personal" (and consent-requiring) person. The "a" is very important, clearly. It means giving people relevant digital experiences based on their assumed membership in a defined customer segment, not on who they are or what they need as a person.

There is some acceptance of this argument among the marketing community. Although let us not forget that Gartner is a commercial entity, redefining a term for anything short of altruistic reasons could be questioned, as in all walks of life.

As Speero's Paul Randall suggested a few pages ago, the personalisation maturity scale has been so distorted by this preconditioned account that we feel that, in order to deem that we are employing personalisation, we have to be really specific about the variables to be classed within that bucket. In reality, as Tideman suggested, personalisation can be something as small as what resonates with an individual. This is now a conversation about art rather than science, which, in my opinion, is a much better reflection of what personalisation is intended to be.

On my quest for definition, I realised that we didn't necessarily need to define it but rather understand it. The why is more important than the what. Society conflates personalisation based on marketing principles; namely segmentation and optimisation. Seeing it at the far right of a mythical, alliterative maturity scale. It doesn't have to be one-to-one to be personal, and so I argue that it shouldn't sit on this scale. Instead, I believe that personalisation sits above it because it is a communication principle, not a marketing discipline. It is intended to speak to individuals personably, taking into account their context, designed to form the basis of a relationship.

You see where I'm going with this ...

Chapter 9

Connection & Conversation

"You're having a conversation. All your job is to listen and respond. That response is personalisation."

Siobhan Solberg, Founder & Consultant, Raze[1]

It is my opinion that personalisation is rooted in connection and conversation. The clue is in the name: personalisation.

All of us – consumers included – must take personalisation personally, or risk calling it something else entirely.

The -isation just allows us to form a noun corresponding to the verb to personalise (with an S, not a Z, by the way; we're not animals). Therefore, if the noun is to be personal, why are brands and retailers deliberately forgetting this?

Personalisation is necessary to be personable. The two can't live without each other because, spoiler alert, they are one and the same. Understanding that an individual has a qualitative response and that they are humans and not just figures on a spreadsheet. Brands need to recognise individuals for who they are.

When meeting a friend for coffee in real life, for example, knowing intimate elements of their life and remembering previous conversations, and even how they enjoy their coffee, perhaps, predicate a current conversation in simple recognition and relevancy. We recognise them, and we create relevant conversation topics that resonate with them. I'm fairly certain that when Brent Smith and Greg Linden, who wrote famously about Amazon recommendation systems and the future thereof, wrote that "discovery should be like talking with a friend who knows you, knows what you like, works with you at every step, and anticipates your needs",[2] they didn't mean plonking a series of products below the fold on a product detail page that matched black t-shirts with white t-shirts.

How is that an example of being familiar, relevant, liked, or trusted? Those are the foundations of connection. Consumers require a relationship with brands – even intimacy at times. And that brand relationship, like a human relationship, requires a lot of hand-holding, eye contact and whispers of sweet nothings.

The truth of the matter is that science — the rise of data and AI — has been placed at the heart of personalisation to reduce this effort. And doing so has diluted its purpose. Assumptions not predictions, impersonal algorithms not personal conversations, and relationships with screens not people.

Creating connection with people is not hard, so long as it's rooted in authenticity. In one study, just using the customer's name in brand communications was something that 57 per cent[3] of marketers believed to constitute the bare minimum of achieving a status in personalisation. Saying "Hello [First Name]" to a customer in a coffee shop is simple common courtesy. Simon Sinek goes one level above that and says it's not only "the greatest gift you can give someone" but it's "the acknowledgment of their existence".[4]

The start of a short-term relationship, sure, but by no means a guarantee they'll return, no matter how good the coffee. Retailers want us to have sex on the first date and convert in just one visit, so they assume they don't need to mention our name or create that connection.

The real reason why Starbucks writes customers' names on their cups isn't to piss you off by deliberately misspelling your name. David "Moon-heim" is the best I've seen. It's to establish a spark, a first impression and a connection. "Starbucks has a role and a meaningful relationship with people that is not only about the coffee," said Howard Schultz, CEO and founder of Starbucks.[5] This is similar to Howard's famous quote: "We're not in the coffee business serving people, but in the people business serving coffee."[6]

Wait. Starbucks is a personalisation business?

In the case of Starbucks, they use your name and the concept of personalisation to dovetail off what is known as the "Cocktail Party Effect" (Cherry, 1953),[7] a phenomenon whereby a human brain has the ability to focus its auditory attention on a particular stimulus while filtering out a range of other noises. This is selective hearing at its core, based on the principle that people can hear their name being mentioned even if they are far away in a crowded room. In the case of Starbucks, despite what we might think, the selection of what we pay attention to isn't random, it's based on what resonates with us most. There's that word again: resonance. Their own brand of personalisation is designed to grab customers' attention and establish a connection. It may feel much more than segmentation because it's rooted in the individual themselves.

Calling an individual by their first name is, of course, easier to do in real life than on a screen. How can that be replicated? It's not just a question held only for the purpose of a name, but in all online walks of life. Most practitioners who work online tend to relate their offline experiences in real life and ask how they can be replicated in their field of work. "What would happen in a store?" is a staple question from most middle-aged execs in all digital marketing workshops. This is the barometer for personalising an experience online.

Best Buy drop the "e" in "eCommerce" because they don't see the two as mutually exclusive. "It's not about bringing one to the other, but how the two work together. We just call it total retail because we're just one Best Buy. We're focused on helping customers shop on their terms".[8]

Practitioners who personalise are familiar with how we communicate naturally in an offline world. In stores. In coffee shops. Over the phone. The Internet has only existed for 40 years. It's old enough to know better, but young enough to still not care. (Just like me.) OK, let's give it a break, the Internet was also only popularised in 1995, so make that 28 years. But brands should be able to learn to simulate a good first impression online after 28 years of trying, should they not?

I had to.

What's fascinating about these conversations is that we're trying to emulate the personal experience of shopping in real life, but online. The adverse is also true. We're also trying to simulate the feeling of shopping online, but in the store. To shoehorn the world's most overused and ridiculed word — "Omnichannel" — has never felt more appropriate here. Burberry, for example, uses technology[9] that identifies if a consumer has purchased an item on their site before as soon as they walk in the store, allowing shop assistants to greet visitors by name and use knowledge of what items they've bought previously to direct them to things they might like. Of course, with this, permission is required. It's a bit creepy though, isn't it? Although perhaps it's just new, and consumers automatically fear things that aren't familiar.

Dropping the "e" in "eCommerce" as per Best Buy may have helped sales grow by 174 per cent,[10] but an emphasis on the delivery mechanism, the store or online, is a de-emphasis on the customers themselves. Whether it's the store, online, a kiosk or a watch, it doesn't matter; it's about providing a connection and sparking conversation between the brand and customer.

"Through more efficient online-to-offline connections, more personalized engagement and shopping experiences, we will enhance the customer experience and deepen brand loyalty."

Davis Lin, Vice President, Tencent[11]

According to Lin, what is rooted in real life is the premise of how to connect with customers. That's why customers gravitate toward conversations with brands that are more live. A study[12] by the Harvard Business Review confirmed this finding, where consumers are motivated more by the emotional value of a brand than any other factor. Social media being a mere simulation of the communication of that brand value where a co-creation value is enhanced by social customer engagement (Nadeem et al., 2021).[13] There's that word again: communication.

Making a connection feel real and authentic should therefore be every brand's objective within personalisation, regardless of delivery mechanism; connection is just the foundation stone. If we're debating where personalisation comes in the sequence of optimising something, it wouldn't be absurd to suggest that perhaps personalisation is just a solution to segmentation rather than a mirror discipline that follows it. Something that sits above it, or below it, not necessarily next to it. After all, you can personalise a segment. Whereas segmentation is the process of carving up your audience, personalisation is about making those audiences feel more human. You're doing something in segmentation, you're making someone feel a way in personalisation. Definition solved, Manjunath.

A Definition for the Ages

The term personalisation has been so rooted in taking a large audience and splitting it up that perhaps a redefinition *is* on the cards, despite everything I profess against. It's a scary word after all. Personalisation with a big "P" rather than just a little "p". And in the interest of putting the person back into personalisation, being more personable with our audiences, redefining it as "humanisation" wouldn't be too crazy an idea. It's part of the reason why Gartner wanted to redefine it as "personification" back in 2015. It has good intent. If we just watch and listen to how people behave in front of our eyes and try to be more responsive to what we're seeing, that's one of the most human things around. Brands simply don't listen enough to be able to respond appropriately. Brands want to sleep with consumers on the first date and so move to the younger model more quickly.

There is a lack of clarity as to what it is because personalisation has only this overly-generic, fit-for-all dictionary definition. This provides little understanding of its purpose. The purpose can change culturally, evolve societally, or differ from organisation to organisation. For example, personalisation for Google Drive is different from the purpose of personalisation for the BBC. Whereby, perhaps overly simplistically, the former is about access and speed and the latter is about membership loyalty and relevance. Their definition of personalisation might well be the same as others', but their purpose is specific to them.

So, what have we learned here?

Definitions of personalisation are either incorrect, quirky, or commercially self-serving, and more than a little divisive. And so, we continually discuss it because it provides us with a modicum of entertainment. But they are necessary, or so we think. Personally, I question the whole value and purpose of what a singular definition of personalisation brings to this quest. It feels oxymoronic to provide a universal definition for something that's supposed to be individual.

To finish, the soul at the centre of personalisation is about building relationships. It's about a connection. It's about communication. It's about acknowledgement. It's about familiarity. It's about loyalty. It's about ensuring that brands do not forget the first three syllables of the very word they yearn for so much: per-son-al. The truth is that brands place so much value in having a singular definition that it becomes excusable to do anything but have that singular definition. And so they rarely move past the point of implementing personalisation as nothing more than a tactical add on to say they're doing it. Or on the mythical scale, seeing personalisation as formulaic and overly scientific past the point of segmentation. Where segmenting is an act of doing – cutting up one problem into multiples – personalising is an act of communicating. It's not sequential, it's an approach to how brands connect with their consumers. A genre of art, rather than a specific painting; a communication principle, rather than a marketing one.

Therefore, it's not the definition that matters, but the purpose. *Why* brands personalise is an infinitely more powerful question than *what* personalisation is. To understand why, and the reason why the expectations are set as they are and the insensible parts that led consumers to want personalised experiences so much, we must understand what makes being personable so desirable to begin with.

Part III

Paradise Lost

"'How do we know that personalisation will work?'
And the replies were usually, 'It's personalisation, innit?'"
Simon Elsworth, Global Head of Experimentation, Whirlpool[1]

There's a constitutional belief that personalisation will just work. After seeing what personalisation is currently defined as, what it should be seen as, and the variety of excuses that live within the minds of practitioners, it was important for me to understand where this unshaken belief in it comes from.

Personalisation's complexity has created continuous fragmented conflict. It's a boxing fight where even the ring girls throw in a few punches. When asked why personalisation is the best thing since sliced bread, all I've ever heard as a response can be distilled down to Elsworth's answer: "It's personalisation, innit?" Such a simple, beautiful Millennial phrase.

But I need more than that to complete my hero's quest. I need a dragon's head on a plate.

Today, brands don't just want to personalise, they see it as a necessity. They see personalisation purely as some Metaverse-like fad that won't flush – but it's lasted twenty years and is only getting more hyped. Without getting any better.

Why has personalisation been allowed to stay the same?

When I spoke to Andre Morys, CEO of German optimisation consultancy konversionsKRAFT,[2] he spoke about brands having this utopian idea of relevance and emotional resonance, always looking for the world to accept those ideals – that's what personalisation is to them. It's creepy, with religious overtones. But it's true.

"Personalisation is the only solution to achieve the highest level of an experience. With great personalisation you can really deliver something that people did not expect and make others love your brand. But that's how it is seen, not how it is done. I see a big gap between the two and that makes me sad."

Andre Morys, CEO, konversionsKRAFT[3]

It makes me sad too, Andre.

Before I begin to explain the paradox, the optimist within me wants to understand, and share out loud, why brands and practitioners peddle the personalisation piece over and over to sustain the hype. I want us all to understand *why* every year is called the "Year of Personalisation" when no year has ever lived up to that. Isolating a belief system for a single year seems almost desperate, akin to a last-ditch attempt to resuscitate it from death. It's been deemed by those in power unable to die, and so it remains like Schwarzenegger's Terminator — always f*cking coming back. In this chapter, I equate personalisation to *Paradise Lost*: an attempt to understand something that has clearly fallen down.

The history and evolution of marketing as a practice goes some way towards helping us understand why personalisation is where it is right now. As marketing has evolved, so too has its sophistication, both in terms of how brands sell, psychologically how buyers behave and, of course, the technological advancements. It just makes sense. Not just that, though, but it feels as though vendors and brands have hijacked personalisation and turned it into something that's more utopian, more paradisiacal, than what it's meant to be, which in turn means it will always fall short of its true purpose ...

Chapter 10

Don't Believe the Hype

"To me, we passed the year of personalisation within the hype cycle, and we're in the times of deflated expectations, and now we're going back up again to the plateau of productivity."

Ton Wesseling, Conversion optimisation and experimentation consultant[1]

If every year is the year of personalisation, which year is the *true* year? To help us understand where personalisation actually is in terms of hype, we can turn to the Gartner Hype Cycle. This graph – a bell curve with a tall rise, short dip, and long plateau; think of a Nike Swoosh followed by an inverted Nike Swoosh followed by another Nike Swoosh – depicts how consumers adore technology but care little about its adoption. Hence the (over) use of the word "hype". The cycle is designed to identify the risks and opportunities associated with technology and whether society adopts something too early, too late, gives up too soon, or hangs on too long. In short, it wants to know if all the hype is real. It feels extremely pertinent for personalisation where the hype seems to never fade ... nor actualise.

First introduced in 1995, the Gartner Hype Cycle consists of five inflection points:

1) Technology Trigger
2) Peak of Inflated Expectations
3) Trough of Disillusionment
4) Slope of Enlightenment
5) Plateau of Productivity

They feel like beautifully crafted milestones inspired by the likes of Hollywood. *Harry Potter and The Trough of Disillusionment* would make for a great film about the once boy-wizard as he enters middle age.

Anyway, according to the digital marketing hype cycle (one of 95 hype cycles designed by Gartner) personalisation popped up on *Indiana Jones and The Slope of Enlightenment* way back in 2015 before vanishing mysteriously. *Evanesco!** That was eight years ago. It now languishes, I guess, in detention with *Harry Potter and The Trough of Disillusionment.* The slope, the fourth stage, is when early adopters see additional benefits and start to adapt the technology to their brand. It hasn't been seen on the cycle before that point and appears to have arrived on the scene like an overly familiar yet introverted, reclusive neighbour. Dynamic Yield, a world-leading provider of personalisation software, concurs. They outwardly noticed a change in the vernacular of how people talk about personalisation in that same year of 2015 when personalisation appeared on the Hype Cycle. They wrote: "Three to five years ago [between 2013 and 2015], the word personalisation barely appeared in any RFP."[2]

Something happened that year.

A friendly reminder, though, that there is still only a 5 per cent adoption rate by the time the product hits this stage (Fenn, 2007).[3] So, despite the assumption that others will start to adopt it, and 2015 was the year of personalisation, the reality is that barely anyone actually has to date.

What's curious here is that Gartner classified personalisation as a technology with a two-year lifespan before becoming mainstream. And so, by 2018, it had gone, vanished into thin air, just as Keyser Söze would do. Past, or well into, the meandering oscillation seen within *Indiana Jones and The Slope of Enlightenment,* and almost all but skipping *The Good, The Bad and The Plateau of Productivity.*

Wait. Stop the bus.

In 2018, did brands not yet realise the benefits of personalisation? *Still?*

While personalisation's hype may be perpetual, its sense of success is always on the horizon. A certain narrative within understanding perceptions of personalisation for this book is the notion that the value isn't worth the effort. A good chunk of the pooh-poohers of personalisation** continually referred to the juice "not being worth the squeeze". Personalisation has therefore remained in *Harry Potter and The Trough of Disillusionment* for the past twenty years, which feels rather appropriate, as Wesseling concluded. After all, Fenn (2007)[4] described this stage as one where "the technology does not live up to its overinflated expectations, [and so] rapidly becomes unfashionable". Like all future *Star Wars* films, no doubt. According

---

* I know you already know this, but *Evanesco* is a vanishing spell in the Harry Potter wizarding world.
** This was a genuine contender for the title of this book.

to Gartner, by 2018, personalisation had become unfashionable and had all but been discarded.

That doesn't mean that's how all consumers or brands felt. It's just their interpretation. Gartner's research methodology appears to be a closely guarded secret. They use language, such as "consensus" to position technologies based on hype.[5] To that point, like any treble-Nike-Swooshed model, the hype cycle isn't without its critics. If at the *Indiana Jones and The Slope of Enlightenment* only 5 per cent of a certain technology has been adopted, we must question whether there is enough sample size for descriptive empirical research. It feels as though there isn't.

Just when hope had all but gone, in the same year of 2018, the familiar saviour of personalisation came back into the fold – the engines that run it.

Personalisation engines give you the ability to accelerate personalisation as a marketing practice on your website. They came storming into the Hype Cycle, immediately thrown into the abyss – the *Harry Potter and The Trough of Disillusionment*. This is the phase where there are identified concerns about problems implementing the technology, or what Fenn (2007) describes as "Things Gone Wrong".[6] How fascinating that as soon as the concept of personalisation was to leave the hype cycle, it is only to be replaced by the very thing that makes it function.

Even more curious is the slow, winding crawl of the big brother of personalisation, the arbitrarily named "personification".

We've identified that Andrew Frank, a distinguished VP Analyst at Gartner, first coined the term "personification" in March of 2015. He wrote a blog post titled "The Personification of Digital Marketing", in which he describes the need to classify audience segments that have been irreversibly de-identified. That is, targeting personas and anonymous users without the need for personal identification, in a bid to put the customer back in control. A valid argument, and one that still holds true today, nearly eight years later. That very same year, in 2015, personification entered the mixer, straight into the technology trigger – the very first stage. This was at the same time that personalisation was starting to squeeze its way out. The phrase that Gartner coined jumps straight in at number one, in the diagram that Gartner created, whilst personalisation is on its way out.

The plot thickens.

Personification meandered its way through hype cycle space and time. It originally had a two-to-five best before date until mainstream adoption. Fast-forward three years later to the year 2018 and we find that personification has barely moved forward. Its classification had increased from a two-to-five-year plateau to a five-to-ten-year plateau. Someone believes it should stay alive, clearly.

Even now, in 2023, personification has only just entered *Harry Potter and The Trough of Disillusionment*. This is when early adopters report low returns on investment and predictable performance issues, so the hype starts to wear off. Personalisation was here eight years ago, in 2015. In marketing years, that was an aeon ago. David Bowie was still alive.

The curious case of personalisation in the Gartner Hype Cycle reads like a murder mystery — more of a whydunnit, than a whodunnit. But a page-turner nonetheless. Its sudden appearance in the fourth stage, *Indiana Jones and The Slope of Enlightenment*, in 2015 only to then just vanish and suddenly be replaced by personalisation engines three years later — only to be followed by the rejuvenation of it with a new brand name of personification, arguably the same thing to many, is beyond curious. Not even Indiana can solve this one. Once again, it's a question of definition. That very same thing was coined by the same people who make the hype cycle itself.

The cynics among us might believe that the constant redefinition of personalisation is a bid by those selling it to keep it alive. That's not to suggest that the Gartner Hype Cycle is incorrect in any form; it has a purpose and, like most frameworks, has its critics. If anything, it spotlights the very same thing that we are debating here and now: the paradoxical positioning within the market. Is personalisation designed for good or for evil? Is it used for the benefit of the customer or for the benefit of the brand? Should we segment like this or like that? Ohhh the Hokey Cokey ...

Even if this is true, constant redefinitions seem to resuscitate and rejuvenate personalisation. We must grap our whips, not forgetting our fedora, and ask what the motive is. Why do people want to keep personalisation alive? If used verbatim, the Gartner Hype Cycle doesn't help us much to understand the why. To know that, we'll need to peer into a potted history of personalisation and make inferences from there.

Chapter 11

Origin Story:
The History of Personalisation

"When WebTrends-Optimize came out 22 years ago, we did personalisation but
we just called it targeting."
Sandeep Shah, Director of Product, WebTrends-Optimize[1]

To understand where the personalisation hype train started from and its
subsequent journey, we must first return to its origins and trace its earliest steps.
Only at its inception can we perhaps predict its future.

Back In The Day

The principles underlying why we interact with others have remained consistent over
the past century, it is only the manner in which we do so that has changed. The way we
need and want to interact with other people has altered because of how technology
has changed. These philosophies have extended to brand communications, too –
modern-day advertising, if you will.

Johann Gutenberg, who made the first printing machine with movable type, is
often called the "Father of Mass Communication".[2] Prior to Gutenberg, most trading
and advertising was done by word-of-mouth. After it, newspapers, the first form of
mass-media publication, soon came hot off the press. In doing so, it ushered in an
information age geared toward mass media and advertising. When the rise of the
Internet truly took off in the mid-1990s it was a moment that was so game changing
that it was spoken of with the same reverence as Gutenberg's invention.

"What has died is the mass-media business model – injuring, perhaps mortally,
a host of institutions it symbiotically supported: publishing, broadcasting, mass
marketing, mass production, political parties, possibly even our notion of a nation.
We are coming at last to the end of the Gutenberg Age."
Jeff Jarvis, Journalist and CUNY professor[3]

Turn of the Century

As society developed and shaped its marketing sophistication, a one-size-fits-all form of messaging that appealed to as many people as possible felt impersonal. Conceptually, academics began to recognise the heterogeneity of marketplaces that comprised of similar groups of people based on their requirements and desires (Smith, 1956).[4] In reality, individual requirements were only extended as far as Henry Ford famously saying about the Ford Model T, "You can have any colour you want as long as it is black."[5] It was seen more as advertising a product by creating awareness than creating some form of relationship. Was one needed as a prerequisite for the other? Did brands even need to create a relationship in order to advertise? Back in the day, the answer was almost certainly no.

General Motors, Ford's biggest competitors at the time, pioneered market segmentation strategies as an alternative to Ford's one-size-fits-all. In fact, it is still one of the biggest examples in the world of doing so. President Alfred P Sloan, famously stated, "A car for every purse and purpose," where each car and its product line were intended to appeal to a different segment of customers. A buyer might start with a Chevrolet and gradually trade up to a fancier Oldsmobile, Buick, or Cadillac. This is still how the car industry works today. And society too, as it happens.

Tail of The Century

That was segmentation, not personalisation, however. A distinct difference covered in the previous chapter. This was the era of segmentation, according to Richard Tedlow's *The Story of Mass Marketing in America*.[6] In the 1980s, however, there was a shift towards hyper-segmentation. In other words, even more narrow market segments. It was mostly seen as a tool to increase the response rates of mail surveys. Researchers were mostly looking at ways to improve the response rates, either qualitatively or quantitatively. No wonder hyper-personalisation is the next step up from personalisation, it was stolen from Tedlow.

Anything beyond segmentation was difficult and expensive, and it wasn't until the advent of computer power that we moved towards this famed concept: hyper-segmentation (Petrison et al., 1997).[7] It allowed marketers to communicate with individuals or very small groups of customers. A particular inflection point and use case was the rise of email marketing in the 1990s. It made it one of the first channels in which personalisation became truly established. With easily available data at your fingertips, segmenting audiences was simple, and personalising was as simple as entering the user's name into the email. Rasmus Houlind, CXO at Agillic, a marketing automation platform, appreciates this and gives a subtle satirical hat tip to it in his book about how to personalise, *Hello $FirstName*.[8] Great title. Not jealous at all.

Regardless of whether it was called segmentation, personalisation or one-to-one, it was seen as a marketing milestone. In 1995, Leonard Berry, a marketing professor at Texas A&M University, went on to coin the term "Relationship Marketing",[9] dovetailing from the works of Dale Carnegie.

"The impetus for its development has come from the maturing of services marketing with the emphasis on quality, increased recognition of potential benefits for the firm and the customer, and technological advances," Berry wrote.

Another watershed moment occurred a year prior, in 1994, when gilet-wearing new-billionaire Jeff Bezos founded Amazon. They were significant catalysts, as we've already identified. Bezos wrote to shareholders in the early days, citing that "through personalisation, online commerce will accelerate the very process of discovery".[10] You can't get more overt or clairvoyant than that.

In the later stages of that decade, the focus shifted to personalisation within service delivery, too. It was no longer just about response rates from mailing campaigns but customer satisfaction (Grove & Fisk, 1992[11]; Hornik *et al.*, 1991[12]) This was a cornerstone in the movement towards relationship marketing and, thus, a movement towards the true objective of personalisation.

The Millennium Age

In the decade that followed in the 2000s, customer focus and centricity was the buzz. It still is. Personalised marketing studies conducted inside the limits of the Internet arose, describing the growth of the eMarketing mix, the use of technology, and expanding on the evidence of relationship marketing. The emergence of technologies helped this era with decision support systems, mobile advertising and those beautiful things we now know as recommender systems.

The "Big Netflix Prize" was a 2006 competition that outsourced building the Netflix recommendation algorithm for personalising content.

Fun fact: the first and second teams on the leaderboard reported exactly the same 10.06 per cent uplift in root mean square error (RMSE), but because the first team, BellKor's Pragmatic Chaos, submitted their entry 24 minutes before the second, The Ensemble, they won.[13] And despite that, they never even used it! "It did not seem to justify the engineering effort needed to bring them into a production environment", apparently. Once again, we discuss whether the juice is actually worth the squeeze.

The Decade of Personalisation

In the 1990s, it was Amazon. The noughties belonged to Netflix, who crowned themselves the new kid on the block of personalisation. They tied their success into it, too, regardless of how well, or poor, we now deem them to be at it. And in the 2020s, it's about that TikTok.

Technology has interrupted our connection with others. In some cases, it's accelerated; in others, it's dampened, even prohibited. There is no greater impact than that of social media, especially when we think about our relationships with friends and family. At first, it was meant to help us keep the relationships we already had while giving us the chance to make new, deeper ones. Such technology has had a demonstrable impact on our social lives. Good or bad, we'll leave it to the economists, activists and politicians to figure that one out. Given that TikTok may be banned in the USA before the end of the year, perhaps it is the politicians who are figuring that out on our behalf.

Sure, there are those who complain about the deterioration of social ties due to social media. But those people also complained about radio, motion pictures, television and — the closest previous technology to Internet adoption — the telephone. Magazine articles, such as "Does the telephone break up home life and the old practice of visiting friends?"[14] appeared with concerns that this new technology would hurt relationships and isolate people. Sound familiar?

It begs the question: How do we build and maintain relationships with others while at the same time living with and accepting this technology? We are living in the decade of personalisation. It's too late to turn back. We must embrace it. I'm curious, though, is there a specific year where this accelerated beyond recognition? That we can pinpoint where that embrace will happen or has already happened? A year that we can finally crown "The Year of Personalisation"?

Chapter 12

The Years of Personalisation

"Personalization is a term for customer centricity in the digital age, with the goal of replicating our 'in real life' store associate experiences."

Nathan Richter, Vice President Program
Strategy & Insights, Dynamic Yield[1]

There are dates that might be of some historic importance within the timeline of personalisation. Such as the earliest use of personalised direct marketing letters,[2] which dates back to 1870. Or fast-forward to 1940, when *Time* magazine found that the first use of personalised salutations, *Hello David*, increased the response rate by six times.[3] These moments are cool, but they don't seem useful to us in modern times. I just want you to know I've done my homework.

Of all the historical inflection points within personalisation, 2015 seemed to be the biggest for some reason. It's hard to guess where personalisation first precisely entered the fold. In my quest, I'm not much interested in when it started precisely, only when it accelerated. There was something about this year when "Netflix and Chill" became an actual real thing, the Jedi ushered in a new hope with *The Force Awakens* and Donald Trump was unlikely to become US President. How quickly things changed.

2015: The Year of Personalisation

Human civilisation may have discovered water on Mars in 2015, but they also discovered personalisation. This was the year. There was something about this year that felt right – one of the main reasons is that it was this year where the term first appeared within Gartner's Hype Cycle.

Whilst the hype suggested one thing, it was the advent of technology that made personalisation feel more real. Google introduced its latest artificial intelligence algorithm, *RankBrain* which was hailed as a game-changer by many in the industry. This update interpreted the intent behind a user's search terms, making for a more relevant result: the good first impression of personalisation.

In addition, take the now-famous, and then-recently acquired, personalisation platform Dynamic Yield. Although they were founded in 2012, even sources suggested that it wasn't until 2015 that they began experiencing "sustained hyper-growth". While that sounds like something you might hear before going into warp speed, or a GP's consultation room, there was something about this year. An investor in Dynamic Yield, Aviad Ariel at Vertex Ventures, called the market "nascent and noisy" and cited the evident opportunity as a reason for part of their $22 million investment round. "Moving away from point solutions, towards recent developments in machine learning and AI that amplify the personalisation opportunity," was the reason, he said.[4]

The market was certainly noisy. The number of MarTech companies that existed, in general, was double that of the previous year, hovering around the 2,000 mark. Personalisation, of which had its own category with "chat", was a title that was undeserving of the methodology. It included vendors such as Monetate and Evergage, both of which were acquired by their larger counterparts of Kibo Commerce and Salesforce five years later.

The very same Marketing technology landscape evolved to include over 3,500 a year later, in 2016. This time, however, personalisation was not under the accompanying category of chat. But instead it was within the "Optimisation, Personalization and Testing" category. Bringing the personalisation fanboys into the more mature and popular group of optimisation and testing. This seemed quite pivotal, recognising its importance in marketing society, and has remained so since.

2016: The Year of Personalisation
"If 2015 was the personalization warm-up; 2016 is game time."[5] So said KickDynamic.

In 2016, Guy Yalif started Intellimize, a no code experience optimisation platform, with Jin Lim and Brian Webb after spending 15 years in ad tech. He watched marketers invest heavily in personalising the right message to the right prospect at the right time (there's that phrase again) in ads and email ... and then forget all of that when those same prospects reached the marketer's website to buy. Ironic given that that was the place where conversion happens. Websites typically show everyone the same thing all the time. Yalif, Lim, and Webb validated this need by talking to more than 100 marketers and at a CXL conference[6] the previous year. Since then, the team at Intellimize has been powering personalisation for loads of brands, creating custom experiences for each unique visitor based on where they are in the funnel at the point in time. They're clearly onto something because Intellimize have received $52m[7] in funding and has since been recognised in 2022 by Inc. 5000 as one of America's fastest growing private companies.[8]

So, 2016 was definitely "The Year of Personalisation".

2017: The Year of Personalisation

Not quite.

Business2Community.com stepped up and crowned 2017 year "The Year of Personalisation". It was also in 2017 that Amazon was presented with the Test of Time award, an homage to the paper Liden and Smith wrote in 2003, "Two Decades of Recommender Systems".[9] It marked twenty years since Amazon first introduced recommendations back in 1998 and established its core principles of recommendation systems such as item-based collaborative filtering — still used today (hence, the Test of Time award).

Segment first published their now famed "State of Personalisation Report" in 2017, too. As did Epsilon, a global leader in digital experience service providers, who published their research report, "The Impact of Personalization on Marketing Performance".[10] Both found that 80 per cent of respondents indicated they are more likely to do business with a company if it offers personalised experiences, and 90 per cent indicated that they find personalisation appealing. Numbers like that don't lie. And cannot be ignored.

2018: The Year of Personalisation

In 2018, it wasn't just Prince Harry and Meghan Markle walking down the aisle towards global hysteria; so too did personalisation. There was something about 2018 that seemed more pivotal than most years. If 2015 was the first baby steps of personalisation, 2018 was the first word.

There was certainly some movement among the big players. Salesforce, jumped on the annual tradition of naming personalisation as the next big thing. Netflix talked about their artwork personalisation for the first time at the Vancouver RecSys Conference. Amazon's Personalize was announced at AWS as the new recommendation engine, a fully-managed service with no machine learning experience required.

Technology helped brands facilitate personalisation, of course. The majority of brands were already there, apparently, with one study suggesting that 45 per cent of businesses had already tailored their websites to individual preferences, with another 40 per cent planning to do so.[11] Despite that, the state of the industry felt underwhelming. One of the angel investors in Mutiny, a no-code AI personalisation platform, claimed that websites were still just an "afterthought" when really they were "the most important marketing asset".[12] Quite a déjà vu moment – this is the same pattern that Yalif saw three years earlier with Intellimize. It is interesting that the same industry issues transcended three years seemingly impervious to the march of time. The quirks of progress.

According to Jaleh Rezaei, co-founder at Mutiny, in 2018 the current state of the personalisation market was a mix of two different types of products. The first: personalisation is merely a minor feature of a larger platform. Every product tends to have some level of personalised offering. The second: genuine personalisation products that, as she calls it, "enable the plumbing of personalisation" but at the same time, still require a tonne of expertise to figure out how to operationalise it.

Given that the dynamic duo found that the average marketing team didn't have access to such wealth of resources or experience required to personalise, Mutiny was born designed to reduce that effort. It is one of the fastest-growing platforms in the space, backed by Sequoia Capital and receiving over $70 million in funding.[13]

2019: The Year of Personalisation

In 2019, *The Mandalorian* came bearing gifts of a *Star Wars* series redeeming the prequels, a Baby Yoda and the promise that this year was *the* year of personalisation. This time, I mean it. There was a vote and everything.

According to the 341 members of the ANA, the Association of National Advertisers, personalisation was awarded the Marketing Word of the Year Award.[14] They found that questions from members on personalisation really ramped up in the previous year, accelerated in 2019 and was worthy of such a title.

It was this year, too, that Liad Agmon, founder of Dynamic Yield, sold Dynamic Yield to ...

McDonald's?

Many in the industry were surprised by the $300 million acquisition, as SaaS platforms are typically acquired by other cross-functional platforms to create synergies. But a fast-food retailer? It's rare, although it's becoming more common. Walmart established its own technology incubator in Store No.8.[15] And in the same year as this acquisition, Nike acquired Zodiac Metrics, a consumer data analytics firm specialising in predictive analytics.[16]

But McDonald's? That surprised the McHell out of everyone this year.

Even if McDonald's were to sell Dynamic Yield to Mastercard in 2021, their rationale for the McPersonalisation was clear. They did so to serve recommendations in more than 12,000 drive-thrus in just six months as part of their growth strategy, "Accelerating the Arches", which I go into more detail about later on, don't worry. There's that recommendations narrative again, though.

2020 onwards: The Years of Personalisation

From the research I found on my quest, the pivotal moments for personalisation were certainly in the years between 2015 and 2019. Sure — there were moments thereafter, but the adventure to find the year of personalisation was put on hold for a couple of years. I wonder why. Moving away from a period of mass marketing towards a period of mass hysteria, there was a lot going on, if you can remember.

In 2020, Boston Consulting Group researched that the No.1 goal for digital transformations was still customer centricity and personalisation, cited by 9 out of 10 executives.[17] A year later, Gartner also found that 32 per cent of 350[18] marketing leaders expressed that personalisation was among the top three of their digital objectives for this year, "creating and delivering personalised experiences for customers", to be exact. Adobe agreed. IBM agreed. Personalisation at scale will top enterprise priorities in 2021, they said.[19] It was clearly still at the forefront of people's minds.

It wasn't just the statistics that showcased personalisation as the thing for the year, but academic research, too. In their 2022 study, "Personalization in Personalized Marketing: Trends and Ways Forward", Chandra et al., analysed 383 publications by popularity and recency. They found that 2020 was actually the genuine year of personalisation as it contained the highest number of publications published about the topic — 57 to be precise.[20] Up from 41 the year earlier, and easily setting records for not only the number of publications about personalisation, but the number of contributing authors. It certainly seems as though the topic was the most popular it's ever been and that the industry was more curious than ever. Or, there were loads of researchers with a lot of free time for some reason.

These years also saw an exponential increase in the number of software vendors offering and acquiring personalisation. VWO created their personalisation product called "Personalize". Attraqt, a platform in AI-powered search, was acquired by Crownpeak Holdings.[21] AB Tasty purchased Epoq, an AI-driven recommendation and smart search solution.[22] In a head-scratching move, Mastercard bought Dynamic Yield, from McDonald's, staking a claim away from the retail-owned personalisation product space, to the financially-owned personalisation product space. Qubit, a leader in AI-driven personalisation since 2010, was acquired by Coveo, a cloud platform for search and discovery. Optimizely, the well-known experimentation platform made their personalisation product generally accessible, aptly called "Personalization". The list goes on.

> "The potential is really exciting because if you think about it, ten years from now people will look back at today and be shocked at how impersonal and generic and one-to-many we call the 'web'. And, in the future, if you look at companies like Amazon or Google or Facebook, they're really pioneering the idea of using data about an individual to give them a better experience. And part of the reason we took this round of funding was to really invest in web site personalization and enable businesses to show exactly the right thing to the right person at the right time."
>
> Dan Siroker, Founder, Optimizely[23]

The reason for this increase in personalisation engines was thanks to the advent of AI. After the pandemic panic of the year before, in 2021, global venture capitalist investment into AI technology shot up by 48 per cent,[24] reaching all-time highs. Investors with deep pockets have never been more bullish that AI will be a disruptive technology. Jasper, an AI copy platform, raised $6 million in a seed round after just being born in January of that year, only to raise a further $125 million a year later.[25] AI is the lord and saviour for personalisation, and the answer to the eleventh-hour prayer, "we need to personalise at scale".

2023: The Year of Personalisation

Coincidentally and equally hilarious, in early 2023, Inc.com just published why 2023 will be the year of personalisation.[26] Another clairvoyant within the marketing industry.

Let's just call 2023 the year of personalisation, OK?

One of the reasons for this constant clairvoyance of calling every year the year of personalisation, apart from the obvious click-bait headline, is the pandemic. It felt as though the pandemic created a shift, or acceptance, of a heightened customer experience, and personalisation was the answer to that.

"The biggest shift — other than the massive disruption caused by the pandemic — is a move toward true, multi-touch omni-channel experiences driven by customer expectations."

Gregory Ng, CEO, Brooks Bell[27]

There has therefore been a shift in consumer expectations, but I still see 2023 being like every other year. AI is on the rise with the advent of ChatGPT, and every tech provider on the planet is falling over themselves to replicate the commercial success of it.

The point isn't in the *when*, it's in the meandering away from the purpose. The fact that 65 per cent of consumers say personalisation earns loyalty in 2023[28] is a step in the right direction towards creating relationships. It moves the narrative away from tactical add-ons.

If we can find that every year is the year of personalisation, it means all years are — or no years are — and we have to just accept that with each new year personalisation keeps getting re-defined to include more definitions. Hyper-this, and one-to-one-that. More recently, and perhaps a sign of the times, I've even heard personalisation being called p13n. The Alpha generation really does have to abbreviate everything nowadays, don't they? There are 13 characters between the first "p" and the last "n", hence the name. Although this feels a bit seedy to me, as this is just one "s" short from being a SMS-influenced countdown conundrum for "penis".

It doesn't matter if the ANA gives it an award, or if it shape-shifts again, personalisation is the red wine stain on a white carpet. It's going nowhere, figuratively and metaphorically. Sure, it might have its critics. And sure, if we believe what we see with the definition-rejuvenation paradox, it might morph into something else. Hans Hoogenboom, Head of CRO at Search Laboratory, and one of my favourite cynics, told me when discussing this future: "I think personalisation will get a new jacket. We'll probably call it something else and it will be re-marketed in a never-ending circle, pretending it's something completely new that you can charge money for."[29]

It's not the definition that keeps personalisation alive, it's the belief. If Jedi can be called a religion, so too can personalisation. (Please let that make me a Jedi Master.) This hype is clearly not going away. For the past eight years, at least, companies have been bullish on personalisation capabilities, as demonstrated by the acquisitions, the funding and the quotes and comments of experts around the world with a particular inflection point coming in 2015 and again in 2018.

When this hyper hype of personalisation started no one thought it was pertinent to ask *why*? *Why* do brands need to personalise? And *why* do consumers want it?

Answering this question may help us better appreciate its current position in the market and what brands can do to truly harness it.

Chapter 13

Vendor-Tinted Glasses

"Personalisation's popularity has been largely the result of MarTech companies successfully promoting their own personalisation technologies."

Samuel Scott, Columnist, The Drum[1]

That's some statement, Samuel. And it's one that plenty of the practitioners I interviewed agreed with.

I understand that when a certain approach gains popularity, it can lead to the creation of new businesses. Brilliant for the economy. These businesses aim to assist those operating in the market and make the very thing they are selling more accessible. Undoubtedly, in recent times, the concept of personalisation has gained a tonne of traction, especially in the context of creating marketable products from third-party vendors. This is where the personalisation hype train has accelerated.

The question surrounds the ethics and practice of these vendors. Addressing the taboo idea that such marketing is a factor of exploitation, not explanation.

In an interview, a source (who shall remain nameless) recalled a story of how a third-party vendor in an adjacent space already had the ability to personalise experiences. Indeed, that's how their users were already using the platform in some instances. The vendor saw dollar signs. To monopolise on this opportunity, the vendor decided to rebrand a part of their product dedicated to personalisation, repackage it with the same features, and sell it as an additional upsell – jumping on the proverbial bandwagon. That platform and upsell still exist today.

These vendors create case studies, commission research, and evangelise the wonders of personalisation almost as a religion, such is their raison d'être. They are all perfectly entitled to market their own products based on their independent research or experiences. This is advertising 101.

However, when products get oversold, it can start to become a problem. Recall the last time you bought a car. You've probably seen an advert on TV. A handsome, suburban, mid-30s man not unlike myself, alone, driving at speed in a shiny, clean car through some long and winding road towards a mountain peak, looking smug. "I want that!" you yell at the TV. The expectation that that car will change your life because of its dynamic manoeuvring capabilities built into the steering from the ground up is how it starts. Of course, it's bullshit. After three weeks in that new car, the new car smell has disappeared. You still loathe your two-hour daily commute on a congested M4. Your kids are screaming at you, "Dad, I dropped my ice cream!" They're kicking the back of your seat with their muddy boots. "Not the leather interior!"

This is when advertising does not meet expectations.

The car didn't change the reality. All it did was set unrealistic expectations.

Just like personalisation.

We've all heard of 150 per cent increases in conversion here and 500 per cent increases in revenue there. The fallacy of accurately attributing revenue to personalisation is one that's not only misunderstood but just plain incorrect. It shifts the conversation away from being a story about relationships and towards a story about how thick your wallet is. A commercialised story – a dragon we will seek to vanquish later in the book. If Dynamic Yield found that only 35 per cent of brands were able to tie their work to quantitative results in their 2021 annual maturity audit, what are the other 65 per cent doing? How can such claims of unrealistic increase in revenue be accurate? In the same study, 22 per cent of respondents said that their personalisation success stories were completely non-existent.[2]

"As the tech tools started releasing personalisation as functionality. A lot of the hype and visibility came from technology saying both how great, fast, efficient and easy it is. It was over sold. It's a major problem over the past six years that I'm still seeing in 2022. Saying you don't need a web team because of how easy something sets bad expectations. This leads to the second problem thinking that personalisation sucks, because we didn't do it well, because we were lied to."

Jeremy Epperson, Chief Growth Officer, Conversion Advocates[3]

The belief that technology will fix our problems is a fallacy. The word "facilitate" is missing from that phrase. Technology will facilitate fixing our problems, but nothing is plug 'n' play, despite what the tech provider may profess to be. Everything is a one-script, five-minute integration; yet nothing is. I interviewed examples of businesses waiting years to just implement personalisation technology, let alone use it. A large media company in the UK wanted to personalise with their vendor for almost two years, but they couldn't get the stack to work together, so they bought Optimizely while they were still under contract with the other vendor. There was another large UK high-street brand that purchased a piece of personalisation technology but was unable to integrate it for four months because their platform was built on React*, which supposedly worked with this technology but it clearly wasn't the case.

It is a brand's right to advertise their product and create more awareness for the wider personalisation market. It is also their obligation to realistically manage expectations. The technology vendors aren't alone here, it's also the services side of the personalisation market. Those selling services that purport to meet unrealistic expectations with minimal effort. The two — services and vendors — can be conflated when it comes to quality control. According to Jeffrey MacIntyre, Principal of Bucket Studio, a personalisation consultancy,[4] that is for one main reason. "A lot of these tech companies took venture capital, so they have a structural disincentive to cater to services work," he told me. "I've heard this many times from vendors, where if they were to do as much service work as there is market for, it will put a damper on their valuation, diluting their exit prospects." There is a method behind the madness of lies, or so it would seem. Speaking of lies ...

Statistics Can Lie

Alongside vendor-tinted glasses, another notable issue to mention is statistics — or the accuracy thereof. When research is undertaken to highlight the state of the market, usually by a vendor of some sort, I'm certain it's done with the best of intentions. To create awareness in the space and, by virtue, their brand.

However, as I discovered in my research, there is zero evidence to suggest that personalisation is *not* a good thing for businesses. In fact, revenue increases purported by technologies ranged from 10 per cent[5] at the lowest to 1,189 per cent[6] at the highest. The sceptics amongst you will raise an eyebrow. It's nothing but positive.

Not one statistic I found was negative. Not one.

Any research can become myopic and ignorant of context. The narrative starts to become statements based on opinion, not evidence. Sometimes, when evidence does exist, it disregards even the rigour of science. This is especially true in our

---

* React is a free and open-source front-end JavaScript library for building user interfaces based on components.

data-driven world, where false-positives are often misunderstood and causation and correlation are commonly mislabelled.

With more and more vendors purporting the same increases in a piece of technology, personalisation becomes more of a necessary fashion statement than a genuine use. Expectations are inflated, and subsequently, not even a new car smell can shift the feeling of reality.

Most of the "Year of Personalisation" chat is pure conjecture. They, too, are pieces of opinion that are based on little evidence besides statistics that are usually collected by third-party vendors. Not that there's anything wrong with that, but those vendors are selling a particular service, and that service just so happens to be the new and improved formula of personalisation. If you're relying on wider research about personalisation demand, it's funny how the statistics are always positive for those selling the service. Particularly those based on such conceptual issues.

Methods used to conduct personalisation studies require rigour and bias. While it is difficult, there is no evidence to suggest that some research firms that have been doing this for years are asking biased questions. Not at all. But the concept behind the definition is one that cannot be avoided: *what* is personalisation?

As we've already explored, asking one hundred marketers on the definition of personalisation will result in one hundred different answers. This is thanks to the lack of alignment in understanding, context and use case. Each is rooted in an opinion, experience and knowledge area. Remember that there were three different applications and four different implementations and each held its own interpretation. We should not expect a linear interpretation of what constitutes personalisation and, therefore, we should not take these consistently positive statistics at face value. Unlike Shakira's hips, numbers can lie.

It's not just the question being asked that can be biased, the answers being given can also be subject to interpretation. When it comes to asking about personalisation, the benefits are so obvious that the answers are always going to be inherently positive. Being asked if you prefer content that is personalised to your needs is similar to being asked if you prefer oxygen in the air to breathe. Or if you prefer tastier food. It's going to be a resounding yes. And if it's not, it's because of a lack of oxygen in the air you breathe. In other words, you're an idiot.

Heli Vainio, who manages one of the largest shopping malls in Northern Europe, has gone a step beyond. "People respond to questionnaires in a way that makes them look better. I don't care about lies. I'm interested in facts," he has said.[7]

Because of this cynical approach towards qualitative feedback to drive improvement in her mall, she's equipped her shopping centre with Wi-Fi equipment that can track visitors in the immediate vicinity of the building with an accuracy of two metres. The goal is that instead of the visitors giving feedback, their actions should do the talking. Or walking, as the case may be.

When it comes to personalisation, a concept that's rooted in relevance, no one wants irrelevant products. We all know we are living in the McDonaldisation of society – hell, we all ordered it! – a world where everything must be served to go and delivered in minutes. In a universe of online choice, relevance is a necessity. And if someone were to take away our nuggets from us, we'd miss them enough to go mad.

Chapter 14

The Fear Factor

"If we don't do personalisation, we will lose customers."
Harsimrat Kaur, CRM insight manager, Costa Coffee[1]

Personalisation is peer pressure. Many brands only do it because everyone else is doing it. And if they don't do it, they'll miss out. They're not sure what they'll miss out on, but it's better to be seen doing something than nothing. That's FOMO, folks. And we all get it. And from speaking with industry leaders, FOMO seems to be a big part of their personalisation decision process.

"With the growing consensus that a one-to-one content approach is table stakes for success, marketers are worried about falling behind, and so there's often a rush to preach personalisation, even if they haven't yet figured out how it makes sense for their brand."
Neil Ripley, head of Corporate Communications, ComScore[2]

A brand's fear of missing out is what drives it, not trust. The statistics reported by vendors in the previous chapter and others are designed to educate (or exploit, you decide), but in doing so, it can be argued that they also incite fear. "We have more data than nearly everyone in the world. We're making heavy investments in artificial intelligence and machine learning to grow our business. Why? Because we have to," Galagher Jeff, VP of Merchandising Operations and Business Analytics, Walmart[3] – one of the world's largest companies – has said.

"Because we have to" is such a profound, yet simple, declaration. Apart from the necessity derived from others doing it, Galagher does not provide many other reasons for embarking on a journey of personalisation other than FOMO. And fear should not be the main purpose that fuels personalisation forward.

What is this term besides a lazy acronym? According to the World Journal of Clinical Cases, the term "Fear of Missing Out" started to gain traction in 2004. It was first associated with the rise of social media sites such as MySpace and Facebook. It soon expanded to other walks of life, taking on a more commercial context where the potential of unlocking more revenue opportunities created impulsive behaviour. "[Brands] feel as though there's an unlock there," Paul Randall, Senior Experimentation Strategist, Speero[4] told me. "And if they're not in the space of personalisation they feel as though they're missing out."

For FOMO to exist, it requires a comparable behaviour, usually one that is popularised. And popular behaviour comes from success. Therefore, when a good idea occurs and the results are evident, it gets copied.

Exhibit A: Innocent Drinks

If you turn a bottle of Innocent Drinks upside down, you'll find a humorous tone of voice designed to engage you with the brand packaging. The creator of this concept for Innocent was Paul Burke, an ad man working in London, along with the founder of the drinks company, Richard Reed. In 1998, Burke helped Reed create not just the brand name Innocent (because it contains 100 per cent fruit), but also the distinct tone of voice of the packaging. Inspired by the likes of Paul Newman, Burke created the tone of "a naïve and affable ingénue, extolling the freshness and purity of their smoothie". Innocent disrupted a stale fruit drinks market beyond even the drinks industry.

Seeing the success of Innocent, brands copied it using what was known in the industry as "wackaging" or wacky packaging. Years later, the award-winning copywriter regretted the Frankenstein he created.[5] "It followed me everywhere," Burke said. "Mass-produced milkshakes telling me to 'Get in, fella!' and smug middle-class muesli telling me, 'I like it in the cupboard'."

I hope Jeff Bezos regrets the personalisation Frankenstein he, too, has created. Even if it is from the poop deck of his 127-metre-long superyacht.

The concept of ideas being created, copied and then homogenised creates a set of expectations. This brand was successful in this thing, and we will be successful by virtue. Not just the brands but the customers — now all consumers expect brand packaging to have some sort of tone of voice, just as we all expect our web experiences to be designed individually for us.

Exhibit B: Amazon

Bezos' baby's rampant success has resulted in every retailer virtually snooping around their business model ... so as to be seen to be doing the same. Their recommendations were the first form of personalisation, in some sense, where people could see a visual representation of what items chosen for them.

Amazon was far from the first to offer recommendations, but they are frequently called the pioneers. It's no wonder. They created a system known as Item-to-Item Collaborative Filtering. Two researchers at Amazon, Linden and Smith, published an award-winning paper that told the world about this pivotal system used to power their recommendations. So pivotal, in fact, that it won the IEEE Internet Computing award for the technology that has withstood the test of time.[6] Can you name another methodology that has withstood over 20 years of innovation? Their paper, "Amazon Recommendations: Item-to-item Collaborative Filtering" has more than 4,200 citations in Google and more than 12,700 downloads. It's influential.

And, therefore, worthy of replication.

It has been imitated and influenced by YouTube, which cites item-based collaborative filtering as their primary function within their recommendation algorithm – even seven years later. Their industrial recommendation system, built from the jump-off-a-cliff manta of "we should copy Amazon", is dealing with one of the largest and fastest growing datasets in the world.[7] They know recommendations work. Some 81 per cent of YouTube users say they at least occasionally watch the videos suggested by the platform's recommendation algorithm, including 15 per cent who say they do this regularly.[8] In 2010, video recommendations accounted for 30 per cent of overall video views in 2010. Eight years later, those recommendations accounted for "more than" 70 per cent of all watch time.[9]

That doesn't mean to say it's a good thing for the user, of course. Sources suggest that within a few clicks, a search for Saturn can easily lead to pro-Putin propaganda. Mozilla built RegretsReporter, a browser extension that allows people to donate data about the YouTube videos they regret watching on the platform for this very reason. It found that recommended videos were 40% more likely to be regretted than videos searched for.[10] Who cares if it makes money, he says sarcastically, depressively putting his head in his hands.

Copying from Amazon's success is warranted. Being the world's largest retail chain gives you a level of credibility. Making over $1.29 billion revenue each day gives you a sense of aspiration.[11] If a company grows quickly, it is natural for others to follow, copy, or use its methods as inspiration.

It's not just the "famous by association" fallacy, either. When brands are successful, other brands imitate. By the same token, because of that success, consumers expect other brands to offer something similar. The amount of traffic that Amazon receives alone means that customers from across the globe are preconditioned to how things are and behave. Everyone has visited Amazon – they had 2.4 billion visitors to its site in the month of May, 2022[12] alone (a peak). That many people use Amazon as the barometer for what is good and what isn't, setting their own expectations for other brands. They're used to it and, in becoming accustomed, expect other websites to offer things such as next-day free delivery or a one-click buy button. There's a compelling case to suggest that if Amazon jumps off the bridge, all other brands should follow. And consumers expect brands to follow. It's therefore no wonder that recommendations and personalisation receive the level of hype that they do, given that our Lord and Saviour, Jeff Bezos, created and uses it.

In Bezos we believe.

It could be a very different world if Amazon never detailed their personalisation approach in their 1998 paper, "Recommendations: Item-to-Item Collaborative Filtering". The Bible of personalisation.

Since then, reportedly, a third of all Amazon sales have come from recommendations.[13] This created a copycat gold rush. So much so that the recommendation engine market is now worth more and growing faster than the personalisation engine market, at a 33 per cent growth rate and $1.7 billion respectively.[14]

The marketing industry now only needs to look at free delivery to see how quickly others can catch on to something that perpetuates and sets an expectation. It was something that was virtually unheard of before Amazon came along. Everyone now offers free delivery because they have to keep up. That expectation is embedded in society now, and it's only getting more loaded. What's next? Going from free delivery to free one-day delivery, to free-same day delivery, to free-get it in the next hour delivery by drone and then, perhaps, no delivery using 3D printing your own home.

"There's a need to enter personalisation too quickly. A run before you can walk mentality. There are loads of things that suggest they're not ready. Symptoms like the lack of data, lack of resource. But the excitement of doing personalisation as a feeling, individual or collective, is generally just attributed to fear of missing out."

Emma Travis, Director of Research, Speero[15]

The question of personalisation's purpose rears its head once more: it's less about what you're trying to achieve and more about *why*. The why sets those expectations and standards, which will ultimately help brands understand what success is. Without it, they default towards commercials that drive the personalisation purpose away from the customer and towards the business. As Travis suggests above, it is this rush to the finish line, the desire to use something zeitgeisty, and over-expectations that creates the misrepresentation we see today.

Common Sense

Before we spiral further downward into the personalisation paradox vortex, let's introduce a little bit of common sense. Thankfully, the cavalry is coming ...

"If you come from a place of believing that diversity is a good thing, that fundamentally leads you to the conclusion that all people are different and therefore personalisation is a force for good. You're making your messaging resonate more with personas, so commercially you should be more effective."

Leon Andrews, Head of User Experience, RICS[16]

This feels like common sense, doesn't it?

The nebulous argument of moving from mass media messaging to segmented messaging to personalisation feels natural. And inevitable. Bogomil Balkansky, a partner at Sequoia who invested in platforms such as personalisation software Mutiny, mentioned about the benefits of personalisation as being, well, rational. "Personalization has always been the holy grail of marketing. You don't need to explain to marketers that if you personalise messages, you'll get better results. That's a given."[17]

"The last decade in marketing was about top-of-funnel. The next decade will be about conversion, giving rise to a new breed of CMOs that every company will desperately try to recruit."

Jaleh Rezaei, CEO & Co-Founder, Mutiny[18]

"That's a given" makes it feel as if personalisation is pure common sense, as though everyone should be personalising. That certainly wasn't the case in previous decades and so it is society that has shaped this opinion — the example and technological advancements thereof.

Prior to this, for paid ads, for more than a decade, Google would ask marketers to give it five ads, and it would automatically figure out which ad to show whom — the good ones more, the bad ones less. This is the experience that users are used to when buying paid ads, yet no such tool existed on the market in 2016 for website experiences.

Guy Yalif and his co-founders at Intellimize talked to more than 100 marketers to see if there was something within this concept, and they resoundingly saw that there was. Personalising for each unique prospect, showing winning ideas more, starved bad ideas of traffic, and optimised for a goal a marketer cared about. This is just what programmatic advertising does (and 90 per cent plus of display ads are bought this way because it produces better results), so Intellimize found a huge opportunity to create an experience optimisation platform that combined experimentation with personalisation to effectively do the same thing that programmatic ads were doing, except on a website. Lim and Webb had experience personalising at scale as they led a several hundred-person engineering team that optimised and personalised the Yahoo! Homepage when it was the most popular page on the internet for more than half a decade. In talking to marketers, the trio also discovered, in a broader sense, that marketers are very data-driven, accountable for measurable results, and used to personalisation. Marketers have been doing this openly for years with our ads and emails. Despite this, there isn't enough money being spent on solving this problem. Brands spend $520 billion every year[19] driving people to websites to turn them into customers and fail to convert them into customers an astounding 98 per cent of the time.[20] In what world is this OK? How are we all still in jobs? Have our expectations become so low that we now accept this as the new benchmark? When it's spelled out like that, it does echo Bogomil's point above about it being commonsensical.

The concept of treating every customer the same is ludicrous. It sounds ludicrous. It feels ludicrous. Customers are people, not numbers. Doing so removes connection and relationships and replaces it with a standardisation slap in the face. Everything becomes the same because brands treat everyone the same. From my interviews, I felt a common thread in how this manifests itself in how brands currently measure performance on websites: using conversion rate.

The metric used to understand success is highly aggregated. It's an average of averages of averages. It's made up of so many conversion rates (plural) that trying to shift that behemoth metric is akin to pulling a U-turn on the *Titanic* – it's going to take a lot more than a boatload of topless coal trimmers.

The result of optimising for an averaged metric is an averaged approach. For retailers, they split this average into further averages: templates. This is how the majority of retailers optimise experiences. Brands speak about eCommerce websites, for example, as though they are casually split into five very distinct areas:

1) Homepage
2) Product listing page (PLP)
3) Product detail page (PDP)
4) Basket
5) Checkout

What this does is remove the user from the conversation altogether. It's almost the antithesis of personalisation to speak like this. Brands output becomes more optimised versions of generic templates because their metric is a generic performance-based one: template tweaking. Averaged metrics produce average approaches which produce average results. The irony here is that brands speak of this as user experience, when what they really mean is page experience.

The game needs to change away from averages.

Away from Averages
According to one study, most Americans nowadays are exposed to a whopping 4,000 to 10,000 ads every day.[21]

If that's the case, the reason to personalise, at its lowest common denominator, is to help cut through that noise and create a wave of relevancy. The advent of technology has merely allowed us to achieve that. Personalisation feels nothing short of common sense.

The fact that two major brands in particular, Amazon and Netflix, have associated themselves with that belief and made it part of their commercial success has just accelerated others following them. The fact that technology vendors have commercialised this marketing approach has heightened the awareness. But really, it's the concept that personalisation is just an evolutionary part of sales and marketing that has captured the hearts of so many.

"Anything that can tailor the experience to mirror what the person wants or is expecting to get, improves that relationship. Same for dating, flirting, or swapping your prize cow for magic beans. It's a sales mechanism. We're humans trying to deal with humans."

Tim Stewart, Founder, TRS Digital[22]

See. Common sense. Whether it be improving your success rate in dating, or selling magic beans as Stewart suggests, it translates into more for you — be that a more engaged date or more dollars in the back pocket. We feel its purpose in our bones (even if that's a potential symptom of confirmation bias in and of itself).

Just as with humans however, not everything is as it seems.

Personalisation is like Gizmo. Perfect.

But get a little water on him or feed him after midnight — NIGHTMARE.

The hype might be real, yet it is unearned. The FOMO, the vendors, those leading from the front, they're all moulding personalisation to suit *them*. They're turning it into something it was never designed to be. The true reason why brands should be personalising is being forgotten. I'm seeing symptoms where the allure of it makes us forget about its true purpose: to create relationships.

And so, now I am at that part of my quest when I must enter the cave of Three Dragons. Here, three massive fire-breathing reasons lurk in the darkness, stopping brands in their tracks from achieving their full personalisation potential.

And by doing so, warping what personalisation should be and transforming into something it's not.

Prepare for battle ...

Part IV

The Three Dragons

1) The Golden Dragon

"If you ignore the Dragon, it will eat you. If you defy the Dragon, it will overpower you. But if you ride the Dragon, you will take advantage of its strength and power."

Chinese Proverb

The idea of a mere mortal, like you or I, defeating a giant fire-breathing dragon may seem like an unfair fight. It may also sound utterly ridiculous in what is intended to be a pseudo-business book, pseudo-fairy tale. We're talking about personalisation here, and, let's be honest, defeating dragons probably isn't the most ridiculous thing you've ever heard when discussing personalisation is it?

They're used as a metaphor in this personal quest of mine to represent different battles brands must fight. They are the barriers that prevent brands from personalising. We're not all given three petrified dragon eggs as a wedding gift like Daenerys Targaryen. We don't have stunning spells like Harry Potter. Or the Force like Luke Skywalker. We're not Neo, for God's sake.

The trick to defeating, or even simply training, these Three Dragons of personalisation myth – and any metaphorical monster that lurks and lingers in the shadows – is to understand them individually, and then create a battle plan to beat them one by one.

Over Part IV-V-VI, I'll be throwing shade and light at the "Three Dragons of Personalisation", a rather ridiculous concept I've coined to help us reach our final destination, the alliterative Personalisation Paradise. If personalisation is the "height of customer experience", as Andre Morys said,[1] bringing the customer and brand closer together through a deeper relationship is essential. But what are the Three Dragons that prevent such a relationship from forming? Of course, there are three. In marketing, there is always three.

DRAGON 1: The Golden Dragon
DRAGON 2: The Stubborn Dragon
DRAGON 3: The Deepfake Dragon

All Three Dragons represent an obstacle:

1) Perceived lack of ROI and focus on non-customer driven metrics such as revenue
2) The perils of focusing too much on technology and data
3) The perception of human effort and their expectation

First up, the Golden Dragon.

Chapter 15

Know Thy Enemy: The Golden Dragon

"Smaug ruled the Lonely Mountain uncontested. He spent his days within the mountain lying atop his great treasure hoard, which he guarded jealously."

JRR Tolkien, _The Hobbit_[1]

Our first metaphorical mythical beast to slay — the Golden Dragon — is a business's need to make money, first and foremost. ROI is all that makes this beast happy. All it does is eat, sleep, dream and make investors smile. Think of it like the treasure-loving Smaug, arguably the most famous treasure-hoarder in literature, from JRR Tolkien's _The Hobbit_.

However, when brands focus too much on money as the primary measure of success for personalisation, they lose sight of who they are personalising for — the customer. It feels as though another new redefinition is on the cards — "purse-onalisation".

Believe it or not, it happens all the time.

Brands expect a return on their investment and they expect it regardless of whether they do the one thing their customers want — personalise — but don't deliver (see Amazon, below). What is best for the brand isn't always best for the customer, and vice versa. If the metric that brands use to discern personalisation success is purely revenue, personalisation starts to become designed for the business. It's immediately set up to fail. It actually becomes the antithesis of personalisation. Where the true purpose of personalising is to create relationships based on mutual trust, the action of simulating this for profit feels greedy and self-serving.

The way to overcome this treasure-hoarding, I think, is three-fold:

1) Purpose
2) Experiment
3) Retention

If practitioners can really land on a purpose that suits them and their customers, that's the trick to personalisation. Then, if they can give the business a bit of rope, a carrot, an olive branch in the form of evidence – or experimentation – to demonstrate that personalisation is a good thing, they must do so. And finally, they can then defeat this cash-obsessed dragon by including what I found as the true measure of personalisation – *retention*, the only metric that's more customer-first, than business-first.

As you'll discover come the end of this section, the way to defeat this beast is not with a silver bullet, or magic sword – but a combination of all these strategies – purpose, experiment and retention.

There are three tales of brands that have gone up against the Golden Dragon. Each made famous by their efforts in vanquishing the beast. Amazon, Victoria's Secret and Marks and Spencer. There is something to learn from each of them.

Chapter 16

Amazon Versus The Golden Dragon

"Marketers are too greedy, they want too much."

Maurice Beerthuyzen, Director of Marketing
and Sales, ClickValue[1]

5 July 1994.

I t was a dark and stormy night. Probably. A man with a receding hairline was sitting in his dingy garage in Bellevue, Washington. He may or may not have been wearing a gilet. His name was Jeff. He'd recently quit his job as vice president of a Wall Street company, not wanting to look back and wish he had started his own business during the current Internet boom. The wastepaper basket next to Jeff's desk was full of throwaway names for what to call his next enterprise. Cadabra, Inc. was one of those ideas. (That's what Bezos originally wanted to call Amazon, but after hearing a lawyer mishear it as "Cadaver" Jeff decided to swiftly change the title to something less morbid. Good move.)

Within 30 days of that fateful night, the now-named Amazon was earning $20,000 per week in sales. In just three years, it hit (not literally) more than 1.5 million customers. Bezos' concepts on customer centricity were clear — he spoke about the power of word-of-mouth as the host of the party and his obsession with customers. He did so in a way where personalisation, or the desire to be personable, was the engine that fuelled his vision. His first tip-off about being personal with customers was all about creating and maintaining deep relationships.

"In the online world, businesses have the opportunity to develop very deep relationships with customers, both through accepting the preferences of them and then observing their purchase behaviour over time. In doing so, brands can get that individualised knowledge of the customer and use that to accelerate their discovery process," Bezos wrote.[2] "If we can do that, then the customers are going to feel a deep loyalty to us because we know them so well. They're going to stick with us because they are going to be able to get a personalised service."

Bezos saw personalisation as the key to discovery for his fledgling business. He didn't know what Amazon was going to sell, he just knew it would be a lot. He had read a report about the future of the Internet that projected annual growth at 2,300 per cent. Looking back, it probably wasn't that far from the truth. And so, he created a list of twenty categories that had a tonne of products within them and that he felt could be sold over the Internet. The list was narrowed down to CDs, computer hardware, computer software, videos and books. There was a large worldwide demand for literature, as well as, perhaps a telling sign for what's to come, a low unit price for books. And so, Bezos chose this category for his first course. "The rest is history," the multi-billionaire no doubt says now.

Literally.

Bookshops are history because of him.

It was his belief that to sell all of the books in one online bookstore, customers would come up against a form of choice paralysis. That is, customers faced so much choice that they couldn't adequately arrive at a decision. To combat that, therefore, he chose to personalise for his customers and provide a sense of discovery. Although the most famous book on this psychological concept, Barry Schwartz's *The Paradox of Choice*,[3] wasn't released until seven years later, there was some academic discussion on it. Studies emerged in the mid-1990s showing that, as the attractiveness of alternatives rose, individuals experienced conflict and, as a result, tended to defer decisions.[4] It wasn't a new concept by any means. In the 1300s, French philosopher Jean Buridan pondered whether, if a donkey had to choose between two equally appealing options of hay, it would take longer to decide, a quandary now known as Buridan's Ass.[5] If only Jean's surname was "Har" it would foreshadow what's about to come.

It remains unclear whether Bezos wanted to promote personalisation to help customers discover, to combat the paradox of choice, or to just help customers in a bid to get closer to them. What is clear is that Amazon's personalisation engine was first used to recommend new books. You could see this explicitly in Bezos' first letter to their shareholders, in 1997, where he wrote: "Tomorrow, through personalization, online commerce will accelerate the very process of discovery." He continued a year later in *The Washington Post* — a publication he now owns, FYI — by stating: "Amazon might figure out that I'm a nerd; I read science-fiction books. We can do that online. We can make it your store tailor-made for you. If we have 4.5 million customers, we shouldn't have one store; we should have 4.5 million stores."[6]

Bezos didn't predict the future, he just saw what customers wanted: the need for a personal connection. Like a friend recommending something. And he hogtied that philosophy into the core values of Amazon from the very beginning. By 1998, the team had grown to 2,100, and they started to embody these values of discovery and customer centricity. Hereto begins the Frankenstein that was created: recommendations.

Bezos was so clear in his purpose for personalisation that he cited it constantly in interviews. He put his money where his mouth was and applied it practically in day-to-day life. There are too many use cases for personalisation on Amazon today to name them all. In fact, in 2019, Dynamic Yield published *Amazon: The Chronicles of a Personalisation Giant*,[7] where they outline hundreds of these examples. The 118-pages of nothing but case studies are split into areas where Amazon has been personalising. There's the cart and checkout flow, promotional offers, customer loyalty and cross-device experiences. Yet it is product discovery and merchandising that is naturally the largest section because personalisation is just recommendations, is it not? By virtue, Amazon don't do personalisation, but they do recommendations. Nothing is more pivotal than their famed recommendation systems.

Today, Amazon's recommendations drive more than 35 per cent of its revenue[8] — and that's not a cash-cow and/or dragon Amazon would be willing to kill just to increase its personalisation connections. Don't upset the apple cart.

"For two decades now, Amazon.com has been building a store for every customer. Each person sees it differently because its personalised based on their interests."

Brent Smith and Greg Linden[9]

On the face of it, Amazon's intentions were clear. Bezos was customer-driven and there are quotes after quotes after quotes to back that up. But, let us not forget that it was Jeff Bezos who also said, "Your margin is my opportunity."[10] Bezos is revenue-obsessed, he wouldn't have got to where he is today without being so, and here is where the Golden Dragon raises its monstrous head.

In 1995, Amazon raised a Series A of $8 million from Kleiner Perkins Caufield & Byers[11] — the pre-recommendations era. In 1997, Amazon went public to raise additional capital. Just two years later, the value of the Kleiner Perkins Caufield & Byers investment in Amazon generated returns of over 55,000 per cent. Yeah, you read that number right. It's an important note as this could be described as an inflection point in, not just their evolution, but how Amazon perceived customer value.

Amazon believed so much in their item-to-item filtering recommendation system that they patented it in 2001. In and of itself, that isn't a bad thing, Amazon patents a lot. The altruists among us, however, perhaps feel as though creating a restriction on preventing other brands from helping their customers find stuff is self-serving. And hardly doing what is best for the customer.

Unlucky for them, Amazon got into hot water in 2022 when they became the subject of a £900 million class action lawsuit against them.[12] It was recommended to them – see what I did there – that their fabulously patented recommendations pushed customers toward offers that benefited the online retailer but were not good deals for customers.

I'll let you read that line again.

It begs the question: Should the consumer ever stop and question the real purpose behind personalisation for Amazon? Is personalisation, as Bezos said, meant to help customers find stuff and build deeper, more meaningful relationships? Or is it, as he also said, to create an opportunity by extending profit margins – where maximising shareholder value to increase customer spend comes first and adding customer value comes second?

It's not necessarily an either or … it's a balance.

While the two are not mutually exclusive, companies that succeed in personalisation do so not solely because of their resources, but because it is inextricably linked to the real reason why personalisation should exist: to build better relationships with customers. This is their purpose. It's more than a strategy and infinitely more than a tactic: it's a *value*. All brands have a personalisation purpose. The real question is trying to uncover what that true purpose is, not the PR-stunt that most tell others (or themselves), including Amazon, and then relate personalisation efforts, authentically, through that purpose.

One of the most discerning ways to reveal that true purpose is to understand what metrics the brand uses to define personalisation success. Amazon's battle with the Golden Dragon feels like a tail (yes, I spelled it like that on purpose) of personalising for revenue uplift, and, as such, one couldn't be criticised for feeling as though it was inauthentic.

Chapter 17

Victoria's Real Secret

Money makes the world go round, and no brand should be judged for wanting to get fat on rich and tasty treasures. No one's blaming Amazon for that. But let's not use personalisation as a shield to deflect how money-hungry we all are, either.

Take Victoria's Secret as a shining example.

Rather than simply slay the Golden Dragon — and lose revenue — the brand has used experimentation to give confidence in the strategy that they use. Or rather, they have used experimentation to give confidence that what they are doing provides a revenue uplift; a metric they seem to use to discern the success of personalisation.

Victoria's Secret is the No.1 lingerie brand in the US, with more than 700 million website visitors a year and more than $2.4 billion in global eCommerce sales. That's a lot of knickers. Or I should say, panties. Their personalisation journey started in 2018 — there's that famous year again — and is going great guns, all thanks to one major factor: their willingness to experiment.

Victoria's Secret personalisation strategy is supported up by three main pillars. It's always three. Unfortunately, despite how hard I tried, they're not alliterative.

1) Product Recommendations
2) Personalised Content
3) Individualised Offers

It is the former, as you'd expect, that appears to be the most prominent. Starting in 2018, the brand experimented with several tests on its homepage, targeting different audiences with different content without being overly-promotional. "We spent a lot of time on how to better target offers to the individual at the right time and place versus the total site audience, which was historically all we could do," said Jenna Brunner, Director of Digital Products, during a summit. On the back of its proven personalisation successes, the retailer is now experimenting with what they call auto-personalisation. Ah, auto-personalisation, how romantic. And another redefinition for the history books.

One of the first things Victoria's Secret did, even before selecting a technology partner in Adobe, was settle on an aligned definition for personalisation – much like what Manjunath* originally wanted me to do. That definition was outlined by Brunner as "Connecting with each of our customers in a relevant, personal way to continue to drive brand loyalty and value."[1]

A definition can indicate what the purpose of personalisation might be. In this case, their purpose seems, on the face of it, altruistic and designed solely for the customer. I love the words "connecting", "personal" and "loyalty". If any brand were to create a definition that they wanted to use as their purpose, this is a great start. That being said, it is reminiscent of what Bezos set out to do ... before he perhaps got lost in the jungle of recommendations. Amazon's personalisation purpose was predicated on relevancy amid breadth of choice, whereas Victoria's Secret seems more aligned to connection and loyalty. For what it's worth, I prefer the latter's approach because it's most deeply rooted in the actual purpose of what personalisation is designed for.

Let us not forget, however, that L Brands owns 45 per cent of Victoria's Secret. It also owns Bed, Bath & Beyond and is listed on the New York Stock Exchange. The other 55 per cent is owned by Sycamore Partners, a private equity firm. That's not to assume uber-corporate intentions or a clear focus on revenue and margin. No one is saying that – with or without a raised eyebrow. Yet, one can't help but think that while the process of proving incremental value is an important one for some businesses, it could seemingly be more important for businesses backed by firms that demand a 10x on their investment.

Phrases emerged such as, "Try to squeeze out as much juice as we can out of personalisation." These were overheard in webinars between Victoria's Secret and Adobe when they joined forces.[2] Or, "One of the biggest goals in our business is to sell total outfits."[3] "Squeeze" and "sell" often go together. And if a definition can indicate what the purpose of personalisation might be, a metric cements it. In all my research with multiple leaders, a core learning is that how you measure personalisation is how you deem its purpose. The true reason why brands personalise is hidden in how they answer the question, "What does success look like?"

---

* In the Call to Adventure, Shiva Manjunath set me off on a quest to find out what the perfect definition for personalisation is. He recommended this unity amongst the personalisation community was needed prior to any strategy being implemented.

The task of proving this metric — revenue growth — became difficult for Victoria's Secret. While experimentation can isolate individual variables, cumulating multiple variables together doesn't work so well. The sum doesn't equal the parts. So, while they were finding single digit growth with their automated matchbacks — a section on the product page that highlights matching items — "How do we sum this up and understand what the true impact of all of our efforts are?" asked Brunner in one such webinar I attended.[4]

Some level of attribution is absolutely required to answer this. Especially for the private equity boys and girls. Brands need to create a macro impact for what those micro-moments will have done. Yet, when exact attribution is required, it slows brands down and costs them more by making them spend time and resources on the very thing they're trying to prove. No matter how far down the rabbit hole they go, it costs more to attribute more.

The outcomes of loyalty and connection, as firmed out in Victoria's Secret's initial statement, are not something that's directly or easily attributed to pounds and pence. How do you measure a "connection"?

The problem is that personalisation is trying to quantify an intangible feeling, the quality of a relationship. "There's never been a golden metric for [it]," said Nathan Richter, Vice President Program Strategy & Insights, Dynamic Yield.[5] "It's tough to come back on a continual basis to say here's a single number that compiles all the efforts and quantifies what your consumer has done based on personalisation coming to you."

Put simply, while creating a personal connection is hard to do, measuring the value of that is nearly impossible. Sometimes it's easier to say how not to do it, to avoid the awkward question of how to do it. With that, I can tell you that it's certainly not done by attributing revenue to it.

It is this need to attribute revenue that has led brands down a garden path of aggregation and anti-personalisation. For years, businesses have just focused on the numbers: the need to measure customers en masse, usually by a single figure. A figure that measures quantity, but not quality. We're looking at you, "Conversion Rate". Take a bow.

An averaged, aggregated, retrospective, binary figure for customers that is supposed to be heralded as that which defines performance. Trying to understand and mould performance based on a single figure at the end of the yellow brick road isn't going to effectively change the behaviours that came before it. It will result in mass changes in order to move an aggregate metric. It is better known as the antithesis of personalisation, or, if you will, "Genericisation". A redefinition for the ages. Trademark pending. This is better known as conversion rate optimisation, the process of optimising a, you guessed it, conversion rate. What this does is result in brands so-called "personalising" their page templates. Where the solution isn't the solution itself but the location of the solution. Implementing matchbacks on the homepage, recommendations on the product detail page, or a personalised offer in the basket.

Wait, where's the user in all this conversation?

To defeat the Golden Dragon, brands need to change their measure of success. While the need to demonstrate a positive financial return for personalisation is clearly a necessity, to purely associate a financial gain to all executions brings a fear; that brands will create executions designed for themselves, their bottom line, and not the customer.

Chapter 18

Sexy Sparks & Spencer

Marks & Spencer, a major British multinational retailer, has remained a national treasure for most of its 140-year history. With a global footprint, they sell everything from ethical clothes to affordable homeware to outrageously sexy fruit and vegetables. (Their TV ads constantly sexualise the food they sell, and I'm all for it.) For decades, middle-aged husbands across the UK have stood in the lingerie section of M&S department stores while waiting for their wives to choose a bra-knicker combo that delivers on both comfort and look and just a hint of that Victoria's Secret sexiness (but not too much). The brand delivers more than 6 billion digital customer interactions every year, of which 1 billion are across the website and app alone. This huge following resulted in the launch of Sparks, their loyalty programme, a personalisation facilitator that's well admired in the industry for getting seven million of the most loyal M&S customers together and giving back.

In 2018 — there's that year again — as a result of wider economic changes, they announced their Digital Transformation Programme and focused their business growth through digital marketing. Part of that was a re-launch of their Sparks rewards programme to go digital-first, specifically because, as CEO Steve Rowe said, "It builds our relationship with customers through a more personalised experience."[1] Like Victoria's Secret, some of that was the adoption and use of the Adobe software suite to embark on their personalisation journey as a whole. Needless to say, personalisation was the cornerstone of this transformation programme's relaunch.

> "How do we take all of the things that M&S has been known and loved for globally, where every colleague knows all the customers that come in every week, into a digital world. How do you bring those experiences that used to be in our colleagues' heads, into a digital experience?"
> **Alex Williams, Head of Growth & Personalisation, M&S**[2]

Today, everything is set up for M&S to play-to-win in the world of personalisation. They have it all: diversity of the product range, a loyalty scheme that already delivers engagement levels 4x higher than non-loyalty, an advanced personalisation team, smart personalisation partnerships, sexy fruit and millions of tech-savvy middle-aged (and middle class) mums and dads with disposable incomes who know how to use the app, a direct contrast to the previous generation. The brand's belief in personalisation was unwavering. Despite that, did they blindly go full steam ahead into personalisation like so many before them?

Of course not. And why not?

Evidence. The magnificent, magical, and oh-so-misleading mercurial business case.

Despite the want and desire for personalisation, the need to provide evidence of a viable revenue stream is still required. As I identified with Victoria's Secret, this shouldn't be the primary measurement behind why they are doing what they are doing. It's a necessary evil.

Especially the case with a centuries-old retailer that could be more likely to be stereotypically rooted in legacy practices. For M&S, just the desire to change is not enough. Attributing revenue is a proxy for understanding the investment required in personalisation. The level of resource brands need to achieve that needs to be balanced against how much money will be brought in to pay for that resource. Ipso facto — can you prove it works?

To provide evidence of his business case, the first thing that Williams and the personalisation team at M&S did was take away some competitive benchmarking from Adobe. Using their supplier to help build a business case is an often-underutilised crutch that can really be helpful. Of course, M&S aren't the only ones to build such a business case for their finance team. Leaning on others that have personalised before, especially if they are in a similar vertical, with a similar customer base, feels like a sensible thing to do. This would all fuel their business case for the finance team.

Within the business case itself, there was a need to balance revenue gains against costs. The cost is somewhat easier to identify: "Research is a cost and you can easily calculate something like that," Peep Laja, CEO of Wynter, told me.[3] Brands can review cost based on teams aligned to opportunities and payback ROI, phased infrastructure investment over multiple years, cost displacement of agency support — that type of thing.

The revenue is somewhat more difficult. "You can't say something as simple as if we were to get a modest 10 per cent improvement in that segment, how much extra money is that?" Laja continued. It feels like a finger in the air.

M&S were already employing personalisation activities in their offers, CRM, and several digital experiences through tactical experimentation. Taking current gains and ROI from those channels to help the narrative was useful. The concept, too, of shifting from mass offers to personalised ones added to that narrative. They used research from others in identifying this type of opportunity — such as that undertaken by Boston Consulting Group[4] how shifting 25 per cent of mass promotion spending to personalised offers would increase return on investment (ROI) by 200 per cent. Others providing the evidence for you certainly adds weight to the narrative being told.

M&S created that business case on a case-by-case basis, allowing them to pilot specific examples and scale them independently. Recommendations. Paid marketing. Offers. Email. Web. App. The concept of personalisation, although broad in its application, was used in focused ways to help with the business case in its entirety. As I defined in the first chapter, taking a business case to the Board and yelling, "We need to be more personalised!" is similar to asking investment bankers to "Look past the numbers!" It doesn't feel realistic. Breaking it up into its individual components feels like a more logical approach to an illogical problem.

And that's exactly what happened with M&S. After all this hard work, case studies and academic studies acting as proof that personalisation would work — what was the result of taking this business case to the stakeholders, purporting hundreds of millions of pounds in incremental revenue?

No one believed them. The ROI figures felt unrealistic.

The business case and ruthless focus on revenue measurement were a method to allow M&S to further invest in their personalisation efforts. Such as improving their customer data, building better models to personalise, and then orchestrating these personalised experiences at scale through high levels of automation. So much so, they built their own tool — Bullseye[5] — that combines in-house, off-the-shelf and partner capabilities. How do you put a figure on efficiency, scale and kick-ass personalisation software intellectual property?

Such a thing isn't an exact science. Creating this business case by extrapolating current evidence can still be a risk in some instances. It can be an art as much as anything else. While the purpose of a business case is noted, the direction of travel is sometimes more important than the cost of it. It's a reason why President Barack Obama cited that he only needed a 51 per cent degree of certainty in order to make decisions.[6] In all my expert interviews, I found a common thread where there were those revolutionary youths who often questioned the value of such specific revenue attribution beyond just right-sizing the investment needed to achieve the thing itself. Like Obama, is it not more important to know the direction in which you are rowing, rather than how fast you are actually rowing?

The team at M&S went back after finance rejected the initial proposal. They simply pulled some of the cost savings forward while phasing out the steep returns over a longer period of time. In short, "There were lots of healthy haircuts everywhere," Williams said.

The result?

They reached an agreement and hit 1.5x targets in the first year and 2x targets in the second.

Proof that personalisation is an art, not an exact science. The need to be scientific almost derailed doing the right thing for their customers.

Building a business case that attributes a specific level of revenue to personalisation is a requirement for most. I get that. It's irrelevant how sexy personalisation is, or how much common sense it makes. Especially not with investors and shareholders behind the vast majority of brands. It is justifiable that considering that the immediate, specific need for realisation and return, it can not only stifle creativity, but also prevent the brand from doing the right thing for their customers.

Starting the quest of personalisation holds high financial risk because of the effort that's required, sure. Those financial risks are more evident when they are a line item on a spreadsheet. The cost of an agency or a personalisation platform is staggering. You're talking at least £50,000 a year for the majority of platforms, let alone the time and resources required to power both the agency and the tool. Where the risk — money — is tangible, and the reward — customer satisfaction — is intangible, it comes as no surprise that there is a misguided purpose.

To help with any business case, there are plenty of ROI stats out there, and other case studies to benchmark against, despite how self-serving they may or may not be. They are a good starting point for those wanting to learn about the success stories of personalisation. But be conscious of the expectations they may bring. Starting the conversation with myopic revenue uplifts ends the conversation with myopic revenue uplifts. You might find that your first business case is perceived as being unrealistic and you will need those healthy "haircuts" Alex Williams mentioned. I appreciate the need for a balanced argument. Personalisation isn't about blind faith — hoping some finance bods will approve a concept they hold little context about — it's about testing and obtaining proof of life through evidence.

Chapter 19

Defeating the Golden Dragon

I 've chosen dragons, rather than beasts or monsters, as an homage to two of my favourite films when I was a kid — *Pete's Dragon* and *Mulan*. Since becoming an adult, the remakes of both *Pete's Dragon* and *Mulan* leave me wanting to pop on my SPF 10000 sun cream, approach both of them from behind and violently slay both Elliot and Mushu.* Wishing Disney had never remade these classics, I now see dragons in much the same vein as those in *Harry Potter* or *The Hobbit*: the villain.

To defeat our first of the Three Dragons, the cash-obsessed beast, practitioners of personalisation requires three things:

1) The weapon — PURPOSE
2) Making sure the weapon works — TESTING
3) Keeping hold of the weapon — RETENTION

Purpose

The only way to make personalisation work for brands is for them to understand the purpose behind their desire to personalise in the first place. Without purpose, what's the point?

In the 1990s, Amazon originally personalised because of the wealth of products on offer and the need for relevancy and discovery. Customers with better choices, spend more. As a result, they also did it to make more money. Victoria's Secret originally personalised to drive brand loyalty and customer value. They also did it to make more money. Marks and Spencer ... you get the point.

The reason to personalise can be different for every brand, at least on the surface. Dig a bit deeper and review how these brands measure success, and you might find that there aren't many similarities.

Even if purposes are, at a deeper level, the same, is personalisation for everyone?

---

* These were the names of the dragons in *Pete's Dragon* and *Mulan* respectively.

It's a valid question.

There is absolutely an argument to be made about the level of product stickiness that is needed for personalisation to stick around long-term. There's a reason why personalisation for Netflix works; it's a product that encourages repeat visits and user retention. Brands that double down on personalisation like HelloFresh, *The Wall Street Journal*, WayFair and Birchbox all have some level of loyalty or repeat visit tendency within their products. That might either be down to it being integral to their users' lifestyles or the breadth of choice of product that's on offer. But the outcome is the same: there is a large base of like-minded users who are happy to give brands information about themselves. There is so much rich data available that this creates a healthy balance of people to actually personalise for.

Of course, the reverse is true. Where there's no login, no account and people just come and go as they please, perhaps only visiting once, why bother to personalise? Why should a mattress company that sells mattresses that last a lifetime bother? Why should a lightbulb company that sells something as commoditised as a lightbulb bother?

> "I'm a sceptic. I think there's a time and place for personalisation. People think it's for everyone, and I don't think it is. If I go to a restaurant, I want a personalised recommendation for the wine that goes best with my meal. I don't need the plate, the cutlery, or the chair personalised."
>
> **Bhavik Patel, Founder, Causl**[1]

While the argument that "brands shouldn't personalise" exists, I disagree with Bhavik's quote that not every business should do it. The example that Bhavik gives is one of recommending items to go with other items. The belief that personalisation is just a single definition, be those recommendations, or product discovery, is merely one-tenth of its potential. And, as we found from the AIDA model, about one-fourth of its purpose. It's less about whether every business should personalise and defeat the Golden Dragon, but whether they should defeat it right now.

It comes down to *prioritisation*.

If I take personalisation at face value, it is just one of many marketing or product strategies. Sitting above that and more conceptually, I see personalisation actually as a communication strategy; the act of being more personable. Regardless of what type of strategy personalisation is, the question is, is this the right strategy to prioritise right now?

"What about all those things that we would have done with that time before we put it into personalisation before we were ready? Risk versus reward. It's all about prioritisation. Maybe the gain is bigger and we're skipping past the basics?"

Emma Travis, Director of Research, Speero[2]

To understand whether personalisation is a priority for a brand, they must *test* it. Experimentation is a methodology that will help brands understand this. It's what Victoria's Secret did to understand their attribution, as did Marks and Spencer. The majority of brands experiment with it as a strategy because it provides a level of *evidence*. It's absolutely one of the top pieces of advice across all my interviews with experts around the world when starting a personalisation strategy: *experiment*.

A rather existential outlook might be to suggest "Personalisation is just the same as experimentation. When done correctly it's just an experiment targeted to a more specific audience. When delivered, it should be validated against a control group. I don't see much difference between the two," says Oliver Palmer, optimisation consultant.[3] We've moved past the alliterative pecking-order of personalisation model, Palmer.

And, if you don't believe it, let's revert back to the Jump Off the Cliff model of "if Netflix does it, so should we". Netflix first experimented with personalised content in 2006 via their recommendation algorithm for movie ratings. The hypothesis was simply that your friends would recommend movies in a closed, virtual circle – so it makes sense to replicate that online. IMDb, the Internet Movie Database, was a much more popular method, and a site that Amazon acquired in 1998 and integrated the review system of into Amazon Prime a decade later. It just so happened that, for Netflix, after testing it, this strategy engaged only 6 per cent of its members – so they cut it after six years.[4] Gibson Biddle, former VP of Product Management at Netflix, called this approach part of their "DHM model", which stands for Delighting customers in Hard-to-copy, Margin-enhancing ways. It was a model that helped define which product strategies they should prioritise and test, of which personalisation was one.

The purpose of personalisation is a system of beliefs held by the brand. Any brand that wants to create a deeper relationship with their customers based on mutual trust should personalise. Period. As long as they have a clear understanding of this purpose – and the costs associated – they are well on their way to defeating the Golden Dragon.

Being more personal with customers, creating connection, being familiar, promoting relevance, not treating them as numbers but as people — is something every brand should fixate on in today's global economic environment of infinite consumer choice and universal access, should they not?

Once a brand understands its purpose, it must test it. That's what experimentation is designed to help with: evidence. Netflix is crowned the king of personalisation, not because they spend thousands of hours personalising, but because they *tested* to see if personalisation was right for their customers and concluded that, yes, it was. Even if it took ten years to attribute it.

Testing

"Personalisation is an exponential growth opportunity, but Netflix still needs great content, delivered in 0 seconds in 4K, agnostic of personalisation, if they don't do that, they'll go bankrupt. Their core product is outstanding, and that gives them a right to do personalisation — but it is one of many strategies available to them."

Leon Andrews, Head of User Experience, RICS[5]

Having a purpose for personalising is one thing. Testing it to make sure it works is another thing entirely. Having a sword is useless unless you're willing to swing it around.

Trying to defeat the Golden Dragon with only evidence about what others have done to prove value is a step in the right direction. It worked for Marks & Spencer. Sort of. It does resemble the "jump off the cliff" mentality that others before it have fatally fallen to.

From my research, experimentation is the only approach to effectively attribute a return on a personalisation strategy.

In a study by the Harvard Business Review (HBR), between 19 per cent and 24 per cent of respondents did not know whether their organisation's personalisation initiatives had affected revenue over the past two years.[6] They state that this underlines the fact that organisations need to become better at using data to measure the results of their personalisation initiatives. Experimentation is that better way of using data.

But be warned. There are still plenty of fallacies and things to watch out for when testing personalisation. The first of which is appreciating that any experiment is nothing more than a snapshot in time. If you extrapolate it, you cannot see how users react to that variable over time because macro factors are out of your control. You are also using the retrospective to forecast the future without an understanding of unknown future factors. There is a limit to how much such a discipline can tell you. We're not Marty McFly here, betting on sports games already knowing the final scores. We're gambling with little predictive information at our disposal.

As such, annualising returns from experimentation may make the board stand up on their feet but, without degradation or consideration for how behaviours change, would be considered dangerous. The last thing you'd want to do is put your head on the chopping block for inflated expectations, only to be questioned on why those targets weren't hit a year later. Lucky for M&S, they were. And then some.

The second is an appreciation that when testing the impact of personalisation within revenue attribution, what you're doing is shifting an average. On average, an average customer, exposed to an average AB test will perform averagely. These averages change over time based on the composition of users, behaviours and metrics. For example, running the same experiment in something as arbitrary as a sale period versus a non-sale period will result in two very different averaged results. When there are multiple AB tests designed to attribute one single programme, you get what Stephen Pavlovich, CEO Conversion.com,[7] calls "Fuzz". "I'd be hesitant on grouping together multiple experiments and adding up the impact," Pavlovich said. "As each result is a range — and confidence reflects the existence of a difference, not the size of the difference, then you'd be grouping together fuzzy results — which adds a lot of fuzz. It tends to be how a lot of people look at it and it's misleading."

There's really only one way to do it.

"These are never all purely additive, so you need to either take a series of haircuts or use hold out to get cleaner read on the true incremental."

Alex Williams, Head of Growth & Personalisation, M&S[8]

Victoria's Secret learned from Williams' advice. They started a programme called the "Personalisation Back-test" and held back 5 per cent of all visitors from receiving any personalisation at all. Essentially, this was a small control group compared against the cumulatively personalised group — a holdout cell. This is the control. Experimenting against grouped personalised experiences and grouped mass, or non-personalised experiences will help give an answer to how much the brand can attribute personalisation to. For Victoria's Secret, this was a 15 per cent incremental uplift.[9]

One can't help but think what is the cost of this? This was an experiment that ran for 12 months and only stopped a whopping 36 months or so after launching their personalisation program back in 2018. How come? If a brand's primary metric to determine the output of a hypothesis is a continuous scale, such as revenue, you have more variables to be certain of the exact outcome. To have more confidence in the size of the uplift, not just the fact that an uplift exists, you'd have to run the experiment for much longer. For example, you might continue to serve a losing variation A to 50 per cent of your traffic so you can have greater confidence in the value of the winning variation B. Not only is the length of time needed to run the test longer, but the time taken to analyse the results of the experiment can feel and look a lot like navel-gazing. Which, at Victoria's Secret, is a good thing, I guess.

It's prudent to also ask, "What is the purpose of an experiment?" just as it is to ask, "What is the purpose of personalisation?" It is designed to prove or disprove a hypothesis; to validate a variation. Simply put, is B better than A?

Experiments aren't typically designed to show by how much B is better than A. They are designed to show that a difference exists, not the size of that difference. And so, to wrap up this fallacy, handing the mic over to a source I spoke to at Optimizely: "The second you start measuring every experiment on just revenue, you lose the ability to think strategically. You have to balance two things: solving your customers' most urgent pain points and proving your impact to the business. if you let one of these two overwhelm the other, you're headed for a dead end."[10]

Above all, the expectation is clear — 74 per cent of brands expect personalisation initiatives to boost revenue in some form.[11] Seven years ago, two-thirds of respondents said that they expect at least a 6 per cent incremental annual revenue lift from personalisation, with companies in several sectors — apparel, financial services, grocery and wholesale clubs, and technology — anticipating increases of 10 per cent or more.[12] That expectation is only higher now.

The trick is to manage expectations, not fight them. Or, as I call it: *Appreciate*, *Align* and *Agree* — a hat tip to any trio of alliteration — on what levels of accuracy are needed for revenue attribution within your business in order to prove the ROI of personalisation as a whole. The more exact it is, the longer and potentially more expensive it will be. I would recommend appreciating, aligning and agreeing on a scale of return, therefore, not an exact return.

There are perhaps a few lessons to be learned from the giant advertising agencies of our generation on how to sell to stakeholders and manage their expectations. Brands should not question the $10 million Pepsi famously spent in 2018 getting Beyoncé to star in their one-minute "Grown Woman" ad, but should put on their white coats to financially understand the return of the sticky "Add to cart" button they just placed on the product page.

It's worth asking the question of whether exact attribution is even possible without a holdout cell, which is why Victoria's Secret did what they did. The three perils of forecasting results, collating results and accurately measuring the variance in those results should question the validity of experimenting within personalisation.

Like before, I argue that it's better to experiment to know that brands are rowing in the right direction, rather than experiment with how fast they are rowing.

How should practitioners set that expectation? Experimenting as accurately as possible is one route despite its perils, absolutely. Victoria's Secret's personalisation back-test programme "drove confidence to not need this holistic analysis approach"[13] and they continued to personalise, presumably without quantifying exact uplift, just that things were moving in the upward direction. Another is by first acknowledging, and then appreciating, that personalisation is infinitely more than just a revenue opportunity.

Retention

The answer to how to best defeat the Golden Dragon lies in a balance of attribution, which not only sets expectations, but harkens back to what the true purpose of personalisation should be about: retaining consumers in order to grow a relationship.

But wait.

How do you measure, and grow, relationships?

When we meet a friend, the conversation that we have with them is obviously highly tailored to their needs. We pay close attention. We nod. We maintain eye contact. We verbalise confirmation of listening. Yet, attaching a monetary value to the importance of us squeezing in their name five times unnaturally in the conversation or listening and reacting in a personalised manner (compared to a generic one) is beyond absurd.

In a more commercial setting, what about the value of a salesperson doing this to a sales lead? The belief that listening more and responding better to our friends makes the exchange more valuable for both of us. And seeing or feeling that value is not as immediate as a purchase.

Can personalisation therefore even be attributed given that generating revenue is not its true purpose? McKinsey states the attribution of personalisation as a 10 per cent increase in revenue and up to a 30 per cent increase in customer satisfaction.[14] The closer we are, the more we trust, the more we trust, the more we spend. But the disproportionate disparity evidenced by McKinsey between revenue uplift and customer satisfaction suggests that it is the latter that is the clear beneficiary of personalisation. It suggests that, while there are revenue gains that can be made from it, the gains made from the ethereal notion of "having a happy customer" are disproportionately higher. And of even greater value, both in retention and recommendation. The intangible has more value than the tangible.

A proxy metric for relationship is longevity of friendship, or in a commercial setting, loyalty. Ryan Jordan, Strategy Director, Brainlabs,[15] explained it best: "When a business is so hyper-reactive to conversion movements week-to-week, it makes it harder for personalisation to cut through. There's not the desire to wait around to feel the true benefit of something that could take six weeks or six months to come to fruition. That benefit is in the repeat engagement and loyalty of the user."

Ah. So that's why revenue is commonly used to attribute success. It's immediately gratifying.

One does impact the other, however. In my research, I discovered that there is a clear correlation between personalisation and retention. More than a correlation, in fact. Plenty of academic studies, and larger tech brands, use retention as their North Star for their personalisation efforts. In one paper, researchers argued the long-term goal of a personalised recommendation system is to not only satisfy the users' needs within a current session, but also to ensure they come back to the platform more often in the future.[16] "User return, which indicates users' long-term engagement, should be emphasized as an (at least) equally important metric of recommendation quality, and therefore to be optimized in a recommender system."[17]

Most existing recommendation algorithms only focus on optimising immediate responses. Few of them explicitly consider the temporal behaviour of users after reviewing the recommended items. Or they impose a strong assumption that users' return behaviour is consistent with their immediate responses. Or, worse still, the naive view that the probability of user return is independent from the recommendations being made.

I'd go one step further and suggest that those successful in personalisation have a more mature approach — they *only* focus on retention as their key performance indicator for success.

"Retention is probably the most general and common goal of recommendations. Services only survive if people keep using them over time. And returning over time is the best metric of doing a good thing."

Glenn McDonald, Data Alchemist, Spotify[18]

So, basically, if Spotify jump off a cliff, we should all consider doing the same. Given that Netflix also uses retention as their key metric for personalisation success, we better be sure there's someone there to catch us at the bottom.

When personalisation was first introduced as a product strategy at Netflix in 2006, Todd Yellin, then-engineer product leader, hypothesised that a personalised product experience would help improve none other than retention. Retention was his endgame. He saw short term metrics, such as revenue or conversion immediately gratifying but myopic. One example in one podcast was about making a cancel subscription button difficult to find which would reduce cancellations – but at what cost? "They make it super hard to cancel a subscription service because that moves your metrics. It hurts [long-term metrics]. So, we'll do the opposite. Instead of hiding the cancel button, we make it more obvious. Does it help customer trust and long-term brand reputation and in the end, long-term revenue and profit? Absolutely."[19]

For sure, Netflix are in personalisation for the long haul. In the case of determining the success of personalisation, Yellin's metric was the percentage of new members who rated at least 50 movies in their first six weeks with the service. In other words, usage. The theory was that if members were willing to rate lots of movies, it meant they valued the results of their ratings: personalised movie choices.

It was an initial success, clearly. They drove this metric from the low single digits into the high twenties over a handful of years. Over time, Netflix moved the goalposts of those proxy metrics as they moved away from star-based rating systems using explicit feedback. They moved towards using inferences to base their personalised recommendations on. Their metric never shifted, however. It was always more rooted in long-term retention than short-term conversion. Moving on to avoid spoilers, they saw a steady improvement in these metrics, which provided a strong enough signal that they would eventually succeed. As such, they kept "doubling down" on personalisation, assuming that the correlation to retention was real. All of its subsequent proxy metrics were improving, so it made sense to believe this.

It wasn't until 10 years later that they were able to prove that retention was a beneficiary of personalisation. That's right. It took more than a decade to prove that personalisation directly improved retention.

Gibson Biddle, ex-VP Product Management at Netflix, describes the personalisation efforts at Netflix as a decade-long "leap of faith".[20] You'd be forgiven for thinking it was blind faith. Proxy metric indicators and conviction paid off. Netflix proved that it can take a very long time to verify correlation at the minimum, attribution at the maximum.

The metric they chose may have taken a long time to attribute, but they saw that retention was an indicator of success because it best reflected *the customer*.

Think about that for a second.

Why long-term retention isn't largely considered among most brands is not just the lack of immediate gratification as Jordans indicated, but that it's just hard to do. Analysing the impact of recommendation systems within a current session, such as clicks, likes and purchases is infinitely easier than it is in future sessions, such as returning users or churn rate. Is this why brands focus on revenue and other short-term metrics? Because it's easily quantifiable?

When Dynamic Yield's Nathan Richter claimed, "There's no golden metric for personalisation,"[21] I think what he was talking about was the balance between metrics that quantify results and those that infer quality or performance. Human behaviour is more nuanced than bucketing it into a metric that is both binary and retrospective: "Did the customer convert or not?" When we break up the customer journey into its core milestones – of browsing, engagement, product awareness, consideration, desire and purchase, for example, we need to ask what are the users' objectives at each stage? To suggest these objectives are all the same, which is to buy, is grossly misunderstood. Brands only have a 2 per cent eCommerce conversion rate on average for a reason. What about the other 98 per cent?

"Having a one-size-fits-all website that doesn't tailor itself to where someone is in the consumer decision-making process," said Dr Paul Marsden, Consumer Psychologist, Syzygy, to me in our interview.[22] If the metric that defines performance is generic, it is likely that the approach to website design and experience will be generic also. This is one of the reasons I cited early where brands that focus on something as aggregated as conversion rate as a method of optimisation, end up designing for the location of the solution rather than who it is for. Instead of calling it "User Experience" perhaps it would be more appropriate to call it "Page Experience" given that generic metrics of success create generic experiences by virtue. To me, this is nothing more than anti-personalisation.

Chapter 20

Money Makes Personalisation Go Round

"We established a measurement framework that comprised of balancing metrics. Things that work alongside of one another and the balance of going after those two things that give you a good outcome. As oppose to one single metric which can drive you headlong down a certain route without thought or understanding of the implications."

Alex Williams, Head of Growth & Personalisation, M&S[1]

At the start of my hero's quest, Shiva Manjunath[2] tasked me with finding a definition of personalisation. He claimed that it was the lack of definition that holds the industry back from progressing. Those definitions varied so much, and I was left with the feeling that people redefining personalisation do so for self-serving praise and commercial gain. If we're going down that route, I want to stake my claim that personalisation should be redefined as "purse-onalisation". Another redefinition, because why the hell not?

I disagreed that it was the definition that was holding the industry back, but at the time I didn't know what that one thing was.

After seeing the Golden Dragon turns into a pile of ash on its bed of cash, I now see that it's the lack of purposeful measurement that holds it back. Or, better yet, the *balance of purposeful measurement.*

The Benefits of Revenue Attribution

Revenue is imperative to understand how much to invest and, to some extent, the value of that investment. Don't get me wrong it's not the root of all evil, because by understanding the return on an investment, brands can take personalisation efforts to the next level by adding more resources into it. Being a Golden Dragon isn't always a bad thing when you see it through this lens, it allows brands to reinvest.

Netflix, for example, uses personalisation to cost-analyse future content ideas. In what former VP of Product, Gibson Biddle, calls "right-sizing" content spend.[3] Netflix can use its algorithms and knowledge of customer tastes to create predictions of how many users will see what and, therefore, how much to budget. The first season of *Stranger Things* may have been an overwhelming global success. But all future seasons are a known quantity – more than 100 million members will binge-watch it, so Netflix can afford to greenlight a budget north of $250 million per season.[4] And Amazon Prime knew that 2022's *The Rings of Power* – its flagship acquisition – would invite billions of eyeballs to join its streaming service, even if it did cost them $715 million – the most expensive TV show of all time. Indeed, the company reported that 25 million people worldwide watched the show. And that was just on its first day of release. Knowing what personalisation brings in terms of pounds and pence can help give back and reinvest into the back pockets of the top executives at the firm. I mean, into better customer experiences.

I may sound like a cynical old fart, but I am a product of the millionaire millennial world we live in. Brands have every right to squeeze every last drop of revenue they can from personalising experiences. The value is definitely there. McKinsey, the global management consulting firm, stated that the average revenue uplift from personalisation is usually 10 per cent.[5] Boston Consulting Group has evidence that the revenue increase from personalisation efforts can be up to 20 per cent.[6]

We (read: I) must accept that we live within commercial entities in a capitalist world. We can't escape that. If that's what the world is used to, we have to abide by it.

I Want It, I Want It Now!
How you start is how you end, however. The current state of personalisation measurement is imbalanced in favour of the organisation because revenue is the most frequently cited benefit and so brands expected that to be the case.

This expectation is also influenced by the need for ease. It might not be the most cited because money makes the world go round – although it absolutely does – it might just be because it makes it easier to go round.

This is a curse suffered by a lot of modern businesses. Where brands are impatient. Where they generally over-obsess about the things that are immediately quantifiable because they are easy, and therefore under invest in those activities which are hard to put a figure on. Ironically, it is those that are often the most valuable.

Personalisation improves efficiency and decreases costs, for example. Boston Consulting Group (BCG) undertook research that showed that the most sophisticated digital marketers, those that have reached what they call "multi-moment maturity" another allusion to commercial ownership, can achieve cost savings of up to 30 per cent.[7] This is because they are able to give customers relevant experiences at different points in the buying process. It is also a more efficient way of operationally practising marketing as a whole, according to BCG, yet it is often the more immediate "personalisation increases revenue by up to 20 per cent" that brands fixate on.

Personalisation improves customer experience. However, because it is a slower form of measurement, the money is invested more at the top of the funnel than at the bottom. Is paying Taylor Swift $26 million to star in a couple of Diet Coke ads a more effective use of money than tailoring messages to individual people online?[8] It's certainly sexier. Even more so than M&S fruit.

A rather ridiculous addition to that assertion is that this investment isn't necessarily being spent in the channels because that is where they are most effective, but simply because it's easier to prove that it has an effect.

And so, every area of a business is often reduced to the same treatment. Paid search is attributed to revenue figures. Display advertising, the same. Emails, too. (Which, by the way, is one of the most ludicrous attribution models, suggesting that just because someone clicked on something within an email, it means they own that purchase.) And here we enter the world of personalisation. In the land of recommendation engines where brands fall victim to the same last-click attribution without consideration of longer-term satisfaction. The land of tailoring social proof messages designed to gently persuade those ready to purchase where in fact they are generalised to all users, persuading the few and inciting anxiety in the majority. The land of discount codes to help those immediately convert without appreciating the perceptual impact of continual discounting on the brand. I could go on.

This combination of needing to quantify and prove return, and that return needing to be immediate, is what prevents something much slower to attribute, such as customer loyalty or engagement, from really getting off the ground.

Balance

There is of course a link between revenue and customer satisfaction, as Alex Williams of M&S pointed out to me: "If a customer spends more with you (in a retail context specifically), isn't this creating value for them?"[9]

It's less of a link, however, and more of a balance – one of the strategies I discuss to defeat the beast. When tipped too far one way, this creates an inequality in the relationship being created. What about the often-cited customer-first approach? Is that now thwarted because brands have shareholders to appease and growth targets to hit? Does revenue as a metric trump customer satisfaction as a metric? I say yes.

Efforts fail because of this lack of focus on the customer. A lack of appreciation between the immediate, short-term impact of personalisation, and the long-term brand performance is just plain worrying. In my example above of myopically attributing a revenue figure to a recommendation system, for example, it does not mean that customers even engaged with it, let alone purchased from it, let alone increased user satisfaction to a level ensuring they will return again. Over-indexing on such short-term engagement metrics can lead to undesirable recommendations, such as clickbait content or pigeon-holing efforts. These will, in turn, hurt the long-term user experience.

Balance attribution between the short-term and long-term goals of what personalisation really brings, ideally with a focus on the latter. Retention, loyalty, and predictive measurement. Never forgetting why brands should personalise in the first place. Proving revenue uplift is just a necessary evil within the process, but it shouldn't consume the why behind what brands are doing.

Part V

The Stubborn Dragon

"Come not between the Dragon, and his wrath."
William Shakespeare, *King Lear*[1]

The Stubborn Dragon thrives on eating as much data and technology as it can. Like students at an all-you-can-eat pizza buffet. If the Golden Dragon demands to collect as much gold as possible, this dragon survives by terrorising entire villages with its winged wrath, gobbling up as much technology and data as it can before flying to the next village and firing all its residents, without ever really digesting any of the ingredients it consumes. It just shits it out the other end.

Thankfully, this dragon is easy to defeat. But first we must get close enough to it.

Chapter 21

Know Thy Enemy: The Stubborn Dragon

"In digital marketing, there's so much about taking the person out of the equation. Everything has become data. People seek connection. People want to feel like they belong."

Siobhan Solberg, Founder & Consultant, Raze[1]

Our second metaphorical mythical beast to slay — The Stubborn Dragon — is the false desire to have all the data and technology at your disposal in order to get on with personalising.

It's a lie, an excuse.

If they have their defined purpose (as defined in the previous chapter), they just need to get on with it and only collect data and technology related to that purpose.

Currently, there is a false narrative — and I could feel it from all the industry leaders I spoke to — that in order to kill this particular beast, brands feel they need every weapon available in their arsenal dangling off their belt before plucking up the courage to walk up to this dragon. For brands, they feel as though every last individual needs tracking to the nth degree, with all their preferences needing to be understood, and then, and only then, can brands say they are personalising. Not too dissimilar to how brands wouldn't classify their expedition as a personalised one because the outcome wasn't sexy enough.

Thankfully, this dragon isn't a difficult creature to kill; it has very thin skin and doesn't require a cool weapon to do so; it just has to be done swiftly.

Any sharp stick will do.

When I asked the majority of CEOs and business leaders why they can't reach the personalisation paradise we all see in our dreams, data and technology seemed to come out on top. Fifty per cent of retailers say that gathering customer data is their biggest challenge within their efforts to personalise.[2] It can be as high as 67 per cent, depending on other study sources.[3] They're not wrong. It's hard. But it need not be.

There are two common themes that cropped up time and time again within this research about how the Stubborn Dragon remains so far undefeated and why that's the case.

DATA
1) Data Overwhelm:
Brands consume and collect all the data – too much data – and all the technology resources possible in order to personalise anything and everything.

2) Data Regulation:
Brands must collect data in an ethical, legal and purposeful way.

TECH
1) Implementation & Effort:
Personalisation engines and automated data collection – are they worth all the trouble?

2) Ethics & Manipulation:
Responsibility, regulation and manipulation of AI

Get your stick all nice and pointy, it's time to start poking...

Chapter 22

Data, Data, Data:
The Mouse House's Magicbands

"Data! Data! Data! I can't make bricks without clay."

Sherlock Holmes[1]

There is a rumour within the industry that you need a lot of data to personalise. All the data, in fact. "Data is definitely a big issue. In 95 per cent of the companies I've worked with, the data is a mess. Data Warehousing. Data Repositories. Talk about problems with conflating terms and issues. Siloing. Mishandling of data pipelines, and processing – that's the backbone of more advanced personalisation. Garbage in, garbage out," Ben Labay, Managing Director, Speero,[2] told me.

One source I interviewed, who I won't mention by name, put it more succinctly: "Most organisations' data is absolutely shit and their view of the customer is shit too." Speak your mind, why don't you?

While there is absolute truth in both quotes, it is the expectations that come from the responsible adults leading personalisation that influence this train of thought. One of the reasons why Amazon, Spotify and Netflix are so often cited as the responsible parents is because they require users to log in. They have legal, constant and consented data on their users. Not to mention they have all the money. Their data preferences are more easily managed, and those interests can be more easily personalised against. What is the case for retailers and platforms where the vast majority of users are not logged in and therefore anonymous? In the modern era, where the death of the cookie faces its impending doom, how can personalisation even be a thing when the vast majority of users are non-identifiable?

The Magic Data Kingdom

Disney is, perhaps, the best example of the Stubborn Dragon.

It has endless possibilities for personalisation.

And, naturally, that brings with it endless problems.

Prior to 2013, when a visitor entered a theme park, Disney had very little data on how guests moved or what patterns of experiences they had. Did they throw up an extortionately priced hot dog before or after Splash Mountain? What about the super expensive merchandise — was that bought on their way in or way out? This data, and millions of other identifiers just like it, was essentially a black box, arguably worth billions in additional visitor spending. Disney even applied for a patent to collect customer data by scanning guests' shoes to provide more understanding within this black box, such as the most common paths between rides and where guests spent the most time.[3]

That was, until they doubled down on a $1 billion investment in their concept of MagicBands, introduced in 2013. These wristbands are equipped with ID technology designed to connect to an antenna and pinpoint the exact location of guests in the park, all seamlessly integrated with the My Disney Experience app, their latest online booking system. Since then, Disney has been able to accommodate an additional 3,000 guests *per day* through their park reservation system. An operational and guest experience success. No more goofy data collection from Disney.

In 2015 — the famed start of personalisation proper — *Wired* magazine published an article explaining the benefits of the Disney MagicBands whilst highlighting the bright future of data collection at theme parks happily ever after. At Be Our Guest, the eye-wateringly overpriced restaurant at Magic Kingdom, MagicBands use customer locations to triangulate their table so their server can find them; the bands are connected to a central terminal via radios in the table and ceiling. When the server comes to your table, they already know your name, if it's your birthday and who your favourite Disney character is. Mine is Hercules, by the way.

If Disney decides to install those sensors throughout the park, a whole new world — see what I did there — of data collection opens up. The bands already personalise a guest's experience, but imagine next-level opportunities, like having Mickey or Snow White track down guests for a birthday surprise or email a coupon for free ice cream or a fast pass to another ride if they detect you've been queueing for too long already. Park officials could use a myriad of cameras to capture candid moments of your family enjoying the rides, fireworks and any one of the 12,000 gift shops — I'm exaggerating, but not by much — and stitch them together into a personalised film so you never forget what a small world it really is after all. The product teams at Disney called this the *Story Engine*.

Eight years later, seemingly still stuck in a galaxy still far, far away, none of these fairy tales came true. And not just because coupons and free things don't exist at Disney. But because the expectation of using all that data has been not for guest satisfaction purposes, but for commercial ones. Instead of soothing a crying child, the My Disney Experience app will identify you're near a $5 soda machine and promote a $7 soda. Or whether you might want to purchase a fast-pass experience for the *Pirates of the Caribbean* ride that you're near. Location, with a smidge of brand preference, feels as though it has become the predominant attribute in personalising the guest experience, rather than what it should be: *loyalty*. Personalisation is still waiting for its Prince Charming to come along and save it from another unnecessary live action reboot of *Cinderella*.

Happiness often gets lost somewhere between expectation and reality, and, if the above inability to progress forward is anything to go by, Disney certainly isn't the happiest place on Earth. (By the way, that's been the Disneyland slogan since 1955. And it's been stuck in that time ever since given the lack of renovations and investment into new rides.)

In Regulation We Trust

Disney isn't alone. McDonald's has the same problem with data collection, too. There's too much of it and the possibilities are enough to kickstart the Pavlovian response as much as any Big Mac.

Walt Disney World in Orlando receives about 160,000 guests to their parks every day. That's a figure completely dwarfed (a little pun intended) by the 70 million customers that eat at McDonald's every day.[4] Like Disney, prior to McDonald's investment, understanding individuals was a black box. All those purchases are made in person with buying decisions made on the spot, human to human. There was no understanding of who individuals are because no individual ID is associated with them.

Like Disney, it became evident to the personalisation teams at McDonald's that they also had to create some system that applied an ID to each customer. Create data where there was once none. Today, this is regarded as the foundation of personalisation, if not a prerequisite. The assumption is that if identification cannot be made, personalisation cannot be done. When customers are identified, however, it makes the strategy of personalisation infinitely more powerful because it creates a virtuous circle of loyalty and expectation. The more that brands are able to identify you, the more they can personalise to your needs. The more your needs are personalised, the higher the level of loyalty you demonstrate. The more loyalty you demonstrate, the more you expect the brand to personalise your experience. This is the virtuous circle of the personalisation-data paradox.

Simply put, opportunities increase when brands know their audience. Or, perhaps, it's more pertinent to say: opportunities to sell better increase when brands know their audience. The CEO of McDonald's, Chris Kempczinski, openly talked about audience identification: "What happens when you [invest in data collection] is the percentage of identified customers goes up dramatically. That opens up a whole range of things, from service opportunities, pricing opportunities, etc."[5]

Four years on, and although the percentage of identified users is different between markets, sources suggest that about 15 per cent of users on McDonald's kiosks are now identifiable, and 10 per cent in drive-thrus are too.[6] That still feels rather insignificant when trying to personalise for individuals. But it is a benefit, clearly.

How much data, and to what level, is needed? If Disney collects all these data points where there was once no data before, just like McDonald's, what are they going to do with that? The expectation of being able to ID customers by their number plate, as McDonald's once assumed, or Mickey locating bored and screaming five-year-old children in a two-hour queue just to give their parents a moment of distraction was never realised.

As a parent, I'd love that. But musophobics,* I fear, may not.

It's not just the collection of data that's the barrier, but the ethical and legal consequences of doing so. While the majority of Disney guests are now identifiable through their MagicBands (when they decide to spend the extra $20 for the privilege of a piece of rubber around their wrist), there is still a big hurdle to jump in collecting that data ethically and legally and practically applying it.

Think about it.

If personalisation is all about creating and maintaining relationships built on trust, then an exchange between customer and brand is a valuable precursor to that trust. As a result, it's not all about thinking, "What do we, as a brand, want to collect in order to personalise for our customers?" but, "What do our customers want to tell us to enable us to personalise for them?"

---

* Musophobia is an overwhelming fear or mice or rats.

That overwrought customer-first phrase rears its ugly head once more. Sure, there are restrictions being brought into the fold on how to collect data legally to help shift this balance, such as the European Union's General Data Protection Regulation (GDPR) that came into power in 2018. Yet, it is the ethics and customer first principle thinking that holds a greater impact, especially with personalisation strategies. Much more than regulatory change, something that 60 per cent of brands agree with.[7]

Unfortunately, it's just not how the majority of brands are wired. The need for more data to personalise *for* consumers, not *with* them, has created a domineering dead-end street akin to polite daylight robbery. "Give us all your data, and *we'll* tell *you* what to do!"

Where's the two-way street that's built on trust?

Mistrust

"Unless a customer has a long-standing relationship with the retailer that is trustworthy and loyal, they will be reluctant to give them anything, even their email address. Popping out a sign-up window after 2 seconds of visiting a brand's website is not as effective. Sharing data requires a level of intimacy with a brand. Two main rules of intimacy are: one — it is mutual, two — it takes time to build. Two seconds is not enough time."

Kate Nightingale, Founder, Humanising Brands[8]

Right now, there is such an unhealthy scepticism from customers about how companies use their data. What are customers getting in return? What is the value exchange?

Sixty-four per cent of customers are sceptical that brands in at least one sector would safeguard their personal information and privacy online. Fifty-seven per cent of customers genuinely believe companies are not just misusing it but actually selling their data![9] Every day millions of people scream in unison: "Why do you need to know my cat's name and how often she goes to the toilet?"

Where has this deep-rooted feeling of mistrust come from? Our excessive media consumption, particularly on social media, is often held responsible for various issues, with data and privacy concerns taking centre stage in the ongoing debate. This lack of trust in social media technology, recommendations and algorithms has trickled down to other business verticals, mainly retail. This mistrust accelerated after the 2018

Cambridge Analytica scandal – there's that year again – a global controversy that took the headlines hostage and resulted in a $37 billion drop in the market capitalisation of Facebook.[10] The tech giant was caught with their hand in the cookie jar not by telling people how to vote, but almost definitely influencing outcomes. "Fake News!" They were doing so through proven mistruths such as "Turkey are joining the EU!" when in fact there was never any discussion for Turkey do such a thing.[11] Both no one and yet everyone was surprised when both Brexit and Donald Trump's presidential inauguration hinged on just 1 per cent of the electorate. There have been many books written on this topic with Cathy O'Neil's Weapons of Math Destruction[12] really digging into the weeds of the inequality of algorithms. She wrote about the importance of being aware of the potential biases and ethical implications of algorithmic systems, advocating for transparency, fairness and accountability in their use to mitigate the negative impact of "weapons of math destruction" on society. O'Neil fixated on Facebook.[13]

> "Facebook had a 'Verified Apps' program and claimed it certified the security of participating apps. It didn't. Facebook promised users that it would not share their personal information with advertisers. It did."
>
> **Frank Pasquale, Author of The Black Box Society**[14]

These stories – the current values and demands held by customers – are all about transparency and the benefit of a data exchange. Brands want your data so that they can personalise your experience, making it better and more relevant to you. A simple dot to dot that feels as though it's ingrained in authenticity. In general, and although simplistic, yes. One report says that 33 per cent of people are willing to share their online activity in exchange for personalised rewards and engagements.[15] Another report suggests that figure is as high at 87 per cent.[16]

What that exchange is depends on the willingness of data exchange from the customer. Some are more tempting than others: consumers perceive hard-value incentives, such as discounts and free samples, to be more compelling reasons to disclose their data than soft-value incentives, such as access to games or newsletters. Up to 90 per cent are willing to share that data when presented with the right value exchange,[17] although other studies show that is just 35 per cent.[18] Either way, it's clearly possible to build those pillars of trust with the right message.

What data customers willing to give away is the question. That is inherently related to what purpose the brand is personalising for. Clearly if the brand wants to know how often your cat goes to the toilet, I hope that you are on a site that sells such a thing and not just searching for some high heels.* Customers want personalisation, that much is true; we've been down that road. But customers are downright sceptical about providing their data to be personalised with. This inner conflict creates what the industry commonly refers to as the "Personalisation-privacy Paradox".[19] Where two-thirds of customers want ads that are tailored to their specific needs, but nearly half are hesitant to share their data in order to create those personalised ads.[20] We can't have it all.

Whoever said "the customer is always right" only got it half right.

Once again, that tug of war, that conflict breeding drama I mentioned at the start of the book, resurfaces from the ooze. Personalisation is starting to prove itself as the Adam Sandler of the marketing industry: we want a lot of it, yet cringe at the very idea of paying to see it.

---

* I ended up in an endless spiral searching for cat toilets and wow there are some super high tech self-cleaning ones costing £650!

Chapter 23

Too Much Trouble: AI Engines

"Marketers were sold a vision of personalisation that required way too much effort from marketing teams to make it work."
Tom Wentworth, Chief Marketing Officer for RapidMiner[1]

The technology for automating data collection is already here. The trouble is that it takes too much effort to practically apply. Or at least, that's the belief.

Personalisation engines such as Adobe and Oracle were originally catalysts for personalisation as a strategy, especially in the late 2010s. Etsy, eBay and Pandora were all at the forefront of brands using such technology. Having this capability to achieve personalisation has, of course, accelerated brand's ability to personalise. Gartner's Magic Quadrant[2] cites twelve major technological players in the space, which are ranked by completeness of vision versus ability to execute. The leaders in 2022 were Dynamic Yield, Insider, Salesforce, Adobe and SAP. Hundreds more exist that offer personalisation capabilities and even more than that offer recommendation capabilities.

Fantastic. We've reached the heralded technological age of personalisation perfection.

Or have we?

Gartner ran a survey in 2022 and found that marketers who have personalisation engines inside their organisation only utilise a paltry 48 per cent of their capabilities on average. This ranks personalisation engines as the second-lowest in utilisation among 29 different technologies.[3] Add to the woe, details from a study into telecommunications companies by McKinsey suggests only 5 per cent of companies are fully utilising their data for personalisation.[4] It's like having a Ferrari in your garage and only using it to drive to the corner shop. Which is something I would totally do; I wouldn't want to scratch it. Not in the dodgy area that I live in.

Why on earth aren't marketers taking full advantage of these powerful tools? If the technology is there, why is it not being used? Do brands assume it will just sit there and do it all for them at the touch of a button?

A source I spoke to who, for his flippant comment preferred to remain nameless, summed up and mocked brands' current belief in personalisation technology as: "Recommendations. Plug in this algorithm. Plug in your data. Plug in your contents. Go on holiday."[5]

The answer to this quandary is simple: the level of effort required. Just the thought of brands having to personalise gives them a headache.

In 2020, Peter Weinberg ranted on what he called "the worst idea in marketing" where he suggested: "The goal of marketing isn't to provide relevant content to customers; it's to make money. Most advertising is irrelevant (such as the Geico Gecko), but still effective. The costs of greater 'relevance' (micro-targeting is more expensive, micro-content is more expensive) almost certainly outweigh the benefits."[6]

The rhetoric was something that kept cropping up in my research: the argument that the costs of personalisation outweighed the gains. Or, as Weinberg put it, "Personalisation is an unscalable tactic that massively increases creative and media costs, which nullifies any so-called efficiencies."[7]

What is the cost here? People are a big cost. Publications like *Perfecting Personalization* cited having too few staff to undertake personalisation as the number one organisational barrier to achieving it – because, clearly, people cost money.[8]

There's a different type of cost, too, and that's a mental expense. The more effort required to do something, the more it will inherently cost. Not just in terms of doing time but also thinking time. Within personalisation, there's a belief that it's more complex to create content and journeys for hundreds of segments when one good journey or message for all segments will do. Of course, this is a more ubiquitous problem than one that just sits within commercial organisations. Personalisation is akin to going to the gym. We buy the membership ... then make excuses to never go ... and then go to Burger King... and then complain when we're still overweight.

Dare I say it, we – most of the world at large – is simply too lazy to personalise.

"That's a problem with human beings and the concept of magic bullets. We just want to take the tablet. We don't want to go to the gym three times a week because going to the gym is really hard. Instead of going to the gym, all I really want to do is look at Snapchat and take a magic pill to make myself look better. It's systemic within society."

Leon Andrews, Head of User Experience, RICS[9]

As a result, is it any wonder that the big tech firms are the only ones reportedly doing personalisation well, when really, they are the only ones with that type of cash to create teams to go forth and do it? Is personalisation therefore a strategy reserved only for the elite? Where 95 per cent of brands, mere peasants if you will, are unable to reach the lofty heights and expectations set by the industry simply because they lack the cash? Perhaps when Google reported that retailers invest just 0.7 per cent of their revenue into personalisation it's not necessarily a figure that seems low, instead it's a figure that seems relative. Google noted that the best-in-class retailers are investing 30 per cent more than those who aren't considered as part of the elitist social circle.[10] Of course they are investing more and are better at it, they have the capability to do so; more money equates to more resources. And of course, that statistic comes from a commercial entity in Google that just so happens to sell personalised advertising and experimentation software.

Regardless, even if the resources were raining down and always available in some form, does that mean that the revenue generated from personalisation outweighs the cost? Not necessarily. Once again, we hear that same theme tune ringing in our ears: ROI, return on investment. Or the expectation thereof.

Technology should be the answer here. The weapon we slay this dragon with. AI is the sword in the stone, Thor's hammer. But who's worthy enough to wield it?

The tech absolutely helps, sure, but that doesn't explain its under-utilisation as quoted by Gartner. The effort to wield the personalisation hammer, especially in earlier software, required marketers to create if/else business rules in order to design solutions. That is, for every personalised experience, a set of rules had to be set up, along with pieces of content for each rule. RapidMiner's Tom Wentworth noted that whilst this was attractive it was completely unmanageable. Brands would have to manually tag every piece of content to get it in front of the right person. "Almost no one," Wentworth said, "went through all of that effort, and personalisation was rarely implemented because of it."[11]

The Age and Ethics of AI

Enter the world of AI.

As the capability of artificial intelligence has grown rapidly, so too has the ability to personalise by automating this process. Generative AI can create content in any style the brand wants, and machine learning can identify segments based on their intent and potential to target them with that content. Bringing these two things together effectively silences the protesters yelling "Personalisation is too much effort!" while holding up generic handmade signs.

What attracted investors to the likes of Mutiny and Intellimize, both automated personalisation software, is that they reduced the level of human effort required. "Personalisation usually requires large growth teams heavily staffed with engineers," one investor in Mutiny said. "It has always been the holy grail of marketing. We just have never had good enough, simple enough tools to do it at scale."[12]

Until now.

"AI is the new currency in personalised customer experiences at scale. Our AI Content Studio is another great addition to our AI-powered platform making it easier for marketers to get their jobs done faster and more efficiently," said Tracy Sestili, Chief Marketing Officer at Intellimize.[13]

Without AI, the challenge of personalising thousands, if not millions, of experiences was too daunting. This relatively new technology has allowed us to move past the archaic if/else rules into something that requires much less effort — something that's *more* automated. Eighty-four per cent of digital marketing leaders believe using AI enhances marketing as a whole by delivering real-time, personalised experiences to customers.[14] Maybe we can have a magic pill instead of going to the gym.

This resurgence probably warrants a new term to keep our beloved personalisation on Gartner's Hype Cycle for another five years — personal-*AI*-sation, if you please.

Microsoft Xbox, for example, uses personal-AI-sation in many aspects of the gaming experience across layout, content, and suggestions within games, community engagement, and online video. Personal-AI-sation uses a reinforcement learning algorithm to analyse players' behaviours (such as when they last played, accomplishments and gaming style) and context (such as location, weather, friends online and date). That combination of behaviour plus context is the very nebulous of being more personal with customers. Sources at Forrester suggest that this approach has significantly enhanced player engagement, up to 40 per cent. Without AI, just having business-rules-based techniques wouldn't have been able to build such data-driven experiences.

It may seem like the answer to all personalisation problems, but it's not like a microwave popcorn setting that magically pops out perfectly popped kernels. There's no big red "insert artificial intelligence" button. There's a big hump to get over — the ethical ramifications of using AI within the personalisation space. That could be a whole book itself, but I've tried to keep it to three alliterative salient points.

1) Responsibility
2) Regulation
3) Rigging

1. Responsibility

"Even the largest of tech companies and algorithmic experts have found
it challenging to deliver highly personalised services while avoiding
discrimination."

Alex Miller, Doctoral candidate in Information Systems &
Technology at the University of Pennsylvania's Wharton School[15]

With great power comes great responsibility. And there is nothing more powerful than AI. Apart from Disney.

Who is responsible for automated personalisation? Is it the recommendation engine, the people who create the engine, or the people who sell the engine? Take Apple's new credit card, recently accused of gender bias by awarding women lower credit limits than men. Such limits are determined by algorithms. Who's to blame for these sexist credit cards?

The more complex the mathematics and levels of configuration brands need for the algorithms driving personalisation, the greater the chances are that things will go wrong without their knowledge, and so, it requires constant oversight. That doesn't sound like less effort to me. AI for personalisation is like my five-year-old, focused only on reaching his objective without caring about the consequences. They can end up behaving in discriminatory ways that even their human designers never saw coming.

Where the brand, such as Apple, might be accountable for *why* something is being recommended, it is the recommendation engine itself that is responsible for that. And given that humans code the models, it is not unreasonable to think that the data humans use and choose to train their models with could have some bias in it, intentional or not. Fifty-three per cent of people agree that it's possible for AI to show bias in its decisions. In a study by Pegasystems, because of this, they found that only 9 per cent are very comfortable interacting with AI itself.[16]

Microsoft recently laid off their team that taught employees how to make AI tools responsibly; what does that say about their responsibility? Although they suggest that the team "is not going away, it's evolving", it is businesses business to be responsible in their handling of AI.[17]

2. Regulation

As a result of the responsibility being placed on them, businesses have joined forces to regulate AI.

Private companies, research institutions and public-sector organisations have issued over 84 principles and guidelines for ethical artificial intelligence. They include details about transparency, which is the most cited of the guidelines, appearing in 87 per cent of them, as well as fairness, non-maleficence responsibility, privacy, beneficence, freedom and sustainability. Adding to this, early in 2023, Elon Musk and more than 1,000 other tech researchers and executives called for a six-month "pause" on the development of advanced AI capabilities.

The intent is certainly there, few lawmakers are seeking legislation, according to the New York Times.[18] The Biden administration is currently seeking public comments on potential accountability measures for artificial intelligence regulation, but there doesn't seem to be any rush to do so.[19] India also recently announced they don't plan to regulate the growth of AI within the South Asian market.[20] What is going on?

If there is no centralised regulation for AI, personalisation doesn't stand a chance – Hell, I'd do it for free if somebody asked me in addition to my cult leader position. What is stopping a retailer from using an algorithm to promote the highest margin items within the confines of our preferences and motivation systems, potentially manipulating our choices? Something that Trivago have recently been accused of in 2022. They used a personalisation algorithm that placed significant weight on which online hotel booking site paid Trivago the highest cost-per-click fee. This determined which ratings it would highlight on its website. That doesn't sound as though it highlights the cheapest rates for its consumers based on their preferences or loyalty. The US Federal Court agreed, and ordered Trivago to pay penalties of $44.7 million for making misleading representations about their hotel room rates.[21]

There doesn't need to be such a thing as the recommendation police because the societal impact of buying a dishwasher with a higher margin isn't as great as the misinformation being spread on social media networks. But once it is understood why social media networks create echo chambers, intentionally or not, the same self-serving, capitalist reasons can easily be applied to retailers and their personalisation efforts. It's a conversation that's particularly prevalent because of the omission of a personalisation gatekeeper. There's no central body in charge, and because there aren't any rules on how brands should personalise safely and ethically, both good evidence and personal opinion weigh the same, and the two are often conflated.

With this lack of regulation, and what appears to be an ignorance towards responsibility in favour of a quick buck, this can only lead to a one-way street: *manipulation*.

3. Rigging

"Data should give us information about who these people are, but empathy is going to build more relevant experiences. Without empathy we're left with this vacuum where we might shoe-horn personalisation in for the benefit of no one. Can you do empathy at scale?"

Steven Shyne, Co-Founder and COO, CXperts[22]

Using AI in a commercial context, where brands can automate a process that tailors an individual response to make people buy more, feels inherently dangerous and open to manipulation. The idea that a company's AI can mould how its consumers see the world could be classified as discriminatory. Should brands and businesses even be seeking to assume and dictate what customers like and want? Does that not miss the point of building relationships through genuine connection? Putting automation in the hands of algorithms feels like it's lost what personalisation is here to do: help people make choices that are right for them.

Let's jump back briefly to February 2013.

Eric Loomis has just pleaded guilty to driving a car used in a shooting. The judge used a piece of software called COMPAS (Correctional Offender Management Profiling for Alternative Sanctions), rather than human judgement, to determine the sentence for the crime. The software was designed on the principle that an algorithm can better understand whether, based on a 137-point questionnaire, criminals would reoffend and, if so, recommend a proportional judgement or sentence. The system has a 65 per cent accuracy rate.[23] Is this better than human judgement? (Is human judgement actually any good to begin with?) Trusting a new system, in the face of a judicial system that has been tried and tested for several hundreds of years, certainly invites scrutiny.

Loomis was sentenced to six years.

(For what it's worth, Loomis filed an appeal, and the Wisconsin Supreme Court ruled that the sentence would have been the same if COMPAS had not been consulted.)

This is not particularly a question of commerce, although it is developed by a private company called Equivant, who has a parent company Constellation Software,

Inc. – a publicly traded company on the Toronto Stock Exchange raking in $1.67 billion in gross revenue every year. I'll say nothing more. Yet in such instances, bias is called into question more than any other factor when it comes to this type of recommendation system. According to journalist Julia Angwin and colleagues at ProPublica, the COMPAS algorithm is "irresponsible". In an assessment of more than 7,000 arrestees, they found an inherent bias against African Americans. "Blacks are almost twice as likely as whites to be labelled a higher risk but not actually re-offend." This false-positive was countered with the false-negative: "Whites are much more likely than blacks to be labelled lower risk, but go on to commit other crimes."[24]

It's assumed that such bias in COMPAS is unintentional. The Equivant website even addresses it within an FAQ. "No, COMPAS is designed to assess numerous factors, but race is not even considered when a COMPAS score is developed."[25]

It's not as though that's a defence against these algorithms. But the argument that their use case involves automating and shaping an outcome is an important one. It's particularly important when that outcome results in some financial gain for one of the parties. $1.67 billion annually.

Any outcome is intrinsically associated with trust, which is the foundation of a relationship. To get it wrong, or to insinuate that it's something that it is not, is to damage the relationship with your customer, which is the antithesis of what such algorithms in a commercial context are designed for. It looks a lot like lying.

Therefore, giving the responsibility of managing relationships between brands and consumers to algorithms can do more harm than good. As I learned in the interviews conducted for this book, a clear picture emerged that personalising experiences using some form of automation is exponentially easier than the alternative approach – if/else rules – yet equally dangerous.

Easier does not mean better.

Relationships are hard to build because the reward is so valuable. I respect you, dear reader, too much to start quoting Dolly Parton and rainbows here. The question comes in the form, once more, of balance. Specifically, how do brands balance their need to personalise for their customers in a way that's authentic without being overly onerous?

Chapter 24

Slaying the Stubborn Dragon

"What I often find when I talk to organisations who are starting a personalisation project, is instead of focusing on identifying those all-important differences in user needs at key moments of the journey, they purely focus on what's possible within the tech tool."

Chris Gibbins, Chief Experience Officer, Creative CX[1]

The Stubborn Dragon is called this because it takes a purely numbers-based approach to personalisation. A myopic focus on the need for data and technology to automate and perpetuate something.

We defeat this dragon by using art and creativity to represent the human touch. To put the person back into personalisation. The belief that the only way to scale personalisation is to just press the big red artificial intelligence button, risks losing the essence of what it should be. Personalisation is about being personable, and there's something incongruous when brands remove the person from the equation in favour of trying to do it at scale.

So, to risk losing that essence, I've developed a three-pronged attack spork. Or a trident, if you're feeling fancy.

1) Personalise
The art of being personal is more important than the science.

2) Perpetuate
Automating personalisation is still necessary to make its implementation realistic.

3) Prioritise
Selecting and prioritising the right data and technology to use.

1: Personalise

"Don't throw tech at the problem. It will never solve it. Personalisation to date has just been the tech and that's why we've never cracked it."

Marianne Stjernvall, Founder, Queen of CRO[2]

The best way to articulate this personal point is to get up close and personal with Thread.com, a fashion retailer in the UK. Their intention was one of art, but science reigned supreme.

Thread uses personalisation as part of its core value proposition to curate styles and match outfits for men. Kieran O'Neill built Thread.com in 2012 on one simple premise. "The goal was to build an experience that worked for the customer, and then work on the scalability second."[3] We've heard this tall tale before, haven't we, Amazon? But O'Neill meant it this time.

Online fashion is a tricky beast to get right, though. Firstly, there are no physical fitting rooms in sight. Sure, styles can be moderately matched to tastes and preferences, and AI is helping brands get better and better at learning that. But tastes are universal and varied. Matching outfits adds a layer of complexity as it stitches these two elements together. Allowing for the nuances of individuality to come out and be represented in clothing is, believe it or not, highly intricate. For you fashionistas, it's not as simple as picking something off the hanger because it looked good on a model. It's about identity, comfort, fit and context all rolled into one. Can such a personal experience really be achieved with just recommendations, despite the intelligence being artificial?

Thread.com didn't seem to think so. So, they made sure their business model involved blending the empathy, experience and expertise of actual human personal stylists with the advanced data intelligence of machine learning. What could go wrong?

In 2016, *The Guardian* quoted Thread.com as having just eight expert personal stylists — "Sophie and her team" — working with more than 480,000 customers.[4] There's no way that Sophie can handle 50,000 clients *on her own*, regardless of how great she may be. I've done the maths — it's 136 clients a day for 365 days without a day off (which humans require by law), and training the models on the intricacies of fashion taste and matching takes time. It's far more complicated than just stumbling into correlated matching, i.e. if a man buys white t-shirts, he's also highly likely to buy black t-shirts. The behaviours are highly correlated and accurate, sure, but the cause and meaning behind them are rather useless. Herein lies the debate of causation vs correlation.

How does Thread.com bring empathy to the table and circumvent this problem?

The stylists — Sophie and her team of humans — feed the hungry models with lots of delicious data. The algorithm models, not the real models. A combination of the experience of the stylist working with the automation of the algorithm.

Seven years later, Thread.com has more than 90 employees. Eight of them are still personal stylists, but ten are data scientists. Simon Leesley, managing director of Stitch Fix, a competitor to Thread.com, claimed that their algorithms, "Serve as a recommendation engine for our stylists so they can be curators, rather than scroll through and pick from thousands of pieces."[5]

So, the recommendation engine serves as relevance for the stylist, which in turn serves as relevance for the end user? This begs the question: if an algorithm is making recommendations to the stylists, how much personalisation is actually happening from the stylist? Or is true personalisation being purely ring-fenced by AI?

"The algorithms understand fit nuances that humans can't and remove any selection bias. They provide the science, and our stylists provide the art," Leesley continued.[6]

There's that conflict point again: science versus art.

Leesley's comments would suggest the former is best. But used in combination with an art, such as human experience, it helps create a $10 billion business at its peak in 2021.[7] Maybe this is where personalisation needs to go to succeed: the foundation of science with a cherry of art on top — adding personal touches to a scaled and inherently impersonal process? Without the creativity of the individual, I side with the wisdom of Andre Morys, CEO at konversionsKRAFT: "If you automate bullshit, you'll get automated bullshit."[8]

When the personal becomes part of personalisation, just as Thread.com and Stitch Fix have utilised, success follows quickly ... even if Thread.com did unfortunately go into administration and the latter has a market cap one twentieth of what it used to be.

2. Perpetuate

"I'm sorry to say, the technology is already a good 10–15 years in front of us. So, what's the problem?"

Jeffrey MacIntyre, Principal, Bucket Studio[9]

Too many people think that personalisation is impossible and that the juice isn't worth the squeeze. So many of my interviewees pointed this out to me.

Jaleh Rezaei and Nikhil Mathew, co-founders of Mutiny personalisation software, wanted to prove that personalisation's juice was squeeze-worthy and created a platform that allowed others to scale their personalisation efforts. Mutiny is now a runaway success story, valued at $600 million in less than four years.[10]

When working at Gusto, the cloud-based payroll solution with over 2,400 staff, Rezaei and Mathew were perplexed that everything they wanted optimised had to be built bespoke. This in turn pulled engineering resources away from other parts of the business. Every improvement was a slow, incremental adoption on their site which they saw as wasteful and inefficient.

"We solved this by creating a growth engineering team that wrote a lot of custom code to drive customers to buy — from optimising our website and signup form to driving upsells and referrals in-app. But most companies don't have the engineers or know-how to do all that."[11]

The power couple immediately understood the benefits of optimising individual parts of the journey for individual segments. Rezaei and Mathew felt that every company needed an approach to personalisation because sending one message to all doesn't create the resonance needed to convert. They also recognised the problem on the other end: the effort required to take such an approach was vast, nearly impossible, and required the hiring of hundreds of engineering resources and capabilities. Some of Gusto's $140 million in seed funding in 2018 certainly contributed to this.[12] See, even the elite can't keep it up.

As a result, Rezaei and Mathew developed a way to make this approach more accessible and give marketers the ability to personalise segments automatically, or, as Rezaei described it, "Your own growth engineering team in a box."[13] Mutiny plugs into customer data and uses AI to create thousands of different versions of the brand's website for all the different customers.

Some form of automation is required to perpetuate personalisation as Razaei found out. But the juice is even sweeter now that the squeeze is automated. Thread.com found this. So did Stitch Fix. As did DocSend, the document sharing start-up that was acquired by Dropbox for £165 million in 2021.[14] Alex Poulos, the then-CMO of DocSend, discussed how the business had so many different customer personas. Startup founders, like myself, used the software for pitch decks, while those in sales used it for proposals, and investment bankers used it for transactions and so on and so forth. "I wanted to do personalised marketing all the way down to the bone," Poulos said in an interview with Forbes.[15] Rather than making something so generic that it catered to the "lowest common denominator" in a way that wasn't impactful to any specific group, Poulos said Mutiny allowed DocSend to show different types of customers a website experience based on their individual use case. That led to him running 100 different versions of the same website. Not quite the same as Amazon's 4.5 million stores for 4.5 million customers, but AI certainly levels the playing field.

There's no question that technology can perpetuate personalisation efforts. They get brands over the hump of "it's too much effort". But it's not a panacea; if anything, it can actually become a shiny distraction. When stakeholders purchase technology suites for personalisation, the question shouldn't be "who" but "why". Why should brands personalise, let alone personalise using AI, is the biggest question. Has a board or CEO just agreed to purchase something without knowing what it was? It happens. Did they do their due diligence properly? It doesn't happen. Did the vendor lure them under a false pretence with an unrealistic set of expectations by showcasing competitors generating hundreds of millions of pounds in, quote unquote, incremental uplift at a price that's just too good to be true? That's because, more often than not, it actually is.

It is rare that brand founders and management step back and ask, "Why are we personalising?" Too often, a piece of technology is purchased prior to a strategy actually being developed. The why is rarely asked. Sources from multiple personalisation vendors suggested that when new clients are brought on board, those that are starting off on their journey struggle to answer basic questions, such as "Who is our audience?" or "What are our segments?" If they can't answer those questions, they've got bigger issues than personalisation to worry about.

We circle back to the purpose of personalisation. This question is the key to unlocking the approach to it because it directs that approach. In other words, focusing on the problem, which might not even be about personalisation, helps brands and vendors focus on the solution.

Perpetuating personalisation through technology will become useless without answering this question first, because brands are blind to why and what they are perpetuating.

3. Prioritise

"There's a lot of talk of personalisation and not an awful lot of doing. Brands hold off on ever rolling anything out because they can't get to their version of perfect."

Katie Woodhead, Director of Customer Experience,
Advanced Commerce[16]

Can you handle the truth?
Here it is: brands don't need all the data in the world to personalise. And they don't need all the technology in the world to understand it. All brands need to do is prioritise collecting the most important data points related to their purpose and offer their customers an improved experience with those data points. Prioritisation is the panacea, not personalisation or perpetuation.

When Flannels, a high-end menswear brand in the UK, began their personalisation journey, they did so by collecting just one vital piece of information: brand preference. They discovered that their audience was more encouraged, converted better and had a higher propensity to spend more when they were taken through a branded journey. Amit Rajyaguru, eCommerce manager at Flannels, said so himself: "We found personalising the branded journey for our users to be the most valuable to the business."[17]

Of course, other data points were important, like if the user had purchased with Flannels before or not and, if so, how many times. Despite that, evidence suggested that the affinity between customer and brand was so strong that collecting data around this would help improve the overall journey. They didn't need all the data at that exact moment like Disney; they prioritised. Flannels MagicBands doesn't have the same ring to it, either. Brand preference data was already in existence and easily accessible based on the behaviour of their customers online. For example, visiting Hugo Boss for the twelfth time suggested some degree of affinity towards that brand. They tested their assumption over six months and over hundreds of iterations. "Through testing," Amit continued, "we found that we can take a general experience and personalise it to the user based on what brands they are actually interested in, giving us an average uplift of 17.5 per cent."

One such branded experience was changing the filters on a product listing page to be more focused on the assumed brand preference of the individual. The idea was to provide quick brand links on these pages that were relevant to the customer's inferred preference. Flannels compared this against just showing the top five generic brands, those that had the most items by default. By changing this content to be personalised based on an affinity towards brands, Flannels saw a 5 per cent uplift in conversion rate post engagement and 9 per cent more users clicking on a filter.[18] That's boss.

In my opinion, there is no more valuable priority than asking the Everest of all questions, "Who is ready to buy?" Understanding the intent of an audience can help brands identify where users are in their purchase decision-making process. Do they know what they want? Do they understand the benefits of what they want? Have they reviewed alternative options?

These questions are rarely asked and even less frequently answered. But they give brands the ability to prioritise customers in a way where they can de-prioritise the window shoppers and tyre kickers and focus on those with the big wallets: those with the product already in their arms standing at the till. A rather overly commercial and greedy outlook, but it works for those in the retail world.

The concept of intent was explored recently at a high-value retailer in the UK (who shall remain nameless because I was told I'll get in a lot of trouble if I mentioned their name) under the hilarious codename "Cats and Dogs".

This retailer was trying to understand if there was value in offering discounts to those who were going to purchase regardless. These were called dogs. The most loyal of all animals. Why give a discount to someone who was going to buy regardless of intervention or persuasion and thus didn't require one? The cats were those who were "winnable" and needed some level of price movement in their purchase journey – a discount perhaps. Separating the "cats" from the "dogs" helped the retailer better understand the potential margins to be had without giving a discount code to every Garfield, Lassie and Snoopy. Not only did this help to prioritise customers based on their value, but it also protected the brand's perception, not to mention its margin.

They were not the first to use this tactic. Kevin Ozan, CFO at McDonald's[19] talked about prioritising offers to guests by personalising them based on geography. "We'll continue to have some national offers, but we've moved more toward a local approach, which then becomes, ultimately, a personalized approach. We're in the middle of that evolution – going from national to local to personalized."

According to Forbes,[20] the benefit of transitioning to personalised value offers is to avoid sending promotions to customers who would otherwise be willing to pay full price; the dogs. This understanding of who will and will not buy, or their likelihood to do so, is a question that helps prioritise whilst also benefiting profits and influencing margins. Gartner reported in 2016: "In four years, smart personalisation engines used to recognise customer intent will enable digital businesses to increase their profits by up to 15 per cent."[21] Whether or not that has been accomplished given that was six years ago remains to be seen.

The Stubborn Dragon is the fire-breather who consumes data and technology all day, every day. To defeat it, it's not about starving the dragon of the thing it wants — there is an absolute need for both data and technology. We don't want to kill this dragon. What we want to do here is put it on a diet. And ask it why it does what it does. By asking about the brand's purpose and not go in the dragon boardroom there all guns blazing á la Disney and creating unrealistic expectations, brands can start to prioritise exactly what data and what technology are needed. Don't let the shiny toy distract. Always remember that this is an art, not a science — brands can't place numbers on being personable with their customers.

Whether its money, data or technology. They all have one thing in common. It's the way they are seen and used by the people who see and use them. Last but not least, next up is the daddy of the Three Dragons we must defeat, the Deepfake Dragon, the biggest and baddest of them all.

Part VI

The Deepfake Dragon

"He who fights too long against Dragons becomes a Dragon himself."
Friedrich Nietzsche, German philosopher[1]

As we all know from mythical tales such as those of King Arthur and the gods of Norse lore, the agent of change is not a magic sword, magic shield, or MagicBand, nor is it the strength required in swinging the weapon; it is the worthiness of those who wield it that inflicts the killer blow.

Yes, you've guessed it – it is the person behind personalisation that is, ultimately, behind personalisation's success.

And, yet, while it is the protagonist, it is also the antagonist. The personalisation-person paradox. The people in personalisation are their own worst enemies. As we found out, putting the Stubborn Dragon on a diet by persuading those in the boardroom and those who played with the shiny artificial intelligence toys to take a step back and prioritise was the main barrier to progress. For personalisation to reach the great shores of Avalon – paradise – it must first look deeply at its own mirrored reflection in the lake and work out who precisely is staring back. And double check that it's not a deepfake.

Chapter 25

Know Thy Enemy:
The Deepfake Dragon

"People are as much the barrier to personalisation as technology is. People just get in the way of delivering brilliant experiences for customers. The more ego and politics there are, the more they become the problem."

Peter Denby, Co-Founder, HyperFinity[1]

The third and final metaphorical mythological monster that requires vanquishing is the big daddy of personalisation's dragons: the Deepfake. We do not know its true purpose, its reason for being, or what it intends to do with personalisation, hence it being a potential deepfake. That, and it's beautifully alliterative. This beast represents the people behind personalisation – those with the power to dictate and destroy it – and how often they'll stand in the way of it reaching its potential. They generally experience, of course, three areas of conflict:

1) Misalignment
2) Unexpecting the Expected
3) Ego and the Needs of the Individual

The complexity of personalisation, and its conceptual constructs require the people behind it to catch up to the technology, not the other way around. "We get this a lot from clients," Karl Wirth, CEO of Evergage, a personalisation software said. "They'll say, wow, I can do whatever I want. Now what should I do? The tech is there, but now you have to think about how am I going to use it? What's my use case? How does that tie to business goals? It's a thinking process. The missing thing is knowing what to do."[2]

As is so often the case, people – consumers, customers, brands, businesses, any living being with a heartbeat – just don't like to think. A handful of my interviewees understood this. Rob McLaughlin at Loop Horizon, who provides omnichannel strategies, agreed. "Technology and data are almost never a blocker in our experience. What there often is, is a failure in alignment. In other words, a strategy at the low and high levels of the business on what they should do to meet some commercial goal."[3] (He casually says, setting up a new chapter on misalignment.)

Chapter 26

McPersonalisation

Misalignment is when the left hand and right hand of a business don't agree. When it occurs, it makes brands look like one of those inflatable tube men you see flailing their arms outside car dealerships. In theory, brands should always seek to be aligned from top to bottom, but in reality, this is almost never the case.

It's clear to those looking out through their car windows in the drive-thru that McDonald's personalisation may suffer from a potential case of misaligned strategy. If the stories and rumours are true, this is between two core parts of its business; the persons orchestrating and operating its personalisation strategy.

The story of McDonald's aforementioned purchase of Dynamic Yield in 2019, the year of personalisation, is a story, not of technology, but of human perception.

Let's take a closer look.

McDonald's acquired them for $300 million. It seemed like an odd move for most in the personalisation industry. At first, it gave me a weird taste in my mouth, as if I'd eaten a Filet-o-Fish. Just joking. I would never order that. I'm a nuggets guy.

McDonald's were already a customer of the leading personalisation platform, so why acquire it? While it might have created confusion for those in the personalisation industry, such as myself, it made perfect sense for those in the fast-food restaurant industry. In short, the purchase signalled the start of a technology-first age for quick-service restaurants (QSR). McDonald's à la carte menu is now seen as the pioneer in technology for their industry, as some sources I spoke to in my interviews have suggested. Others soon followed.

"I feel for so long, tech companies came into this space and tried to get restaurants to change their model to fit the technology ... I think you're going to see a lot more tech companies adjust their model to make sure that it fits the restaurant."

Sterling Douglass, Co-founder and CEO, Chowly[1]

McDonald's Dynamic Yield acquisition was actually an astute one, as Douglass points out. It was part of the self-explanatory "buy or build" argument – do brands buy technology or build it themselves? Not just that, but it set out a clear commitment to those within the organisation. When you push other markets to use any technology, regardless of whether it's personalisation or not, there will be natural resistance. Resistance to change, resistance to control, and resistance to ownership. McDonald's firmly believed that owning the technology, rather than just using it, would make it easier to shape the solution. Therefore, acquiring Dynamic Yield made it easier to work on the financial model to accelerate decision-making, deployment, and usage. That and the technology are outstanding. The leader in the QSR world and the leading personalisation software vendor were getting McMarried.

As so often is the case, the question isn't in the who, but the why. Why would McDonald's want to personalise the customer experience? A simple response is that it makes no sense for 38,000 restaurants to have a single static menu. Different locations have different needs. Different demands determine whether you need chicken nuggets for breakfast, lunch, dinner, or at 2 am. In my opinion, you can never have too many chicken nuggets, but that's irrelevant here.

Macro-events can influence the popularity of items like their limited-edition McFlurry or whether a baseball game is just around the corner, driving up burger sales. The plan to ID these customers, according to some publications,[2] was to use licence plate recognition as identifiers for previous customers and their previous orders. Something that never really came to widespread fruition, as I imagine it would have been a legitimate legal nightmare.

The purchase of the platform was the strategic, not the tactical, reason why McDonald's invested so much in personalisation. Ultimately, they knew personalisation will drive customer lifetime value, as there is a wash of evidence to suggest it.[3] In fact, a recent survey showed that customers now value personalisation more than speed when it comes to customer service, which in turn increases their loyalty towards a brand.[4]

McDonald's wanted both, and their grass-roots idea was that the former facilitated the latter: *how can personalisation accelerate time to serve?* Given the variance in micro and macro factors for each restaurant, the purpose of personalisation at McDonald's was to give customers their order as quickly as possible. It was as much an operational purpose as it was an incremental revenue one – just as was part of the benefit for Netflix in right-sizing the production investments.

Personalisation became part of the company's wider growth strategy. They called it "Accelerating the Arches". McDonald's doubled down on what they called "The Three D's": Digital, Delivery and Drive-thru. Another alliteration apparatus coming in threes.

With this in place, the company expected digital sales to exceed $10 billion in 2020. Just two years later, digital sales in the company's top six markets alone exceeded $6 billion, or about one-third of total systemwide sales, in a single quarter.[5] They clearly exceeded their expectations for what digital would bring, and personalisation was an integral part of that success.

Personalisation technology, among other things, was acquired as part of that digital strategy. The capability to showcase what items are recommended at a given point in time given their availability was clearly beneficial to McDonald's. By virtue, it was beneficial to the customer, too, by getting their order quicker. The ability to tie all that together in a nice, neat loyalty bow was far too appetising.

Not just that, but drive-thrus became more automated after the purchase of Apprente, a voice-automation start-up, and a strategic partnership with IBM. The future of drive-thrus appeared bright, thanks to conversational technologies, personalisation and automation. The capability was in place – so much so that the business created McDonald's Tech Labs in Silicon Valley to house these technologies. The alignment was in place, and their purpose and mission were clear – what could go wrong?

Despite exceeding targets, just three years later, McDonald's sold all Dynamic Yield assets. The headline itself sounds suspicious. Why did the success of the digital side of "Accelerating the Arches" result in an apparent fire sale of its assets? Did anything prevent the mass adoption of personalisation at the most valuable food chain in the world?

According to a *Wall Street Journal* investigation, franchisees – actual people; foot soldiers with boots on the ground – questioned the performance of personalisation just a year after its adoption in 2020. According to them, they expected personalised order suggestions to help boost sales by 1 per cent on average in the US compared to drive-thru transactions without them. Yet, sales fell short of that target.

"The return on that investment is just not there," Vicki Chancellor, a McDonald's franchisee, said in the article.[6]

The *Wall Street Journal* doesn't expand any further on what Chancellor meant when she said return on investment, either in how that was measured or her interpretation thereof. It seemed clear that the original purpose of acquiring Dynamic Yield was one of operational efficiency, not incremental revenue. For example, if there was a surplus of Crispy Chicken Wraps on a Sunday lunchtime in Wisconsin, promoting that item above others seemed well thought-out. How well that was communicated to the franchisees or understood is another question altogether.

The relationship between McDonald's and its franchisees is a curious one and could go some way to explaining the perception that the ROI was not meeting expectations.

The agreement between McDonald's Global in Chicago and the individual franchisees is one where each store must contribute to technology fees. The decisions are made at the top, while those at the bottom must foot the bill, or at least a portion of it, though this decision is not forced. Given this model, there is constant negotiation over what franchises have to pay for and who should pay for what. It doesn't matter whether that's coffee machines, new napkins or ... personalisation technology.

Not just that, consider the interests of each entity. The franchisees are charged based on the sales of the store, not the profit. If the store is pushing for more sales through the use of technology, that benefits McDonald's as a company. But since the franchisee has to pay technology fees, profit doesn't grow proportionally to revenue. It is therefore in the store's best interests to keep profits as high as possible, regardless of sales figures. Franchise costs need to be heavily monitored as a result of this.

These efforts at "Accelerating the Arches" resulted in considerably higher costs for franchisees. Their monthly payment to McDonald's for technology alone was 10 times[7] what it was a decade ago. In a very short amount of time, McDonald's HQ made this investment and the franchisees got into debt because of it. To the point where, in December 2020, after all these acquisitions, the company told its franchisees they would have to pay an extra charge of $5,000 and to move from a six-month payment schedule to a monthly one. This debt amounted near $70 million.[8]

Needless to say, the franchisees were not lovin' it. There was significant misalignment between the left and the right hands. The National Owners Association conducted a survey in which 75 per cent of franchisees said they supported owners filing an injunction to stop the collection of the technology fees.[9] After an independent review by Ernst & Young, McDonald's agreed to trim this fee by 62 per cent in mid-2021.

This case study highlights the errors within human alignment and expectation (more of that in a moment), not capability. The personalisation worked perfectly. It was the people who were misaligned.

What personalisation means for those who use it is as important as the wider personalisation purpose. The reasons for personalising at McDonald's felt purposeful. These benefits, however, must be bought into by the teams, in this case franchisees.

There's no evidence to suggest that this wasn't the case but considering that 93 per cent of all McDonald's 38,000 locations worldwide are franchises, consulting, persuading, and writing a business case – ironic – for them is imperative to the success of their efforts. McDonald's should at least bring them along for the ride.

And then charge them for it.

Just kidding.

That all being said, Dynamic Yield and personalisation are still huge parts of the technological initiatives at McDonald's. So much so, they are extending their personalisation efforts to more channels and more markets. They've clearly identified benefits that have contributed to the $10 billion increase in digital sales per quarter. When talking about digital and personalisation, Chris Kempczinski, the new CEO at McDonald's stated, "We're starting to see the benefits; we just need to go harder and faster."[10]

As suspicious as it seemed to purchase technology just to sell it three years later, it was apparently all part of the plan, according to Kempczinski. McDonald's has continued to spend roughly a billion dollars on digital systems annually, according to the company. "If we do acquisitions, it will be for a short period of time, bring it in-house, jump-start it, turbo it, and then spin it back out and find a partner that will work and scale it for us." Kempczinski said.[11]

This is a story of (mis)alignment – both physical and emotional.

Sometimes it is the physical structure of the brand that causes such individual failure, a lack of cohesiveness. Where things naturally happen in containment. Marcel Rduch, RVP Customer Success, Dynamic Yield agreed: "We're still at a point where personalisation is still happening in silos – advertising, direct mail, website, emails. Those personalising at these touch points are using different data sources or sitting in different departments."[12]

Adobe's 2022 Digital Trends report found that less than half of senior executives believe their marketing or experience teams collaborate successfully with their technology counterparts – just 47 per cent. And of these, 65 per cent don't think their organisations are doing enough to break down these "silos".[13] These segregated teams have individual wants and needs, even competing KPIs. A source from a leading retailer in the UK explained to me how the KPIs of the offline and online teams were vastly different – so much so that it created competition and conflict. To that extent, the online team didn't care whether the offline team weren't hitting targets, and vice versa. "Shit happens," they told me nonchalantly.

According to other sources I spoke to, it took nearly nine months for a leading FMCG brand in the UK, that used the Adobe suite to implement a leading personalisation software, because the data didn't match. The same is true when there are multiple platforms. Specialty Commerce, a direct marketer which sells wigs, knowingly has one tool for website personalisation and another for email personalisation. Those two systems produce different data sets. "The email tool will come up with its product recommendations based on the data it has," says Locky Macdonald, Director of ecommerce, Speciality Commerce. "We've got another tool for the website. We've enjoyed working with them, so we didn't feel the need to make the switch."[14]

Whilst Speciality Commerce knew of this dual purpose, others didn't. A source I interviewed for this book, but who preferred to remain nameless, indicated that there were examples where stakeholders purchased a personalisation vendor for one part of the business only to find out another part of the business – a different market in this case – had a completely different vendor for the exact same purpose.

Paying twice for the same thing: smart. Easily rectifiable though.

It is the emotional alignment that is more frightening than the physical alignment. In McDonald's for example, were the staff and business partners well aligned with the purpose and mission? Did it appropriately set and meet ... *expectations*?

Chapter 27

Unexpecting the Expected

"The first step in exceeding your customer's expectations is to know those expectations."

Roy H. Williams, Author[1]

When personalisation is expected to work 100 per cent of the time and doesn't (probably because of human expectation or misalignment) it is presumed the whole thing must be bad. And it gets thrown out. As mentioned in Part I, personalisation comes attached with such a high level of hyperbole and praise that it is inevitable that it will disappoint.

Expectations need to be realistically managed. And kept fluid. If one element doesn't work, it should be refined rather than wholesale abandoned.

When McDonald's Vicki Chancellor stated: "The return on investment is just not there on personalisation,"[2] she was highlighting that there were a set of expectations that were not met. It clearly wasn't the personalisation platform that she was referring to. In my opinion, it was her understanding of what was expected.

Chancellor isn't alone. Eighty-five per cent of retailers are unhappy with their personalisation performance.[3] Stating you are unhappy represents a preconceived thought as to what that person would have originally expected; the differential between expectation and outcome.

Expectations are set by the overly transparent world in which we live. Instagram has set expectations for what boyfriends and girlfriends should be and behave like. There are far too many over-the-top TikTok engagement videos making every boyfriend feel inadequate when proposing, each one trying to outdo the other in grand gestures and emotional theatrics. Just as there are way too many videos of "perfect" girls "treating their man right", the perfect illusion of modern romance. Thanks, social media, for keeping our expectations sky-high and our self-esteem in check.

Insta-perfect lives create unreasonably high expectations without accepting any responsibility for the fact. The same is true for personalisation. We compare our current performance to that of others, and all that does is distort the wicked truth. Similar to how TikTok moulds what living a life less ordinary *should* be, such unrivalled high expectations are destroying the name of personalisation. In doing so, many brands stigmatise it because they have attempted personalisation, failed to meet their existing expectations, and experienced some form of anxiety from the whole ordeal. Or the newly coined PTSD: Personalisation Traumatic Stress Disorder. Another acronym that will soon be introduced to the marketing lexicon, no doubt. Or as Mark Pybus, Managing Director, Creative CX[4] put it: "There's a bit of uncertainty for those that have been around a while. People who have been around in marketing for 20 years will have encountered a personalisation initiative at some point. A lot of people have got their fingers burned in the past with an initiative that didn't deliver anything."

Didn't deliver anything? Or didn't deliver what *they expected*?

When talking with Leon Andrews, Head of User Experience, RICS[5] he spoke about this phenomenon of expectation within companies: "Brand expectation is 90 out of 100. Their implementation is usually so poor because of their internal alignment. The returns of personalisation therefore always seem to be 10 out of 100 because it wasn't implemented correctly in the first place. And, as a result, people are like ostriches, put their heads in the sand, and ignore it."

Andrews wasn't far off with a 10 out of 100. In fact, according to a 2018 Evergage study, only 12 per cent of marketers are very or extremely satisfied with their level of personalisation, with 50 per cent reporting they are dissatisfied.[6]

Personalisation is still seen as the shiny and new trend that just won't quit, despite its potted history. For those of you who missed the memo, feel free to refer back to this book's "Years of Personalisation" for a quick catch-up. It's funny how this is the case for reasons unknown to us mere mortals. Maybe it's the thrill of something new, the sense of accomplishment, the excitement, or the optimism it brings. I already addressed a number of potential sources on how the champions of personalisation, Amazon and Netflix, have possibly pruned the garden path for others to follow. Those that I interviewed, however, kept coming back to the vendors that peddle personalisation. A 50 per cent uplift here, or a 2,000 per cent uplift there, will raise the eyebrows of any Chief Marketing Officer or Financial Director.

When brands tender for personalisation vendors, they are often caught in a personalisation beauty parade, with such vendors batting their eyelashes and showing off their Rectus Orbitalis Inferior (ROI)*. Generally, these are pitches that are all sunshine

---

* Not a real muscle.

and rainbows, with little mention of the effort it actually takes. Naturally, confirmation bias kicks in, and brands convince themselves that they'll reap undeniable benefits from this shiny new thing. It's not unreasonable to think that the stated returns are inflated in any case.

Just think about the motivations behind personalisation vendors for a second, rather cynically. They are often backed by investors because creating and selling a software product is expensive. Mutiny raised $71.6 million,[7] Namagoo $69 million,[8] Intellimize $50m[9] and Nosto $32.8 million.[10] This raises investor expectations for scale and growth. Perhaps there is a little bit of haste within the selling process between a personalisation vendor and a brand — "Vendors are selling personalisation like a gold rush," Jonny Longden, Conversion Director, Journey Further, told me. "They're trying to sell it quickly. They're going in saying you need personalisation; we can install it on your site really quickly but nobody has thought about why they would do it and what it is for."[11]

This attitude can manifest itself in end-of-quarter or end-of-year discounts in order for salespeople to meet targets. A tip to all the brands out there, if you can wait until the end of the quarter, or better yet, the end of the year, to agree on a platform to work with, odds are there will be a discount at play. Cha-ching.

Equally, if individual salespeople are personally bonused and reimbursed based on how much they sell, it is also in their own interests to sell as much as possible. It is not unreasonable to think that self-interest can come at the expense of altruism, care, doing what's right, or ethics, as so often we unfortunately see in our modern-day society wracked with fraud, greed and selfishness. And the *Fast and Furious* franchise. This, again, is a rather cynical view more commonly shared with those that have had their fingers burnt, which was enough to comment on within the research undertaken for this book.

Is it the brand that gets lost in the weeds when they buy a platform without a clear purpose in mind? Or are vendors leading brands astray by setting unrealistic expectations? It's a dragon-or-egg situation. It's like trying to slay a mythical beast while blindfolded, stumbling through the tangled mess of misguided goals, misplaced trust and mismanaged expectations. Whether it's the brand or the vendor that's to blame, one thing is clear — managing expectations is key to slaying the bastard Deepfake Dragon.

Chapter 28

Vanquishing The Deepfake Dragon

Formulate a well-thought-out plan. Choose a strategic approach that plays to your strengths and takes advantage of the dragon's weaknesses. Coordinate your team's efforts and execute your plan with precision. Strategic alignment is the first method to vanquish the dragon. Ensure those in charge and those on the frontline work together happily for the same purpose, expectations and implementation of personalisation.

Next, gather your allies. You'll need a team with diverse skills and expertise to aid you in your quest. Knights, archers and wizards can all play a crucial role in your battle against the dragon. The second method is one of cultural alignment. Brands should seek to create a culture that's genuine about building customer relationships, elevate the right people and kill off any ego.

1: Strategic Alignment

"Resources, process and alignment is one the main challenges. Companies are very siloed. Every department has their own priorities and personalisation might not be within their priority at that moment in time."
Doron Taub, Director of Customer Success, Dynamic Yield[1]

Firstly, let's not blame the vendors. They have accelerated the personalisation industry by creating hope where there was once none. Even if that hope has morphed into a state of misexpectation, at least it's something to improve. Strategic alignment is the key to slaying this particular dragon and it's the brands themselves that deserve the pointy-finger of blame for dragging their heels, not the vendors.

McDonald's personalisation practices, on the surface, may not have accelerated as quickly as they, or their billions of customers, would have Mcliked. At least not if the franchisee comments in the *Wall Street Journal* are a marker of anything.

What McDonald's, and brands in the same boat as them, require is mutual strategic alignment between HQ – the Boardroom – and the franchisees, those who have their hands on the means of production. Jean Rene Boidron, CEO of software company, Kameleoon, a leading personalisation vendor[2] concurs. "In personalisation, you can have some nice talkers, but they don't know how to implement it, which creates a lack of alignment." That push-pull on the door occurs once more, this time between those in the trenches and those in power; a personalisation-corporate-divide-paradox.

If you can create alignment around a purpose, generally speaking, personalisation is nailed on for success.

Gousto, the meal kit retailer, is an example of a brand where personalisation is in their bones. Timo Boldt, the founder, sees Gousto as having personalisation in its bones. Some publications even talk about personalisation when describing Gousto – "an online meal-kit manufacturer and retailer, using AI and automation to provide extensive choice and personalisation".[3]

Their purpose seemed clear, and their alignment does, too. That doesn't mean they are exempt from challenges, however. "Where we've had challenges is in explaining what drives performance improvements and future plans internally," Robert Barham, Director of Data,[4] told me. "We've sometimes had conversations where we will test an improvement, see an uplift, and say 'Awesome!'. The feedback in response will be based on anecdotal gaps, such as 'I still get recommendations on this, which I don't like', or on experience, such as 'Wouldn't you be better off investing in other data attributes?' Personalisation is always about giving results and sometimes explaining that level of detail takes a long time."

People questioning purpose sounds misaligned on the surface of it. Barham goes on to explain that this is more of a positive than a challenge *per se*: a healthy amount of scepticism and a culture of constructive feedback are what drive creativity. Without this, there would be an imbalance scientific approach which is what got personalisation here in the first place; a focus on the science without an appreciation of the art.

What Boldt did was set these expectations from the start and at the top. He appreciated that personalisation, experimentation, and decision making is a craft; as much an art as a science. In a letter he wrote to his younger self, Boldt said, "Be willing to change and adapt – a fast-growing business requires you to reinvent yourself all the time."[5] He appreciated that personalisation is an exploratory process. It's not like building a bridge. Brands may not always find that elusive revenue uplift because failure happens along the way. I'm reminded of Sir Thomas Watson's influential and equally paradoxical quote – "If you want to increase your success rate, double your failure rate."[6] That was in 1940. This seems untenable in today's day and age, where brands need to navigate the difference between managing expectations and delivering results. Yet Gousto manages that. From all those I spoke to within Gousto and saw first-hand, they represent a business that has an aligned personalisation strategy because there is a purpose that is well communicated, accepted, authentic and was driven from the very beginning.

2. Cultural Alignment

"People think that everyone thinks you should only do personalisation one way. Failure comes from a combination of stupidity, arrogance and ego."

Simon Elsworth, Global Head of Experimentation, Whirlpool[7]

To me, as I have said, personalisation is a belief system, not a single discipline. And ensuring everyone at the company buys into the *why* should be the first objective for any brand. Not just those in charge, but everyone, from bottom to top. Creating a culture about customer relationships, being obsessed with humanising business, and ensuring that customers are not reduced to data points are all cultural "feelings" rather than individual methodologies, but they are equally valid.

Dynamic Yield agreed. They observed what makes businesses successful and what causes businesses to fail in their attempts to personalise on a day-to-day basis. Sources told me that their No.1 cited reason for failure was cultural misalignment. In fact, when they assess brands before working with them, they do so on a maturity scale for personalisation. Their first questions are all about organisational culture, and their second is about resource allocation. In other words: "People first. Technology second."

Even the most successful personalisation practitioners, who have a personalisation purpose like Gousto, the right tech like McDonald's, and the right data like Disney, still face an uphill battle because they don't have what's needed most – the right people. It is not only the alignment between those in the boardroom and those on the ground, but also the inter-debate between those doing the do. "Everyone is competing against each other internally as well as externally," Ryan Jordan, Strategy Director, Brainlabs, told me while we're on the subject. "There's conflict between individual targets and business targets. We just need to look at the trading mentality where everyone has their own category and targets to hit. Of course, they're going to want to put your product on the homepage – you'll get 50 more sales this month. I wonder whether individual category focus and targets trump what a collective business needs?"[8]

The Deepfake Dragon prevents brands from reaching the personalisation paradise. In order to kill it, a brand must have an aligned strategy built on a solid foundational purpose, and the right people who are all aligned with that purpose.

In a study by Gartner, it was found that as many as one third of retailers don't do any personalisation at all.[9] Peter Weinberg, Global Head of Development, B2B Institute, LinkedIn,[10] believed that the reason why this is the case falls into the categories of "Couldn't, Shouldn't and Wouldn't". (Weinberg would also say that due to the number of barriers brands come up against when personalising is so overwhelming that he coined personalisation as the "worst idea in marketing".)

The thread of these three barriers as to why brands couldn't personalise, wouldn't personalise and shouldn't personalise is all in the people; the cultural alignment.

Yes, there is an expectation set by society that personalisation works and preconditioned notions that it can't fail. Yes, there must be an alignment of goals determined by a singular purpose. Yes, the personality, type, and ambition of the individuals in question must be considered. (The themes of ego, greed, ignorance, and arrogance kept recurring in my research.) But ultimately, we must conclude and understand that personalisation is made by people and therefore should be treated like a person, or derivative thereof. It is a person with a set of beliefs, not just one rigid goal. A person who makes mistakes. A person that can learn. A person that needs other people. Whether that's individual traders myopically promoting their own category, the procurement department writing a myopic request for proposal, or even the CEO myopically purchasing a personalisation provider in a biased way.

Why do you think Netflix, Spotify and Amazon remain the princes of personalisation? It's not because of their resources – although having a $2.7 billion R&D budget certainly helps.[11] But because personalisation is fundamental to how they want to do business. Much like Gousto, it's ingrained in their strategically aligned culture, championed by a person at the top and implemented by people on the bottom who are culturally aligned. It is not an add-on.

Only those who have a purpose to personalise at the foundation of their business will be successful within it because only then is it rooted in authenticity. Those that appreciate the need for technology and data but not the reliance on it. Then it becomes strategic, not a short-termist, tactical method to hoard more money. That manifests itself into a question of aligning those within the business to that purpose. If brands follow that strategy, the Deepfake Dragon will be too scared to do battle — and personalisation survives to live another day ...

Part VII

The Six Spells

"A dream doesn't become reality through magic; it takes sweat, determination and hard work."

Colin Powell, American politician[1]

Personalisation isn't a star anyone can just magically wish upon to become perfect. There is no potion that we — consumers and brands — can consume to instantly make it bigger or better. There's no glass slipper we can just slip on. Just because fairy tales always end with true love's kiss, that doesn't mean all will end well in the story of personalisation. There's a lot of frogs to kiss first.

However, not all hope is lost. There are ways brands can make personalisation work.

I call them the Six Spells. If cast correctly, they'll work like magic to awaken personalisation, the sleeping beauty, from its slumber.

And because personalisation is bloody complicated to get right, I devised these six, not three, spells to simplify how it can be brought back to life. That's the key word right there — simplify. Simple spells that are spelled similarly.

1: The Memory Spell
Simply remembering what personalisation's purpose used to be will help the penny drop for brands.

2: The Acknowledgement Spell
In order to start building a relationship with customers, brands must acknowledge them as more than just numbers.

3: The Listening Spell
When brands truly listen and pay attention to what their customers are doing, they can help paint a better personalisation picture.

4. The Observation Spell

We were given two ears *and* two eyes. Looking at what people are doing is just as important as listening to them — if not more so.

4: The Appropriate Spell

When brands know more, they can be more appropriate to their customers' needs. Humans aren't all the same, so they shouldn't be measured the same.

5: The Care Spell

The Horcrux in our spells, when all these things are considered, brands need to care more about who it is they are communicating to.

By forgetting how simple personalisation can be, the marketing industry (aided and abetted by brand bosses and boardrooms) has created a paradox. False narratives, misconceptions, preconceived notions and, yes, even narcissism have moulded personalisation into something it was never meant to be — an overly commercial, purely scientific marketing function that's built for the business, not for the customer.

By understanding and applying these Six Spells, brands will have the tools to awaken personalisation from its never-ending nightmare. Not about shoving arbitrary recommendations for products *the brand* wants to sell down people's already stuffed throats. Not about pushing genericised content and messages that is in no way personal to the individual. Brands just need to remember that it's about one thing: building a relationship with a customer built on foundations of care, competence and trust.

Chapter 29

The Memory Spell

"Within the whole personalisation industry, I think very few do it well because they don't know how to actually sell. Personalisation is best done based on the intent of the user because it's so closely aligned to how we sell as human beings."

Lorenzo Carreri, Experimentation Consultant[1]

Obliviate![*]

Brands have forgotten what personalisation should be.

The first of six stunning spells should remind us that personalisation should be a make-believe we can believe in. Casting the Memory Spell will help brands remember what personalisation used to be. So, let's cast our minds back ...

It was the mid-nineteenth century. Chinese railway labourers worked long days of physical stress and toil. Such hard work, in fact, that they regularly complained of joint pain like arthritis. To cure this, they used snake oil, believing that when the oil was rubbed on the skin at any painful wound, it would bring some form of relief. They had their reasons: it had an incredibly high concentration of omega-3 fatty acids, even more so than salmon.

The Chinese sold it to the Europeans claiming that it was more than just relief for joint pain, that it was a cure-all elixir for many kinds of physical and physiological problems. The web of misrepresentation grew bigger as the travelling salesperson often posed as a doctor, with forged qualifications, selling counterfeit medications with wild marketing hype, typically backed up by bogus scientific proof. Sound familiar? This was commercialised as Snake Oil Liniment by Clark Stanley.[2] Still with all the associated hype and the forgery, it wasn't until 1916 when the Bureau of Chemistry fined Stanley $20 for the "drastically overpriced and of limited value"

---

[*] In *Harry Potter*, *Obliviate*, also known as the Forgetfulness Charm, was a charm that could be used to erase specific memories from an individual's mind.

medical remedy. About the same size of the insignificant fine Meta received when they were found to leak personal data in 2022.[3]

This is the story of snake oil salesmen exaggerating claims, often with confidence and a lack of evidence, for the purpose of commercial benefit. This has nothing to do with eCommerce in any way, but when we talk about technological solutions that make claims about their efficacy as panaceas, the two don't sound too dissimilar, do they? Ubiquitous claims that vendors make about any one solution giving a 500 per cent uplift in revenue in a matter of minutes with one line of code feel rather snake-oily.

Selling throughout the years has obviously evolved. Well, for most. The Ford Motor Company adopted Grant Neblos' "Science of Selling" approach in 1923,[4] believing customers could tell a person's character by just looking at the shape of their head. The bigger the head, the more imaginative and less likely to resist new ideas. OK, maybe it didn't evolve by that much in those ten years, but it should certainly work for Dwayne Johnson.

Psychological selling came a decade later. Henry Link wrote in his 1925 book *The New Psychology of Selling and Advertising*[5] about understanding what makes customers tick and changing your pitch accordingly.

A few years later, in 1936, came Dale Carnegie's famous book *How to Win Friends and Influence People*,[6] which ushered in a new era of relationship selling. It's a self-help mega-classic as much as it is a book about selling and understanding prospects. The importance of empathising with other people is a core component of the book. Finally. We have a reason.

These eleven years between 1925 and 1936 really set the stage for a more personable approach by understanding who the salesperson was selling to and responding appropriately. Sounds like personalisation to me. Maybe 1936 was actually *the* year of personalisation? I'm afraid the Spanish Civil War overshadowed it.

Relationship marketing feels like everything personalisation was designed for. It was further emphasised sixty years later by Brian Tracey's *The Psychology of Selling.*[7] Here, Tracey taught the lesson that businesses will generate more sales if they ask their customers questions and adjust their pitch appropriately to their specific needs. In fact, Tracey suggested that the six most important words in selling are: "Spend more time with better prospects." More time. In a world where brands rush to sell within a session, or carelessly throw that tiny bag of Haribo in their wackaging because investors are breathing down their necks and waiting impatiently for their return, it feels as though that's the one luxury that brands don't have.

It's a question of observation. By spending more time with customers, brands can uncover true customer intent and appropriately respond to it. Tracey encouraged readers to ask really simple questions at the beginning of any sales pitch designed to uncover whether the person is even a prospective customer or not. (Keep that in mind for when I talk about the simple act of listening more.)

Does this all sound near and dear to your heart? It should do. Personalisation used to mean being more appropriate when selling. That's what Carnegie taught us, and Tracey reaffirmed. "Personalisation of the sales pitch" is how Rishi Rawat describes it, optimisation specialist at Frictionless Commerce.[8] "How we describe the product based on the job that the buyer is trying to get done is what really interests me. Because of this, personalisation is the next phase of eCommerce," he continues.

Whilst it may be the next phase, what started off as snake oil, evolved to be more about relationships, and I feel as though it's reverted back to selling the dark arts; omega-3-fuelled potions acting as panaceas. I wish the next phase existed. It's actually a reminder a phase that has since passed.

Remembering what personalisation was originally designed to be – using our Memory Spell – to communicate more appropriate and relevant information will help brands start to appreciate and acknowledge people as individuals.

Chapter 30

The Acknowledgement Spell

"A good reference point for personalisation is simply how you deal with people in real life."

Tom Hill, Co-Founder, HyperFinity[1]

Helloviato!

*Helloviato!**

The Acknowledgement Spell will awaken brands to the simple fact that they must acknowledge different customers differently. Why? Because acknowledgement is the foundation of building a relationship. What do I mean when I say "acknowledgement" though? An acknowledgement is a recognition between a brand and a customer that says:

I've Seen You Before So I'll Therefore Treat You How You Deserve To Be Treated

Within websites, customers knowingly – most of the time – are OK to give up some of their data in exchange for a better experience. Because, on the surface of it, there's little to no harm in it. However, when a customer buys a product from a brand, there should be some acknowledgement of that purchase. Why do consumers live in a world where this isn't acknowledged? Where, if I buy an overpriced pram for my child, I am continually re-marketed more prams. This is lacking any form of acknowledgement that I just forked out over a grand to buy the latest and greatest four-wheeler for my two-year-old.

This impersonal approach undoes all the personalisation a brand has done up to that point, as it proves that it was never that personal to begin with. Basically, it boils down to one simple point: stop stupidly trying to sell products to your customers who have already purchased them.

---

* A completely made-up spell that doesn't exist in modern literature – to my knowledge.

Brands have that data. But they are choosing to ignore it. I use the word choose purposefully, too, as though it's a deliberate act. Rob McLaughlin, Founder of Loop Horizon, agreed. "I think it's rude that businesses would have useful information about their customers and choose to ignore it. Let's recognise people and let them know they make sure we recognise them so they're not offended."[2]

Recently, I was told a story about a big media company who offered customers the ability to watch sports, cinema, entertainment and drama packages on their service. Like the BBC. (But not the BBC.) It was a Monday morning with coffees at the ready. The personalisation team of three were in the boardroom. Excited about showing off their latest sexy personalisation efforts that recognised how active the customer was in the past 30 days. Or the colossal amount of revenue generated by inferring that family accounts created 25 per cent more conversion with specific comedy packages. Their CEO nodded his head in agreement, smiling ear to ear, fuelled on caffeine and commerce. He then sat down and logged in to his account. Taking a sip of his hipster coffee, he turned his laptop and around asked the simplest of questions. "Why is it that I am being promoted a sports package, when I already have one?"

In one swift sentence, the basics of acknowledgement are laid bare. The personalisation team had focused so much on sex that they forgot about the dates that came before it. The simple groundwork that needed to be done before sleeping with the customer on the first date.

Irrelevant targeting, or irreverent messaging, is everywhere, some are just more overt than others.

They're called Persofails, a term that is rooted in superhero-power simplicity, like Batfleck*.

"Persofails are the gloriously awkward, often daft misfires of personalisation gone wrong in the wild," Jeffrey MacIntyre, Principal of Bucket Studio,[3] told me. Usually it is "design [that] is the most common missing ingredient in almost any personalisation failure that we can think of — beyond ethical and creepiness issues, of course". MacIntyre keeps an online collection of persofails handy on his community website Bucket Brigade, because it can be instructive seeing the common ways personalisation does fail: they are interaction patterns of what data scientists call overfitting, or making false-positive audience assumptions, for instance. In talks and publications, MacIntyre is adamant about the role of information management professionals in delivering

---

* When Ben Affleck was cast at Batman, fans referred to this combination as Batfleck.

better personalised or automated experiences, folks adept at marrying data and design considerations.

That might all be true, but I see them as examples of just wanting to get into bed with the customer on the first date.

Examples like receiving an email from a brand we know and love calling us "$firstname" only to receive an apology email 30 minutes later. One story told of some poor bloke receiving an email from a large household brand, which read "Whoops! We weren't ready to send that email!" attached with a 10 per cent off code. The optimists among us would think that's a solid marketing tactic, not a mistake. But it was clearly human error.

One of the more common persofails on Twitter was a guy who bought a pair of shoes on Zappos. A few hours after his purchase, he was then targeted in an advert on YouTube offering up to 70 per cent off shoes on Zappos, including the pair he just bought. He was pissed off and venting, as so many Twitter users like to do. And rightly so.

Are we – the marketing industry – supposed to be proud of this? Of this utterly batshit, archaic, infant-like approach? All the data we could ever want at our fingertips, and this is where we have arrived? It has to change.

Like bailouts, persofails run rampant no more than in banking. Nothing illustrates failure within personalisation efforts, in my opinion. It's fascinating that most customers remain with the same bank for most of their lives which is surely the tell-tale sign of personalisation; ultimate retention. Yet this isn't an example of retention, nor do customers remain out of loyalty. Quite the opposite – it's just a pain in the ass to change banks.

I've had a current account with the same bank for more than twenty years. Yet, every time I log on, the homepage still chooses – yes, once again they choose – to inform me that if I switch to their bank for a current account, they'll give me £100. The bank knows better than anyone else that I already have a current account with them. And a mortgage. And the names of my kids, their birthdays, when my cat goes to the toilet and probably that I spent far too much money on that pram that can also go off-road.

But now, all I feel is that my bank has made me £100 poorer.

The choice to do this is an approach based on the archaic commercial principles of mass acquisition: cast their net wide enough to acquire more fish, and simply ignore the fish they already have. We live in a world where acquisition is sexier than retention. Ironically, according to an Accenture survey, 40 per cent of consumers would switch banks for more personalised service.[4]

By not acknowledging an established relationship with customers, such as in that example, all banks are doing are reminding their existing customers that they are giving £100 (of their money!) to trap a new customer in this twisted loop. How rude. It's effectively punishment for being a good customer.

What happens in these scenarios is that the irrelevant turns irreverent. Presenting a consumer with a very poorly recommended mortgage may seem irrelevant at first, but at its core, it is a form of disrespecting their customers' interests. Just because a customer bought a horse-riding whip doesn't mean they want to see BDSM outfits. Not always, at least. Maybe some of you do.

What happens is that when brands don't personalise in a way that demonstrates even a whiff of context, it decreases consumer trust in that brand. An Adobe 2022 report stated that 72 per cent of consumers believe that poor personalisation execution, such as sending irrelevant information, ignores customer preferences and harms their relationship with that brand — 33 per cent significantly so.[5]

Acknowledging existing customers should not be hard. Especially in this day and age. As customers — people with hearts that beat — we just want to be acknowledged and heard. This is rarely achieved because, perhaps, what once used to reflect acknowledgement is now so easy to achieve that the action has been reduced to that famous phrase, "best practice". Brands want to get to the good stuff and quick. The bare minimum of purely acknowledging a customer is seen as boring and isn't sexy enough to be allowed to be deemed as personalisation. It's actually not that acknowledging someone isn't personalisation, but its rather a reflection on our expectations, since both brands and customers demand that it be so infinitely more.

As Rasmus Houlind suggested in his book, *Hello $FirstName*[6]: "There is much more to personalization than putting a person's first name into a subject line." While there might be much more to it, adding a first name to a newsletter is intended to be a demonstration of acknowledgement, of a relationship, and by virtue personalisation. It's the first step in a 100-step journey to build a relationship with a customer — so don't skip it. Acknowledge acknowledgement. The thought that goes into deciding to use a first name and address of someone personally is entirely intended to reflect familiarity and acknowledgement. Studies have proven this, suggesting that saying someone's name over and over creates relationship and connection.[7] And it's even backed up by the influential American writer and lecturer, Dale Carnegie, who once wrote, "A person's name is to him or her the sweetest and most important sound in any language."[8] Carnegie is slowly becoming the protagonist in our quest.

Tim Stewart, owner of TRS Digital, calls this communication device "The Mental Enema".[9] Using someone's name grabs their attention and clears their mind from other distraction. It sounds disgusting, but it's true. And it's a concept that can be built on to elevate acknowledgement and familiarity. Remembering someone's name is a demonstration of the Acknowledgement Spell because it shows people the brand was listening and signals that their intentions to help are, on the face of it, genuine. If cast right, this spell will awaken the customer's attention ... and encourage them to be more susceptible to the next spell ...

Chapter 31

The Listening Spell

"If God intended us to talk more than listen, he would have given us two mouths and one ear."

Mark Twain, American Writer[1]

*Muffliato!**

The third spell brands can cast to awaken personalisation from its slumber and make it feel new and improved is ... *Listen*.

That sounds trite and obvious — and, ugh, clichéd — now I've written it down, but yet the point, ironically, still falls on deaf ears to most in the personalisation game. The simple act of listening to what customers are saying, or rather clicking, tapping and typing, then responding in a way that lets the customer know they've been heard lays an even deeper foundation for building a relationship.

In 2012, the year of personalisation, a Microsoft research paper was published that highlighted that there was a "widespread problem with search". Without naming names, they coughed, winked and pointed a few fingers probably at their biggest competitor, Google. Microsoft suggested the problem with any type of search query was "... to reveal actual user intent, provides little data about uncommon queries, and omit many interactions."[2] In short, they were suggesting that Google, and search in general, needed to listen more.

Three years later, Google evolved their search engine to do just that. To be more contextually dependent. At that time, about 15 per cent of all search queries were new[3] — phrases that Google had never "seen" before. This is generally known as the Cold-start Problem where there was no context for those queries. While a logged-in Google account provided some understanding of who the person was, there was little appreciation for what they wanted, and therefore zero compassion. Searching

---

* The Muffliato Charm was used to fill the ears of any person in the vicinity of the caster with an unidentifiable buzzing sound so as to allow for conversation without being overheard.

for "Hot Dog" has different meanings and purposes for different people. For some it's food, others, it's pets. For some people in China, it's both.

What is the context behind *why* the person is searching for what they are searching for? That's the real question.

To address this, Google introduced their pioneering algorithm update, RankBrain. It was a machine-learning system that took Google to another dimension by listening more. This is to say, instead of reading literal characters, RankBrain saw the entity they represented. "By discerning the searcher's true intent, Google can deliver more relevant results," an author from Moz[4] wrote. It was nothing short of a game changer.

Let me give you an example ...

If I were to type in "Disney tickets" (again) into Google, RankBrain would not see 13 characters across two words. Instead, it would discern the context available around "Disney" and "tickets" and then provide results based on that perceived context. For example, because I've searched for it multiple times before, and previously clicked on the Orlando theme park in context, the tickets are location specific and more about buying than educating. It knows I'm a Disney devotee. By doing so, search results instantly became more relevant, more personalised. Put simply: Google *listened*.

> "RankBrain changes the whole search experience and landscape in profound ways. As Google begins to understand which pages and content solves user problems — beyond them just mentioning the right keywords — different websites and brands start to show up in the search results. Users find what they're searching for in new and unexpected places, and the balance of power shifts. In many ways, it levels the playing field."
>
> **Jono Alderson, Head of SEO, Yoast**[5]

RankBrain paved the way for other algorithms to deliver contextualised search results and listen more. In the years since their introduction, the algorithm evolutions of "Medic" and "BERT" have doubled down on this concept of understanding user intent through advances in artificial intelligence. "We have a hunch of what Google tried to do with this Medic update: it seems to try and show results that better match the intent of the search,"[6] said Yoast.

Whilst that was a hunch, no algorithm update was more overt in its purpose of understanding intent than BERT, which stands for Bidirectional Encoder Representations from Transformers. It helps a machine understand what words in a sentence mean, but with all the nuances of context. Google's Vice President, Pandu Nayak, gave an example of what this context looks like to distinguish the intent of the phrase: "2019 Brazilian travellers to the USA need a visa." The word "to" and its relationship to the other words in the query are particularly important to understanding the meaning. It's about a Brazilian travelling to the US, not the other way around. Previously, our algorithms wouldn't understand the importance of this connection, and we returned results about US citizens travelling to Brazil."[7]

It was heralded as the most important Google update in five years. It affects one in every ten searches. That's 100 billion searches a year, just to be clear.

This update immediately changed the way search works because it centred the Google algorithm on the vital concept of listening more. In turn, they can offer more relevant results. This is personalisation is it not?

Although Alderson suggests that: "Google are very careful to avoid using the word 'Personalisation' (while providing localisation, utilising historical data, and tailoring based on other status), but definitely a rise in the number of types of places that Google provides interfaces, tools and systems for helping you progress on an individual user journey. Whether that's buying a car, or researching homework questions, they're trying to provide tailored support for your needs, not just to return results for your keywords."[8] So, yes, basically it absolutely is personalisation. It's one of the best examples I could find in all my research.

In a service setting such as Google, relevancy was clearly of the utmost importance. What about a commercial setting? Not that Google isn't a commercial entity – it absolutely is with its $279 billion empire. It's perhaps more a question of whether commercial entities appreciate the need for listening more, for context and appreciation of different stages of a user journey? I don't think so. But there is one industry that has that appreciation.

Businesses selling to other businesses (B2B) have been trying to listen to customers for years. Most likely because they are generally much more complex selling cycles than those just selling to the layman consumer. Buying a six-figure piece of computer software is clearly more complicated than buying a pair of Kermit the Frog socks. There are way more stakeholders involved, so the sales process often takes longer. Marketing materials, such as white papers, varying pricing options over different product comparison tables, the need for a live demo, then there's the dreaded procurement getting involved – there are just many more touch points. This process has gotten even longer over the years, too, to the tune of about 22 per cent[9] thanks to even more choice than ever before. More touch points equal more interaction. And more interaction gives those businesses that are selling the opportunity to ask more questions and *listen*. If there was an industry that was built for personalisation, B2B is it.

Like Google's ability to provide more relevant results, the key to selling is listening. This enables brands to respond appropriately, as well as prioritise accordingly. Brands can ask questions to customers or inferring actions from them. In either case, their goal is the same: to listen as much as possible, to gain as much context as possible in order to sell as effectively as possible.

You have two ears, and as such, there are two ways to listen. Ask questions or infer actions. Also known as *explicit* and *implicit* forms of listening.

FAQ It

When selling products, it's essential for brands to understand their customers. One way to do that is to ask explicit questions and encourage explicit feedback. By asking customers explicit questions, what brands are generally trying to discern is whether the customer is explicitly satisfied with what was sold. No room for vague ambiguity here. If they were, or weren't, the brand has explicit data to understand why and then learn and improve. When was the last time, for example, you bought a product online and didn't receive a follow up request for feedback asking, "How did we do?"

Lorenzo Carreri, experimentation consultant, believes that the best personalisation lies in this explicit form of listening. "When I think of personalisation, I see it as users give me an input and based on that input, I show you what matters to you,"[10] he told me. When you think about it, asking a question is one of the easiest forms of listening because it's direct and accurate.

Domino's personalise their pizza business based on geo-location and ask me to confirm my address. Many D2C (direct to consumer) brands personalise by using product quizzes. Butternut Box, who serves tasty meals for dogs, asks what breed of dog you have, their size and eating habits. Lovingly, an online flower retailer, asks who the flowers are for and where they are going. There are hundreds of examples and explicit product quizzes have become a staple in helping customers find relevant products.

There are limitations with this approach, however.

Not least is that quizzes have become popularised with exactly that – relevant products. They are usually referring to customer preferences to help find a product. Remember how we spoke about the AIDA model (awareness, interest, desire and action) and that finding products is only application of the first "A"? Recommendations, people.

The second limitation is that customer satisfaction is contextually subjective. For example, if someone states they are satisfied with an outcome or the completion of a task, it lacks all sorts of permutations, both situational and contextual. Different people will have different opinions on what satisfaction actually means. Being satisfied is not the same thing as being happy, just ask my wife. Nor does it warrant repeat business. At its lowest level, satisfaction is scalable — 1 to 10, 1 meaning bad and 10 meaning good. It isn't binary. And because of that, it's equally subjective. The answers of different users to the same result or task may be very different. Cue riots against the famed and equally generic NPS (Net Promoter Scores).

This situation and context are as important as the answer itself, if not more so. What people say isn't always what they mean and what people say isn't often what they do. For example, good UX researchers will "pay much less attention to participants' webcam video during remote sessions and focus much more on the screen they're sharing," said Jim Ross, Principal UX Researcher, AnswerLab.[11] In other words, they focus more on what they do than what they say.

This is because 93 per cent[12] of what someone means is communicated through the non-verbal. Body language, tone of voice and pitch constitute the majority of what someone is trying to communicate. Seeking just one form of that feedback, what people say, feels problematic in and of itself.

Albert Mehrabian, a professor of psychology, devised the 7:38:55 Rule, which stated:

— only 7 per cent of meaning is communicated through spoken words
— 38 per cent is through tone of voice
— 55 per cent is through body language

And so, when a person explicitly says something, it is therefore only 7 per cent of what they really mean. Again, ask my wife. Or try to infer what she means when she says "the dishwasher isn't loaded properly" through her angry growl. In an interaction with another person, or demon-angry spouse, there are simple verbal cues such as "Hmm", "Go on" and "Uh-huh" that are expressed to indicate that the other is listening. This is what brands need to learn. If they won't demonstrate to customers that they are listening, at least simulate it.

Learn from humans. We are excellent mimics capable of expressing a tone of seriousness with a burrowing of an eyebrow, a frown, a nod of a head to insinuate that we are listening. Or, at least, pretending to. Like my children. On the other hand, just moving your head up in an upward inflection can denote genuine curiosity.

We can hear what another person is saying through explicit feedback, but not understand the true situational or contextual understanding of what they really mean. That's all well and good in face-to-face interactions, but we don't have that explicit level of meaning online. How can online brands understand what customers truly want in a face-to-screen relationship? To that point, how can brands truly understand whether users are satisfied when what they say can clearly be different from what they actually mean?

The answers lie in obtaining explicit feedback to acknowledge what the person has said and mixing that with implicit signals to fill out the other 93 per cent of what they actually mean. A picture is worth a thousand words, and all that. Brands must listen as well as observe.

Chapter 32

The Observation Spell

Oculus Reparo![*]

Asking questions is a great way to demonstrate brands are listening – absolutely. But what I've learned is that observing as well as listening is the only way to truly understand the customer. To truly be appropriate. To demonstrate genuine care and, therefore, provide a better service. Brands need to do more than just hear if people are sneezing, they need to observe that glorious scrunched-up sneeze-face first. The unnecessary wrinkle of the nose, the pause in discussion, the closing of the eyes, the weird look up at the bright fluorescent light – all the signs before the sneeze of release – *ah-choo!*

We are talking about the intent to sneeze. Purchase, I mean. Like Google identified over seven years ago with RankBrain, how can brands better understand what customers mean rather than just what they say. Context is just as, if not more important, than content. Casting the Listening Spell is a great way to ensure brands do more than just listen …

Actions Speak Louder Than Verbs

"We take in not just what people watch, but also what they saw and didn't watch which can also be an important signal. We're also constantly looking at the particular context of the experience. If you're watching a short, you actually might be in the mood to watch another short, not necessarily invest in a long movie."
Laura Evans, SVP Data, Disney Streaming Services[2]

---

[*] In *Harry Potter*, Oculus Reparo is used to repair eyeglasses.

While the user's first and last actions — what they searched for and what they clicked — are important parts of purchase success, they don't tell the whole story. Like Laura Evans said, it's almost what the user doesn't do that's more important. There is so much more behaviour that sits in between the first and the last actions, just as body language and other non-verbal cues account for 93 per cent of what a person says. So, while the expression lies at the start and end, the meaning is hidden in the in-between. Observing these movements will increase chances for brands to build a deeper relationship with their customers. Their ability to personalise will therefore proportionality increase.

Think of your last actions on a website. Cursor movement, hovers and scrolling. These have all been proven to accurately imply some level of intent to purchase because they gives clues about user context.

Studies have shown how cursor activity can be used to estimate the relevance of search results and to differentiate between good and bad search abandonment.[3] For example, the rate ratio of cursor movement to reading time is a good indicator of page quality, which in turn can imply a measurement of customer satisfaction. A common pattern for online customers is to read with their mouse. The patterns of purely cursor behaviours, such as reading by tracing text, can predict future behaviours with a stunning 79 per cent accuracy.[4] More so, actually, cursor travel distance and the overall length of time that users spend on a page are metrics that are very common to use to denote quality in day-to-day analysis for customer engagement. Otherwise known as the arbitrary and wholly aggregated scroll engagement and time spent on page within platforms such as Google Analytics.

Within the context of mobile, there is no such thing as a cursor, clearly. But similar patterns of relating intent to signals such as swipes, dwell time on landing pages and zooms have also been identified.[5] Plenty of studies have evidenced the effectiveness of these patterns combined with customers eye movements can identify user preferences, too.[6] Overall, these non-explicit actions have been proven to help more accurately imply searcher intent and interest.[7]

Time, too, is one of the biggest factors in determining customer satisfaction and intent.[8] On the one hand, the quicker a customer clicks on an item, the higher the inferred intent. When you go to the supermarket and want a pint of milk, for example, you head straight to the milk aisle. You get there quicker. Yet, on the other hand, there's been work done in the field of web searches to understand user satisfaction showing that long dwell time clicks (> 30 seconds) are highly likely to indicate satisfaction.[9] Which is it? Quicker actions lead to high intent, or do they lead to low satisfaction? The answer is rooted in context.

Craig Sullivan, owner of Optimise or Die, said to me, "The best way of personalising a journey is through reflecting user context."[10] He cited the example of using an airline app which makes perfect use of all the relevant contextual information about you as an individual. Whether you were planning your trip, on your way to the airport, checking in, passed security, used your boarding pass, or were sitting down in your seat choosing a meal, the ideal app should be showing the most relevant options for the actual context the user finds themselves in – not the boarding card again! Clearly no such app exists for boarding flights – yet. I wonder whether this is because the Golden Dragon prevents such an app from being created because it holds little commercial value. God help brands for ever wanting to create something that just helps people.

Not only does time play a role in intent, but so does search. If a customer wants this pint of famous milk and had the option of searching for it at the supermarket, they would be more specific in their search query. "Famous Milk". Where if the customer were less sure of what it is that they needed, they might ask for "dairy" or "cereal supplements". Specificity is the other main factor that indicates a very high level of intent. Doug Rozen, CEO, Dentsu Media Americas[11] agreed: "Search is one of the best intent signals, and adept marketers will continue to unlock how search behaviours can drive personalization at scale across other channels and media decisions."

It's not just the specificity of the query itself. Studies have suggested the number of queries, the number of clicks, the number of satisfied clicks, the number of clicks resulting in a dwell time above 30 seconds, the number of dissatisfied clicks, the number of clicks with a dwell time less than 15 seconds, and the total time (seconds) before the first click in the search dialogue[12] are all as vital as each other to correctly infer intent.

The long and short of it, I think, is that there are plenty of inferences to consider that could imply customer satisfaction. Time and specificity are two obvious ones, but movement and behaviours between the start and end of actions can hold so much information about intent. Brands just don't listen enough or observe enough, hence the importance of both the Listening and Observation Spells.

Implicit Intent

"No matter what you are studying, and regardless of the many flaws associated with a behaviouristic approach, at the end of the day, observable behaviour is the ultimate outcome of any psychological process."

Glenn Geher, Psychology Today[13]

Signet Jewellers is built on a culture of innovation that has seen their sales grow to the tune of more than $5.2 billion across 10 different global brands in 2021 alone. And, since 2017, their eCommerce sales have quadrupled – granted, the pandemic probably had something to do with that. (Clearly, nothing beats the sight of your own reflection wearing a new ring while doing nothing while locked inside your own home.) Their revenue per visit has increased by over 50 per cent,[14] in large part due to their approach to observing more. Helping them understand customer intent has ultimately helped increase sales.

"Consumer intent is the other key lens we consider when defining audiences, grouping visitors into either low, medium, or high intent to buy. Somebody just coming to our site might be trying to decide between buying some jewellery, a new iPhone, or a vacation – their intent to buy is quite low. But then, as they continue working through our site, we're looking for any signals that might warrant moving them into that 'medium' bucket so that we can start to treat them a little differently. And then once they've shown high intent and are screaming that they're close to purchase, it's deciding how we can personalise their experience to encourage them across the finish line."

Craig Kistler, Director of Personalisation and Experimentation, Signet[15]

Signet aren't the only ones who do this. Patrick Fagan, Behavioural Scientist at Capuchin Behavioural Science (and ex-lead psychologist at Cambridge Analytica)[16] told me: "We always profile users on intent in order to see who is most valuable, to see who is going to buy anyway against people who will never buy. Don't forget there are people in the middle. I recommend to always segment on behaviours, motivation and psychology, but always personalise to them on intent." An interesting distinction from Fagan on the difference between segmenting and personalising.

To do that, a brand must first observe.

Better understanding customer's intentions, means brands must know where the customer is in their journey: are they simply window-shopping or are they further down the tunnel and focusing on research and selection? "Once you understand that, you can focus on asking questions or showing them complementary products to drive a purchase," said Ephraim Luft, ex-CPO, FarFetch.[17] "To be there at the moment the customer needs you," he continued, a point reminiscent of being there with a Kleenex when someone sneezes.

Understanding customer intentions at the start is a concept rooted in care and helps them in a way that is relevant to their goal. There's that word "relevant" again. It's personalisation in a nutshell. It's the lowest common denominator and yet the foundational principle of personalisation. And, if that's the case, understanding customer intent is the primary constituent of that. It's probably what led Whirlpool's Simon Elsworth to tell me, "When I'm thinking about personalisation, that's what I'm thinking about. *Intent.*"[18]

And so, I found on my quest that intent is the key to personalising. And no one does intent better than Spotify.

Their concept is focused on the basic premise of both observation and implication. In the case of personalisation online, this is the belief when the actions of a customer speak more truthfully and accurately than their words. Netflix are also a great enforcer of implicit feedback. Remember, in 2017, the year of personalisation, they moved away from star-based rating systems – explicit feedback – in favour of hundreds of thousands of implicit cues that determine what is and isn't recommended to you. Whether you view something, watch it for ten seconds, ten minutes or ten hours, rewind, re-watch, hover and pause on a title, scroll past a title quickly – these are all implicit cues that drive the recommendation system. That very system accounts for 80 per cent of everything you now watch. Spotify are no different. Their personalisation strategy is also inherently rooted in the implicit.

Spotify tries to understand the intent of the audience when you enter their app or site. Depending on the signals that you infer, there are eight different intent profiles that they bucket you into. Whether you might immediately search for Drake suggests that your intent is to listen to a specific song, album, or artist. Or, if you spend some time on the homepage, scrolling through the various "shelves" of content, it suggests that you are in a discovery mode. For example, "to quickly access my playlists or saved music" and "to explore artists or albums more deeply" are some of the intent definitions shown.

For Spotify, the implicit can infer meaning, but that is contextual to the situation. On the one hand, scrolling can be an indicator of exploration, but scrolling back and forth can signal a struggle. If a person doesn't scroll, it could mean that they like the suggestions that were given, or it could mean that they are utterly repulsed that they have been recommended *Let It Go* for the fiftieth time. This drives the need for different interpretations of interaction signals for different intents, or what they call "Intent profiles".

It's not unreasonable to have a mixture of both the explicit and the implicit when listening to customers. For example, Spotify used interviews and surveys to whittle down the types of intent profiles they might see. They asked a selection of their app users "How satisfied or dissatisfied were you with your experience on the Home screen today?" as well as asking "Why were you on the Home screen today?". While this helped bucket individuals into a profile, therefore able to associate implicit behaviours towards, their response rate was just 4.5 per cent.[19] For Spotify, this is fine, as it still equated to 116,000 people. But we're not all Spotify.

And, so, both the explicit and the implicit are useful in understanding intent, but they each have different benefits. What I can say with confidence is that listening to and observing customers can help to signal their intent which may be the main predictor of satisfaction or establishing a genuine relationship.[20]

Chapter 33

The Appropriate Spell

"The notion of intent comes from understanding where the person is in their journey. I'm trying to give you what you want, and I want you to do this in return. There's a value exchange going on all the time."

Tim Axon, Founder, Lean Convert[1]

Tarantallegra![*]

With a sprinkle of acknowledgment, a dash of listening, a pinch of observation and a dollop of understanding intent, brands can be oh-so appropriate with their customers. Being appropriate is hitting the sweet spot of customer satisfaction because it acknowledges people and demonstrates care. These are the foundations of personalisation. The Appropriate Spell helps a brand sell but is also about showing a customer it's understood all its learnt about them in their journey together so far and applied it. The results should now be appropriate to that customer.

What I've learned in my quest is that inappropriateness comes from brands who forget that customers have different needs and goals. They treat everyone the same, and measure everyone the same. Luckily, there are wise souls like Signet and Fagan who acknowledged that customers are different. Who would have thought? So, too, are their needs at each stage of the experience. By acting appropriately with a customer, a brand can demonstrate its first step towards care of duty.

Alex Hisaka, Principal at Fresh and Only Marketing[2] explained this well. "Buyer intent is really all about timing. Too many businesses focus their sales and marketing strategies on expanding the first stage of their funnel — Awareness — and they neglect buyers entering the sales cycle at later stages or in novel ways."

---

* Casting this spell in *Harry Potter* makes the victim dance uncontrollably which, I consider as being always appropriate.

When Hisaka is talking about a myopic focus on awareness, she is tipping her hat to the AIDA model I spoke about in the first chapters. Where the word "Relevant" has been misunderstood for product selection or discovery. A narrative that has been set by Netflix and Amazon in their quest for recommendations supremacy. This is the proposition of affinity. Matching products based on preferences and interests.

Yet, the market is so focused on affinity that it's forgetting about its bigger brother — intent. This older sibling is what helps brands understand appropriateness. Where brands don't focus enough on the *strength* of intent because they are too blinded by the *direction* of it. You might be in the market to buy a Maserati over a Porsche (direction), but how likely are you to buy the Maserati (strength)?

Within Google Ads, for example, they have two features available for customer marketing to audiences. Those are Custom Affinity and Custom Intent; the difference between them is clear. The first is the ability to create audiences based on users' interests. Instead, custom intent allows advertisers to target people who are actively searching for specific topics. Those "in market" if you will. Where affinity can help find, intent can help appropriate.

Because of this, understanding customer intent feels like the most appropriate way to create a relationship with a prospect, does it not? Gone are the days of blanket marketing messages, we hope. A lack of respect for the strength of intent, as Hisaka mentioned, creates neglect for the customer. Or worse ...

"The difference between persuasion and manipulation is intent."
Robin Dreeke, Head of Behavioural Analysis at the FBI[3]

Emma Sleep, the UK's most awarded mattress brand since 2019, are a big business, operating in 20 countries. In 2020, they were acquired by a German holding company, Haniel, and they drove €405 million in sales. That's a lot of mattresses. And that was up from €150 million in sales from the previous year.[4]

In 2022, however, the UK's competition watchdog, the Competition and Markets Authority (CMA), investigated Emma Sleep for misleading consumers through the use of pressure-selling tactics.[5] This investigation, in particular, was about how they used countdown clocks on their website implying time was running out with big discounts. The investigation simply asked the question: does the countdown ever stop?

Here, a clear lack of care can be seen in their approach to marketing and, some would argue, an over-index in competency too. Emma Sleep make excellent mattresses, to be sure, but their technique for selling, and motivation behind the tactic, has been called into question. It feels inappropriate and neglectful to continually pressure customers down a funnel to purchase irrespective of who they are or where they are in their journey – especially if the countdown is pure fiction.

Emma Sleep doesn't hog the bed, however: 71 per cent of people who shop online have encountered misleading selling tactics that signal the brands neglect to listen to their customers appropriately.[6] Booking.com, amongst other booking engines such as Expedia, fell victim to a CMA investigation in 2019[7] over practices that gave a false impression of a hotel's popularity, with claims such as "one room left at this price" and "booked four times in the last 24 hours".

The problem isn't necessarily that these tactics don't work, they do. Very well. Of course they do, they're rooted in psychological pressure – and our old friend, FOMO – and they net out positively if most case studies are to be believed.

The problem is that they are applied universally to every customer, which feels inappropriate because it is inappropriate. Such tactics omit the context or intent of the consumer. Because of this, the pressure tactic is viewed as inciting fear and anxiety in the many rather than gently persuading the few.

Pressuring consumers to purchase with slimy second-hand car salesman tactics – "Lots of people have their eye on this beauty!" – omit any form of care for the customer where the brand is continually stuck in sixth gear; the gear of sell, sell, sell. We're back to the early 1900 days of snake oil salesmen again. Customers who were simply researching a particular product are now being preyed upon, with their own vulnerable psychological impulses and instincts working against them. And applying them to every customer then becomes counter-productive. That is to say, because these tactics are not relevant or appropriate to the customer at their current level of intent, they dismiss it. And so, when the time is right to buy the product, the impact of the tactic is greatly reduced.

But, of course, who cares? All care is largely forgotten in favour of making a quick buck. The Golden Dragon defeats the Knights of Care every single time.

Prediction Over Retrospection

The reason why inappropriate behaviour occurs is because brands measure all customers the same and so treat them the same. They use aggregated, retrospective and binary metrics such as conversion rate to determine success. In reality that might quantitatively be a measure of success for the business, but what of the customer?

What about understanding the quality of their experience? Please brands, let's cut the fluff and focus on real value, shall we? It's time to deliver excellence, not just mask it in marketing jargon that hides mediocrity.

That supremely ordinary way of determining performance is something I've seen many examples of in my time. For instance, brands who often allude to the fact that search is a positive contributor to conversion rate. That those who use search are three, four or ten times more likely to purchase than those who don't use it. It doesn't take Sherlock Holmes to figure this one out. This is an example of a piece of analysis that is not considerate of intent. What about the nuances or the context or the deeper dive that makes this anything more than a surface level piece of analysis? Was the search specific or generic? What were their behaviours during and after the search? These are much better questions to understand performance, not just the results. As I mentioned before, the expression lies at the start and end, the meaning is hidden in the in-between. Such nuance and meaning feels like an inconvenience in the cutthroat world where profits reign supreme.

The circus of aggregated metrics is a quandary that toyed with the football world for years.

In a game of football, a goal is a rare event. Actually, the average number of goals scored in a Premier League game is less than three. Especially if you're a Crystal Palace fan. Like conversion rate, it, too, is an aggregated, retrospective, binary figure. Did Crystal Palace score? Yes or No. In this instance, goals are often skewed by randomness and luck because there are so few of them. How can coaches strategise and personalise styles of play against their opponents when the focus of play is collated in a single, rare and averaged metric?

Similar to customers converting online, there are many behaviours that footballers exhibit that can be used to infer whether a goal is likely to occur or not. The distance from goal, the angle, the freedom, and space occupied by the striker, the number of touches before attempting the shot, the location of the assist — there are loads. These are all things that happen before a goal. Not only can these behaviours they predict whether a goal may occur, but they can help determine the *quality* of a goal-scoring opportunity. The word there is quality.

In 2012, an analyst named Sam Green published a blog post on the OptaPro forum. It was mostly a place for semi-interesting, semi-scientific mumbo-jumbo but on this occasion, Green brought something fully intriguing to the table. He proposed that the idea that the quality of a shot might be just as important, if not more so, than how many shots were taken. He was talking about quality over quantity. About the performance over the result. Green was the first to use the term "Expected Goals" (xG), a metric that predicted whether a goal might occur by modelling all these attributes together. In doing so, he "provided an antidote to the disease of randomness that permeates football",[8] as well as the disease of aggregation one could argue. Can Green also come and provide an antidote for the disease of false narratives within personalisation? And my Athlete's foot.

With the introduction of expected goals, although it took at least five years to hit the likes of Gary Lineker's mainstream analysis on Match of the Day, football successfully moved away from a myopic obsession with the end result – a goal – and instead toward the underlying attributes that drove success. Performance, not results. Since being in the public eye, it has now become the dominant, the only, the one-to-watch statistic in global football. It is the reason Brentford FC have risen from the fourth tier of English football to the Premier League. They're currently sitting eighth and now worth more than £300 million.

Brentford FC, by the way, are the English football equivalent of the baseball giants from across the pond, the Oakland Athletics. A similar story of a team who used predictive metrics to find value where it was once overlooked, giving them the ability to buy players and find themselves competitive with teams such as the New York Yankees, who spent more than $125 million on payroll in a season where the Oakland Athletics spent just $40 million. Do you think the story sounds familiar? It is. The origin of expected goals is not too far away from how Sabermetrics, its American equivalent, was born. Predictive, more appropriate analytics that looked beyond batting average in baseball. (Yes, I've read *MoneyBall*. And, yes, I saw Brad Pitt's movie adaptation. And, yes, it was very good.)

Expected Goals, like getting on base, was the revolution that each game needed.

If we apply the same logic to how brands should personalise experiences on their site, such statistical endeavours will help them move beyond what could be argued is a narrow-minded approach. A more predictive play can help brands place an emphasis on the interactions, attributes, factors and purposes behind the end output without myopically focusing on the output itself.

Instead, it can introduce an appropriate metric that defines the quality of performance – expected conversion. A metric that isn't an obsession over short-term gains, but values the long-term impact of actions. A metric that appreciates the intangible and the intent behind the numbers. A metric that can help flip the mindset from "revenue first" to "quality first" — or at least a rebalancing of that mindset.

B2B have got it down. The evolution of the B2B sales process has seen them move towards data that measures the intent of their customers and helps them prioritise based on this type of predictive lead scoring. They have moved away from data that allowed them to understand who the right prospects were, or who was "in market". If a brand has an experimentation platform, for example, understanding if other potential customers had similar customer experience vendors on their site, such as FullStory, HotJar, or Heap, would be helpful to understanding that retailers maturity and approach to optimisation. Useful yet lacks context.

The future lies in taking a leaf out of the world of football with a move towards metrics that are more predictive, more appropriate. Using intent data, businesses are able to discern the most likely prospects that would buy software. This type of data helps businesses eliminate the guesswork to understand the definition of what a good lead actually is, helping them to be more appropriate at each stage of the journey. Sometimes known as "lead scoring" it is now a standard practice in B2B sales. It works by leveraging machine learning algorithms to evaluate key behaviours of prospects and rank them against a scale that can distinguish between the prospects who are more likely to buy the company's products. Just like how football worked in appreciating the quality of a goal scoring opportunity. In other words, how ready to buy is this prospect out of 10? In doing so, it helps B2B sales understand the quality of their efforts, not just the output of them. Hereto, I reiterate the phrase "performance, not results".

Sephora, the makeup mecca, is one such example outside of the world of B2B, using prediction to help understand a purchase beyond what the user is currently doing. Always thinking ahead. When the retailer's marketing team identified that multi-category shoppers were more loyal than single-category shoppers, they set a goal to convert more single-category shoppers into additional categories; broadening their horizons of discovery. For example, customers who buy liquid eyeliner will provide highly targeted customer and product data used to include personalised recommendations from new categories in post-purchase emails — like mascara or lipstick.

Whilst predictive, these are still, ultimately just recommendations. The stub of personalisation as a whole. Yet, looking at future purchases that were more predictive was an approach to personalisation that focused on more than just the immediate session. Boy, did they nail it. This resulted in an 8.4 per cent increase in revenue per client for Sephora to which everyone in the marketing team threw confetti of glittery eyeshadow.[9] And money from their bonuses.

Brands like Sephora need to take a page from football's playbook. It's a game-changer, pun completely intended. Gone are the days of obsessing over retrospective metrics that solely define quality and output. Just like in the world of B2B, it's time to start valuing quality. This can, in turn, help brands be more appropriate with their customers. Brands that truly care about their audience will measure their intent and create better relationships with them because they will be more in tune with that their customers want at that point in time.

Chapter 34

The Care Spell

"Approach each customer with the idea of helping him or her solve a problem
or achieve a goal, not of selling a product or service."

Brian Tracey, The Psychology of Selling, 1985[1]

Amortentia![*]

In a world of mass-market, mass advertising, mass money and mass opportunity conjoined with the need for speed and cash, brands have lost that most human of attributes: care.

When was the last time a brand actually delivered on their promise to make a connection or make you feel more like a person and less a customer? Thinking back to the reason why I started my quest standing in line at Disney World, that's exactly the feeling I had. Dejection. I don't think I'm alone when I say marketing feels like it has lost its sense of compassion. As Publilius Syrus once said: "We are interested in others when they are interested in us."[2] And usually others are interested in us when we have a spare tenner in our back pockets.

Right now, it feels as though brands have reverted back to the commercial one-way street where it's business first, customer second. I'll take an educated guess if you're reading this book, that you feel the same.

"We don't believe that people and profit are mutually exclusive. We understand the concern, but reject the premise that there is a choice to make between the two."

Chad Dickerson, CEO, Etsy[3]

Etsy did more than just recognise the division between people and profit. It attempted to stitch them back together.

---

[*] Amortentia is an extremely powerful love potion.

Rob Kalin, founder of Etsy, and his band of friends saw the opportunity to "Make eCommerce human".[4] Frustrated with eBay's exorbitant fees, Kalin, a novice furniture maker with a penchant for handmade creations, couldn't find a fair platform to sell his goods. One that demonstrated a level of care rather than a whiff of what he felt was exploitation. So, in 2005, the year of personalisation, he and his cohorts cooked up a small eCommerce store in a matter of weeks and dubbed it Etsy. The concept was simple yet ground-breaking – create a space where vendors could become the "the protagonists of their own [lives]"[5] and buyers could connect with unique handcrafted products.

What a wonderful line: "Making eCommerce human". Etsy became a beacon for those seeking a human touch in their shopping experience, and Kalin's dedication to his business was palpable. He took it personally, unlike others who were solely focused on the bottom line.

Etsy's goal of making online shopping more human and caring for the artisan remains intact today. It somehow survived eight rounds of investment, too. For me, and those who share a similar view, it's inspirational to see such a pioneer create a huge business nearly twenty years ago, reminding us all that business can be more than just dollars and cents.

This was measured by moving towards quality performance metrics, where it was said Kalin regarded real conversations and loyalty as his most important KPIs. A connection that provided unswerving loyalty with his customers. And in doing so, a move away from quantitative results – a view he classed as "ridiculous". Where trying to maximise shareholder value was the antithesis of doing what was right for the consumer and the artisans. OK, he was described as "almost anti-commercial and idealistic"[6] by one of his earlier investors. I'm certain that some of you reading this would describe me as the same.

Yet, like Dickerson said, the two aren't mutually exclusive. This unwavering belief of caring for artisans grew the business to more than 80 million members and made it go public in a $100 million IPO. It's now valued at more than $14.6 billion.[7] Who says you can't scale personalisation?

Kalin's desire for "loyalty" says more than the word allows. In a free-market economy, repeat business isn't always a sign of success, although loyalty is. There is a distinct difference. Recent studies have spotlighted that repeat purchases are actually a poor indicator of loyalty,[8] because they don't account for whether the customer has a strong relationship with the brand or not. The fact that a brand can sell a product at a low price and deliver it quickly may be indicators of competence, trust and convenience, but not a valuable relationship. Just because Tesco delivered your cauliflower rice and baby aubergines to your door on time for the past ten weeks does not mean that you will remain loyal to them.

This reminds me of that fantastic quote from the US version of *The Office*.

"Look, I'm all about loyalty. In fact, I feel like part of what I'm being paid for here is my loyalty. But if there were somewhere else that valued loyalty more highly, I'm going wherever they value loyalty the most."

Dwight Shrute, *The Office*

To encourage this level of loyalty, Kalin built Etsy on care and connection, rather than competence and convenience. People, not profit. He believed that this attribute of care, above all others, helped create a relationship and trust between the Etsy brand and the consumer that would lead them to long-term success.

Trust

"Don't trust the right thing done for the wrong reason. The why of the thing, that's the foundation."

Donald, from the movie *Interstellar* **(2014)**[9]

The human brand. Malone and Fiske talk about how we, as discerning individuals, evaluate the trust of each other based on two critical dimensions: warmth and competence. Warmth is all about whether someone will lend a helping hand or provide assistance, while competence focuses on their ability to actually deliver on that help.

But let's be real, "warmth" feels a bit too touchy-feely for me. I prefer the term "care" instead, because care is a verb, it implies action, it's about doing something. Warmth, on the other hand, is just an adjective, describing how we feel about that care. But regardless of the term, it all comes down to empathy, and if that isn't a central tenet of a brand's personalisation effort then they've missed the point.

So, if care is the act of showing helpfulness, sincerity, friendliness and trustworthiness — when was the last time you saw it in a commercial setting? Of the two — care or competence — it is care that is jettisoned first in the pursuit of a quick buck. Brands can get so stuck in their day-to-day optimising what colour the "Add to cart" button should be that they forget that there are actual real-life people using that button on the other side of the screen.

These two attributes of assessment – care and competence – come down to trust. Do we trust each other as people? Do we as people trust brands? At the moment, trust is perhaps at an all-time low.

The personalisation-trust paradox. Nearly 60 per cent of consumers claim to make purchase decisions based on a brand's beliefs and values, whether it's their stance on climate change or economic inequality. But here's the kicker – a whopping two-thirds of consumers believe that business executives and government leaders are nothing but a bunch of liars.[10] We're stuck in this twisted cycle of seeking brands that align with our beliefs, only to doubt their sincerity. It's high time for brands to walk the talk and prove that their values are more than just empty rhetoric.

In December 2022, the year of personalisation, it was reported that a shocking 98 per cent of all Black Friday deals across most of the big retailers weren't actually deals at all[11] – and get this – could even be found cheaper throughout the year. How can customers trust retailers when the lies are so blatant?

Another example is seen in the wonderfully frustrating conversations with brands, where customer service numbers are hidden on websites or routed through voice automation technology that never works or takes too long. "No, I did not press back!" It's anti-customer service founded in what's best for the business not for the customer – competence over care. Sure, there are the odd examples of brands shoving Haribo sweets into your wackaging, but brands are spending, on average, nearly 4.8 days a month dealing with problems – up from 3.8 days last year.[12] Things are getting worse for the customer, not better.

What about our good friends, recommendations? When a recommendation is offered by a brand – let's use Netflix for the hundredth time again as an example – there is an implied pre-requisite of trust that hangs in the air. To be able to recommend something implies a level of authority, knowledge and intimacy with the customer. It requires all the customer's lovely loyalty (and cash) and trust with that brand to believe that they have the capability, or competence, to recommend it to them. The more valued recommendations they get right, the more loyalty (and cash) the brand will retain.

There's something quite dominating and submissive about that relationship, isn't there? And dirty too – considering customers hand over money at the end of the transaction. Alex Birkett, co-founder at *Omniscient*, called it "paternalistic" when I spoke to him, "When maybe that sweater you found that was sent by a friend, just one data point, means you get recommendations like that from now on and funnel yourself into this sense of style."[13]

This one-way street is implied within the term itself "We Recommend". It's a term many brands use to imitate the bare minimum of personalisation. Why that specific phrase? Glenn McDonald, Data Alchemist at Spotify told me rather cynically that "'We recommend' can feel like 'hold still and we'll tell you which power tool you should be buying'."[14] It's not about talking at customers, it's about talking with them. The "We" implies there is a person behind the brand doing all the talking. The term "recommend" is used instead of "advise" or "suggest". "Recommend" is not a bad word by any stretch of the imagination, but let's consider its implication. It begs the question: who is the verb actually for? Is it the person being recommended or the brand making the recommendation? *Why* is the brand recommending that recommendation? Who benefits most from that recommendation? Can we trust that recommendation? In a retail context, is the recommendation because these items are running out of stock and the retailer needs to get rid of them? Or is it because they are the most popular items and the brand is just promoting them? And if so, are these promoted items the best for the customer or best for the business?

It all boils down to two seemingly similar, yet fundamentally distinct concepts: "giving the customer what the customer thinks they want" versus "giving the customer what the brand thinks they want". But let's be real, it's actually just "what the brand wants the consumer to want". It's like a subtle manipulation game, where brands try to nudge customers in a certain direction, under the guise of personalisation. Cynical smoke and mirrors.

At the heart of it all is trust. If you trust the brand and by virtue the recommendation, the rest is moot.

A lack of care, however, can destroy this trust in a single instance. Generally, examples of irresponsibility such as COMPAS[15] or Amazon[16] are mostly the passing of customer responsibility to the algorithmic: the recommender systems that are seen everywhere. They tend to either ignore context, have an agenda, or have some form of natural bias — perhaps all three. The question might be the intention behind this irresponsibility, not necessarily the irresponsibility itself. Either way, the impact is the same. Or as one academic study wrote: "Some eye-catching recommendations may attract users to click, but after reviewing the recommended content, users might get unsatisfied or even upset. This will hurt users' trust in the system, cause them to return to it less often, and eventually leave."[17]

Promotions, customer service, recommendation systems – it is this imbalance focusing on competence and not enough attention on caring that creates mistrust between brand and consumer. This is no more prevalent than our good friends, the bankers.

Almost everyone in the UK is associated with a bank – 96 per cent hold a current account with a bank or building society, to be precise.[18] Talk about a monopoly. A real monopoly, not just the game. Statistics show that less than one million customers switch bank accounts every year.[19] If less than 2 per cent of adults switch banks, this is surely a reflection on the high degrees of loyalty between them and their bank. Yes?

Nope.

There's a reason why the average banking Net Promoter Score (NPS) is just 18.[20] Switching banks is difficult. It requires time, effort and energy – and all for very little reward. Maybe even just that £100 voucher my bank once promised me. Therefore, a customer's relationship with their bank is predicated on an over-index of competence alone. Satisfaction and happiness with their banks remain low.

This is directly related to customer-brand trust, or the lack thereof. Today, only 32 per cent of UK consumers believe that their bank can be trusted. And 46 per cent say their level of trust in banks has deteriorated over the past three years.[21]

What is driving this trust deficit in the industry, I discovered, is not that customers feel that banks are incompetent at managing our money, it is that they are uncaring. A whopping 63 per cent of the variation in trust can be attributed to how customers perceive their banks to act in their best interests, or in simple terms, how much they actually care. Competence? Well, that only accounts for the rest.

The outcome of which is clear: "to thrive and grow, banks need to become more caring".[22] What this suggests is that care is by far the most important of the two variables.

Sure, there are some challenger banks like Monzo and Revolut that are disrupting the scene with their digitally native approach and customer-centric mindset. But let's be real, overall consumer care in the banking industry has flatlined. Banks have become the necessary evil, the familiar devil you know rather than the devil you don't. It's time for the banking industry to wake up, prioritise customer care as a core value and show customers that they genuinely care about their best interests.

A Caring Relationship

Trust is earned, not given. And it takes effort. It takes genuine care. It's about showing up consistently, being transparent and keeping brand promises. It's about being there for your customers when they need you, and even when they don't.

Without it a brand without trust isn't a brand, it's just a glorified product distributor. In the same way that advertising without trust is just noise. Or technology without trust is obsolete. If trust is the pre-requisite, the requisite is relationships.

Marketing professor Susan Fournier, in her now-famous 1998 paper "Consumers and Their Brands: Developing Relationship Theory in Consumer Research"[23] wrote about the importance of relationship in marketing. In it, she called brands "relationship partners" and maintained that, in order for customers and brands to have a relationship with each other, there must be interdependence between them.

It's because as individuals, we yearn for intimacy. No, not the steamy kind, although that's always fun too. I'm talking about the relationship we have with brands. Turns out, we humans have a knack for forming bonds with the products we buy, just like we do with our friends and family. It's all happening at a subconscious level where our brains are out there, swiping right on brands, looking for that perfect match.

"Your relationship with Spotify is intimate," Kate Nightingale, Founder, Humanising Brands,[24] told me. "They actually listen, like a best friend, they are able to inspire you. You listen to them in return, and there is mutual trust between the two." Spotify even knows your music taste better than your best friend. Their popular end of year campaign, Wrapped, now seals that deal in a tidy bow. It is now one of the most shareable, well-known personalised content vehicles around – everyone pins theirs to the top of their social media come the final festive weeks of December. This marketing device was reportedly created by an intern on their last day. "When I gave the Wrapped presentation at the end of my intern project, it was received really well," the intern said. "They liked the idea. That was my last day."[25]

Spotify would later deny this in a statement. Some best friend.

To become more than a product, brands must say, believe, balance and demonstrate not just "I *can* help you" but "I *want* to help you" in order to develop relationships with their customers. Demonstrating this top level of care results in greater customer satisfaction because it creates the perception of a more intimate brand relationship.

One without the other doesn't work. Competency without care creates a limited relationship, which is why most struggle to have a genuine relationship with their banks – or Amazon. Despite Bezos statements of loyalty and personalisation, their tales of workers that have been treated in ways that leave them homeless, unable to work, or bereft of income distort your bias as to whether they *really* care.[26] Recent research has calculated that, in 2021, up to half a billion pounds could have been lost to the UK public purse from the corporation tax avoidance of Amazon alone.[27] Being propped up on competency alone, the real reason why customers shop there is not personalisation. In fact, just 14 per cent agreed with that statement in a 2021 white paper by the optimisation consultancy, Brooks Bell.[28] It was the markers of competence that took the top four spots: home delivery, checkout, ease of site navigation and returns process.

Amazon isn't alone. In fact, most retail brands struggle to demonstrate care because "Digital is one of the most impersonal things ever. Trying to bring innate human channels into a cold, static digital set of channels," according to Rob McLaughlin, Founder of Loop Horizon.[29]

McLaughlin is right. It's difficult to build a relationship through a screen, no matter how large or state-of-the-art it is. I've had better conversations with my toaster than with some brands. The brand on the other side of the screen is, by very nature of its location, impersonal. It reduces the cultivation of relationships down to a few mouse clicks and strokes that are interpreted as nothing more than a bunch of data. Where's the empathy? Where's the connection and how is that manifested? Like trying to express emotions with emojis — it's just not the same.

Aside from how brands measure performance in generic and a results-driven fashion, it is their excuse of needing to scale that prevents them from demonstrating care needed to create relationships. They measure performance in generic terms, chasing results and numbers, while using the excuse of needing to scale as a barrier to truly connecting with their customers. Mass communication and mass relationships — it's a mass solution that lacks the heart and soul of genuine care. It's like trying to recreate a Van Gogh painting with a printing press.

I get it. Signifying care en masse is extremely hard to do, if nigh impossible as McLaughlin suggested. When attempted, it's more of a simulation than anything. To re-create care is to personalise and to personalise en masse requires automation, which, in and of itself, is impersonal.

Welcome to the ever-spiralling personalisation-impersonal paradox. Mind your step.

Because of this need for scale, brands can therefore be seen to over rely on competency — "How Did We Do?" — and under perform on care — "How Did We Make You Feel?"

This is why the true meaning of personalisation is lost. Brands simply find care too hard to simulate. As such, brands overcompensate on their competencies. Excellent customer service and stand-out product seem to be the staples of every brand's *raison d'être* yet they are both markers of being able to do something, without the suggestion of wanting to actual do something.

A Thoughtful Marketing Movement

"I'd rather have some empathy and lack full scale than have no empathy at all. Empathy is going to build experiences that last."

Steven Shyne, Co-Founder, CXperts[30]

It doesn't matter whether we're stunning dragons in the boardroom or our egotistical peers with these Six Spells. Everyone in the personalisation industry – including me – must begin to appreciate that the consumer pays the bills and brands need to refocus their attention back to the them. We must acknowledge them. Care for them. We must stop just saying brands are customer-centric, the buzzword of the twentieth century and start standing by it.

In 2019, the year of personalisation, the British flower retailer, Bloom and Wild, asked their customers if they wanted to opt-out of a marketing campaign on Mother's Day.

That time of year can be a tough time for some, perhaps acting as a painful reminder of the loss of a loved one. And so, in a bid to be more caring towards their customers, they intentionally reduced their ability to reach them. Not only by opting-out of the pushed email messages around the campaign, but also on-site content too.

In what they called "The Thoughtful Marketing Movement", they saw interactions with the brand on Twitter grow from an average of 5 per cent to 20 per cent on the same day.[31] They also received positive customer feedback via phone calls and emails, with responses reaching 1,500 – 5x the average amount.

What I love about this movement is that it was a deliberate attempt to reduce the number of email opt-ins. It intentionally reduced the number of total customers potentially purchasing. I see it as choosing to be appropriate over profit, or a demonstration of care over competence.

Granted, this is an example of segmenting an audience, which as I learned, isn't a predicator for "personalising". Whatever. It's an example of segmenting in such a personal way, grounded in emotion. That's all good in my book. Whether we classify this under the binary label of personalisation or not is irrelevant. What matters more is that it's caring and contextually appropriate, littered with empathy. More of this, please.

Thank goodness the world is changing. Since the invention of the shop till, the motto "the customer is always right" has protected the consumer, and now thanks to a few inflection points with the pandemic, AI and data privacy regulation specifically, that has been placed front and centre once again.

Today, consumers hold the keys, and businesses are locked out. But there is a huge amount of money to be made from marketing nonetheless. And brands know that, they'll just need to work harder at it. Or sabotage it. It's up to them. But, with these Six Spells up their sleeve, they can at least try to awaken personalisation from its deep slumber. Nowadays, I don't think brands can afford not to. They need it. With the increase in competition and the advent of technology, consumers expectations on brands are at an all-time high, the question is what does the future of personalisation look like? To quote the Beastie Boys, "My crystal ball ain't so crystal clear ..."

Part VIII

The Great Unknown

ow have we ended up here? After ten years or more of procrastination, in-fighting, and a purpose not fit for customers, personalisation – the once-lauded golden child of marketing – has given up the ghost and gone backwards.

Brands and vendors have found ways to commercialise the meaning of personalisation, stripping it of its actual purpose: to personalise. Today, personalisation is effectively monetisation, but in sheep's clothing.

If I focus too much on *how* we got here, I'll throw up. For the past seven chapters, I've given enough attention to the how/why/when and where of personalisation; I established the origin story, the backstory, the hero's quest, defined the dragons and established the ways in which to slay the big baddies. I even gave you the spells to bring personalisation back to life from being the walking dead.

This final act focuses on resolving the story. The what next.

The big question in my mind is … will personalisation survive? Will retailers and consumers ever reach the Personalisation Paradise – the Great Unknown – or will we all remain stuck on a remote desert island, unable to get ourselves off?

You know what I mean.

To some, the future of personalisation looks bleak. I feel their pain. As I've come to learn, personalisation is too complex a riddle to solve unless brands are willing to put in the effort. If there is much of a future, things have to change beyond recognition. Click-bait headlines such as "By 2025, 80 per cent of all marketers will give up on personalisation"[1] don't help the cause. While articles like that don't provide an alternative, their reasons are clear and rooted in the three bad-ass dragons we quested to battle: the focus on ROI, the perils of data and technology and the overwhelming amount of human effort and expectation.

But it's not the media's fault. It's the consumers' fault. They, we, all of us, wanted more choice; we are the ones that wanted to live in a booming capitalist economy. We were Veruca Salt's greed writ large: we wanted it all now.

But then too many choices spoiled us. To help us with that, brands were forced to be more relevant.

The solution to too much choice was, clearly, personalisation. Recommendations and allowing others to make decisions for us turned us into a bunch of Mike Teavees.

Ironically, now we have too much personalisation focused on supplementing choice, and we live in an online world that's impersonal by virtue. It's the classic twenty-first-century personalisation-impersonal paradox of deluding ourselves into thinking we have thousands of Facebook friends when, in reality, you can't recall the last time any one of them gave you a hug?

We can defeat the Three Dragons with our Six Spells. We can reach our Personalisation Paradise. But no hero's quest is complete without learning a little wisdom along the way. For our final journey into the Great Unknown, we must ask what the future of personalisation looks like so we can prepare for it. I've learned that:

Personalisation won't go away, there's just too much money in it.

Instead, personalisation needs time. We're in a technology adoption cycle.

And to accelerate its acceptance as a method of human communication, rather than a marketing method for making more money, these three alliterative things will ensure its evolution in the future:

1) Acquisition costs are accelerating
2) Data privacy is more disciplined
3) AI is more awesome

Chapter 35

Follow the Money: Advertising

"If there's money to be made from the vast advertising estates of Google, Amazon, Facebook and others around the world, you can definitely count on them going where the money is. And the money is in personalisation."

Ian Daniels, Co-Founder, The CX Collective[1]

I agree. Money is in personalisation. Brands just need to know where to look. To quote one of my favourite lines from *Indiana Jones and the Raiders of the Lost Ark*: "They're digging in the wrong place!"

A brand's need to remain relevant and resonate more with customers is never going to fade. It will only ever grow. It's where the money is. Right now, the sea of choice is too much for consumers; they're seasick at the thought of having to choose a movie on Netflix or a song on Spotify, only to revert back to watching *Das Boot* for the fourth time. Consumers need refined messages to cut through all the noise.

Brands, businesses and organisations understand this. In the latest version of Dynamic Yield's "State of Personalisation Maturity Research", they found that 98 per cent of brands believe in the value of personalisation, understand its benefits to the larger business strategy, or have made it the core of their CX operations. This is up from 93 per cent last year, a record-high trend. There's only another two per cent to be squeezed out from the perpetual belief of brands. Its religious undertones are evident.[2]

I don't see personalisation going away any time soon.

The industry and the media that it feeds on will continue to call every new year the "Year of Personalisation". Or some derivative thereof. I personally liked the upcoming "personal-Al-sation" and "purse-onalisation". But I bet there will be some inclusion of the prefix "hyper" involved somewhere. The reason for this revitalisation, rejuvenation or redefinition is simple: there is a lot of money to be made from advertising. Particularly targeted advertising.

There is, in my opinion, a false rhetoric that says generic advertising outperforms segmented advertising. Peter Weinberg suggested that, "Even if we knew everything about the customer, we still wouldn't be able to design creative tailored to their individual tastes. Is Disney making personalised creative? Are movies like *Wall-E* designed to resonate with eight-year-old boys in San Diego?"[3]

Along with the dragons, Weinberg is slowly becoming the antagonist of our personalisation quest. A brilliant debate, but one that ignores the digital advent of being able to segment. Disney doesn't have the capability to segment or personalise films derived from a singular creative designed for mass appeal.

Personalising movies isn't a thing.

But personalising advertising is.

Netflix, for example, recently released its new advertising model in Q4 2022. Because of their background in personalisation, you can bet that these ads will be highly targeted and relate to the psychographics, demographics and mental models of their customers. So much so that they are calling out a CPM of $65 – which is higher than 2022's Super Bowl.[4] "We don't need to think about the ads experience being uniform across all of our members, we can leverage the personalisation capability we built in terms of titles and how we present titles, and also in terms of how we present ads," said Greg Peters, Netflix COO and Chief Product Officer.[5]

Surprisingly, a month later, Netflix's advertising business hit a rough patch. Ad-supported viewership was falling short of expectations, and the company started allowing advertisers to take their money back, though some opted to stick with Netflix and shift their spending dollars to a year later. I fear this example isn't holding up my argument.

Ads are laser-focused to resonate with customers. With Netflix, this resonance is done in real time, and because of the data being held, it can be done at more than just a demographic level but also a psychographic level. Given that demographics change over the course of a series, advertising can be targeted right down to the episode. Or they can be targeted at an engagement level (a hat tip towards "intent") based on how engrossed the audience member is in the film or show. Or, on a more psychological level. Viewers of *Breaking Bad*, for example, describe themselves as thinkers who are withdrawn. They resonate with Walter White because, like them, he is smart and calculating. Having advertising that taps into their preferences and interests at a deeper level – one that resonates based on, perhaps, their OCEAN profile of motivation (Openness to experience, Conscientiousness, Extraversion, Agreeableness and Neuroticism) rather than purely demographics is surely going to resonate more. No wonder the CPM is so high.

The wealth of data available, the experience in applying that to experiences, and the belief that permeates the business make personalisation one of Netflix's core values in how it relates to their offering. Clearly, too, their vast number of resources sets them up for success. It would be ignorant to ignore the $4.56 billion net profit in 2022[6] (though it was considerably down from 2021's figures).

Facebook is in the same boat. A recent study[7] has revealed that when it comes to understanding our likes, dislikes, preferences and even personalities, Facebook knows us better than our own family members. With just a few likes, Facebook's algorithm can accurately predict our personality type better ($r = 0.56$) than our closest friends, cohabitants, or colleagues ($r = 0.49$). There's no wonder their ad revenue keeps on increasing every year — from 2015 to 2021, they grew at an average annual growth rate of 36.7 per cent.[8] It's incredible to think that a machine, powered by algorithms, can outshine our flesh-and-blood relationships when it comes to understanding who we really are. That makes for one powerful advertising model.

The reason, therefore, why personalisation won't wither on the vine is that advertisers have already proven that targeting and relevant messages work infinitely better than the alternative — mass, undifferentiated targeting and messaging. According to the Interactive Advertising Bureau (IAB), they found that targeted advertising based on consumer interests and behaviours led to a 40 per cent increase in brand recall and a 50 per cent increase in purchase intent compared to non-targeted advertising. Studies by Neilsen[9] and Harvard Business Review concur,[10] as do numerous other studies in the field.

Like personalisation as a concept, more targeted advertising as a statement feels commonsensical. And in the commercial language of communication, it's a reasonable assertion to suggest that ultimately, there's just too much money to be made in personalisation for it to simply stop. It's a multi-billion-dollar business. And so, we reach a primary paradox within our story, one where personalisation is being eroded because it's commercialised, but it's only alive because it's commercialised. The personalisation-commercial paradox.

Personalisation is a buzzword that's been buzzing around the marketing world for quite some time now. And while it is not going away anytime soon, it doesn't feel like it's going anywhere either. It feels stuck, neglected and unable to progress to the next level. Ironic to my central thesis, and hence the paradox, the natural flow of personalisation is following where the money is. This is what will ultimately keep it alive, yet it's also what's threatening to destroy it.

Chapter 36

Spin Cycle: Everything That Goes Around Comes Back Around

"The more one knows, the more one comprehends, the more one realizes that everything turns in a circle."

Johann Wolfgang von Goethe, German poet[1]

According to the poster hanging in my office, "Success eats failure for breakfast". I don't know what it means, but for some reason, it still motivates me every morning. I guess it's a witty take on Latrell Sprewell's "Success is just failure that hasn't happened yet."

Part of personalisation's bid for world dominance has been to eat failure for breakfast. There have been lots of mistakes, but rest assured, they are what define ultimate and impending success.

The rise of technology adoption is cyclical, not linear. In his research for "Understanding Gartner's Hype Cycle" Jackie Fenn identified that when technology was in the fourth of the five stages, there was just a 5 per cent adoption rate.[2] Ninety-five per cent of technology fails the first time out. For personalisation to come this far, there must be something in it.

Take QR codes as a handsome specimen of this. They came to be adopted during the pandemic. And now they're a global success. This was their second swing of the bat, and success was supposedly true the first time around – so what happened?

They were first made in 1994 to track vehicles while they were being made by scanning them quickly. They swiftly gained popularity, being seen as the cool kids on the block, and were used in more commercial applications as a quick way to send someone to a website or an app while attributing it. There's always an ROI spin on it, isn't there?

Because of their rise in popularity, QR codes were eventually approved as an international standard in the mid-2000s, ten years later, which allowed them to be used anywhere in the world. The only thing better than commercialism is global commercialism.

They were the cool kids for a while because they were seen as easy. Dr Paul Marsden,[3] a consumer psychologist, describes the benefits of a QR code in the same way that he describes the benefits of personalisation – the ultimate in "convenience tech". As we all know, when cool kids peak in their teenage years, then comes the fall. Trying to take a picture of something instead of going to the website address felt unnatural. Their application on moving buses instead of a URL was about as practical as wearing flip-flops in a snowstorm. The need to take out your phone immediately to recognise or remember something of value felt all too sudden and controlling. The hype ultimately wore off, and typing something into Google, the older, wiser sibling, reigned supreme once again.

That is, until the comeback kids of technology rose once more when COVID came along in 2020. Like a late bloomer, they hit their stride during the pandemic, becoming a global success. This was because a genuine need showed itself – the need to avoid physical contact in places like retailers, restaurants and bars – when they were reopened, of course. They moved from convenience technology to helpful technology. QR codes boomed. Again. To put things into perspective: since Summer 2022 more than one-third of mobile users in the UK and US have scanned at least one QR code.[4] That's bonkers. It is expected that phones will scan 5.3 billion QR codes in retail and online shopping alone in 2023.[5]

Where the first boom was about hype, the second was about adoption. QR codes originally boomed because of that chatter and unevidenced, unwavering belief, but then re-boomed because of a genuine need and have sustained growth since then. And it took over twenty years to do so, from their first creation in 1994 to their widespread adoption in 2020.

There is a parallel here with personalisation, of course. This is what personalisation needs: a catalyst that provides a genuine need. Like Christ, personalisation's Second Coming is long overdue, and its earlier failures will help ensure its boom-time sticks. Of course, in order for that to happen brands must pivot towards an attitude of "we *need* to do this" rather than remain stuck in the current status quo of "we *can* do this (if we can be bothered)".

This type of cyclical adoption curve is all too common. Ben Labay, Managing Director, Speero believes: "We'll continue to go through these cycles where there will be a lot of abandonment of personalisation techniques and technology until the new cycle starts."[6] Like QR codes, it feels like that new cycle needs a catalyst of some sort. The pandemic did help — according to the latest Personalisation Maturity Report by Dynamic Yield, the industry has moved from "Basic" to "Advanced" for the first time, a result they say of increased adoption amid COVID-19's digital awakening.[7] How much this has influenced personalisation to revert back to its true purpose, I'm unsure. Either way, personalisation requires a genuine, widespread purpose or reason to rehabilitate it into what it should always have been: being personable.

Where does personalisation currently sit in these cycles that Labay speaks of? Like everything, there's a model for that.

In 1962, EM Rogers created a model that better understood this adoption of technology, rather than just the hype. He originally reviewed the demographic and psychological profiles of farmers in the late 1950s and created a bell-curve graph that describes five distinct groups. These groups within the model demonstrate the milestones involved in adopting an innovation: the innovators, the early adopters, the early majority, the late majority and the laggards.[8] Its simplification has mostly stood the test of time, even though it has been criticised and adapted slightly since then. What model hasn't?

Given the subjective paradox of both anger at one end and praise at the other, and even the varying definitions that sit in between, personalisation could be placed within any of these categories. Who knows. The optimists would place it in the "early adopters" stage given that those who have adopted it haven't realised its full potential yet.

Those who are slightly more cynical would place it more in the "laggards" stage. After all, it has been around for over 20 years. Amazon's "Customers Who Bought This Also Bought That" is cited as the first popularised use of commercial online personalisation, and that was introduced all the way back in 2003, the same year *The Matrix Reloaded* was released, and the year we all realised we didn't deserve nice things. Here we are, 20 years later, and it feels as though we haven't really moved the needle. Unlike QR codes, of course, which have.

Is the answer, as Labay suggested, just a question of time? Personalisation will continue to go through these cycles, and it is only a matter of time before it makes a better second impression. Or third. Or fifth. Or twentieth. Greg Anderson, Senior Manager, International eCommerce at a large US-based retailer agreed: "Email marketing and social marketing have gotten to personalisation already. What is it going to take for websites to get there? The answer is time."[9]

It absolutely feels to me as though personalisation seems stuck on a spin cycle. Even in the year 2023, which should be the year of personalisation! Why is it that when you ask a bunch of marketing professionals, "Who does personalisation well?" they all struggle to answer? That's what I found when conducting extensive research over 150 interviews: puzzled looks. Why is it that, when you ask the same people to define personalisation, it is met with hesitation and uncertainty. Why is it that when you try and find examples on the topic, it's filled with nothing but positive case studies of false positives and self-serving revenue uplifts. Or when you try to look for literature available on the topic, you're only met with Houlind's *Hello $FirstName*,[10] (and now this book) as the only notable mentions in the realm of personalisation.

Thankfully, it's all part of the plan. It will just take some time.

Where are we? Rogers model was further adopted in Malcolm Gladwell's *The Tipping Point* (2000)[11] and again in Geoffrey Moore's *Crossing the Chasm* (2002)[12] who believed that there was an abyss between the early adopters of the product and the early majority, i.e. the pragmatists. At which point, Gladwell suggested there was a "moment of critical mass, the threshold, the boiling point".

That's where it feels as though we are — the tipping point. In my opinion, personalisation is on the cusp of emerging from a passive state. And so, with that, it's less about understanding the current state of personalisation and more about understanding the catalysts that will guide personalisation out of the awkward teenage years, and into being a responsible adult.

Chapter 37

Acquisition-Cost-a-lot: Accelerating

"We need to stop interrupting what people are interested in and be what people are interested in."

Craig Davis, former chief creative officer, J Walter Thompson[1]

B rands need to adopt personalisation in a more sustainable way. It needs a single seismic shift that can influence consumer behaviour to the point that it forces brands to do something about it, just as the pandemic did with QR codes.

Increasing acquisition costs might just well be that shift. It costs more now to acquire a customer than ever before. Facebook's cost per acquisition (CPA) increased by 43 per cent from 2021–2022.[2] Acquisition might be sexier than retention, as I once said, but it's also getting more expensive than it, too. That might just be the one thing we personalisation pals need to poke people out of prostration.

We know from studies that personalisation reduces acquisition costs by 50 per cent and thus improves marketing efficiency by 30 per cent.[3] Personalisation seems like the answer to this growing epidemic. Better targeting leads to more relevance. More relevance leads to better resonance. Better resonance ends up as resilience.

Over the years, the cost of advertising with Google Ads has grown more expensive. In the past year alone, the cost per lead for Google Ads has gone up in 91 per cent of sectors.[4] An average total increase of 19 per cent. While this is comparable to 2019's increase of 21 per cent, it is substantially greater than the 5 per cent rise and 4 per cent drop that occurred in 2021 and 2020, respectively.

Consider the reasons why.

The pandemic certainly played a role, but let's not forget the insatiable appetite for shareholder satisfaction and the unrelenting pursuit of growth. After all, the world would come to a screeching halt if the money-makers stopped making money. Or paying taxes. Wait.

Take Google, or Alphabet as they're fancying themselves these days. Their ad revenue skyrocketed from $41 billion in 2019 to a whopping $70 billion in 2022, with expectations to hit $76 billion in 2023.[5] But alas, shareholders are a fickle bunch, crying foul at the mere prospect of a paltry 8.5 per cent growth forecast after a blistering 70 per cent increase in the three years prior. The woes of big business.

Google, the master of revenue growth, knows the drill: there are only two ways to grow those numbers. First, get more people to click on more ads. The pandemic was a boon for them, with everyone glued to their screens at home, but even after the world has started to open up again, the growth has sustained.

The second option is simple: increase the cost of advertising. After all, why settle for small change when you can milk those ad dollars for all they're worth? The pandemic has created rather unrealistic expectations for shareholder returns on their investment. Google must abide by that in some form, either by getting more people to click on more or by increasing the cost of advertising in and of itself. They have already proven the hypothesis of being more relevant with the introduction of their RankBrain and BART algorithms, so it would seem logical to double down on this level of personalisation. Thank you, pandemic.

Chapter 38

Data-Mine-Your-Business: Disciplined

"When you look at the data privacy trends, personalisation will become more and more challenging to achieve successfully. That will put blockers in the way that might not even make it possible."

David Keown, Digital Product Owner, Screwfix[1]

Where the pandemic has created a singular shift in brands and investor expectations, there is another move to discuss that may impact the wholesale adoption of personalisation – the regulation of data privacy. Data collection, integration, management, and regulations are the main reasons why Gartner believes that 80 per cent of marketers will abandon personalisation by 2025. Twenty-seven per cent of marketers agree, and they specifically cite the Stubborn Dragon as the main beast personalisation must conquer.[2] Specifically, the regulations around data privacy management.

"The difficulty is that currently there are so many challenges regardless already – data architecture and legacy systems – adding a further blocker of legality of being able to track, might diminish the values even further of whether the juice is worth the squeeze," David Keown also told me. This is circling back to the concept of effort. When I spoke with a source at Optimizely[3] they agreed. "Personalisation? I don't see it happening. It just keeps getting harder."

As third-party cookies are being phased out in 2024, advertisers and platforms are facing increased regulation that impacts them in two significant ways: cost and effort.

Meta, for example, has been hit by Apple's App Tracking Transparency Regulation, which has reduced targeting capabilities by limiting access to iPhone user identifiers. In 2022, Meta acknowledged that this feature would result in a decrease in sales for the year to the tune of about $10 billion.[4] As a result, their CPA has climbed by a staggering 43 per cent compared to just 2021, a clear passing of costs onto the customer.

Not just that, but Meta's advertising practises were considered illegal under EU law. In the UK, data protection is governed by the UK GDPR (General Data Protection Regulation) and the DPA (Data Protection Act) 2018. A breach of that agreement could result in fines of up to £17.5 million or 4 per cent of annual global turnover, whichever is greater. Clearly the latter garners more money when it comes to big business for the governments regulating it, and so Meta Ireland was fined €210 million for breaches of the GDPR relating to its Facebook service and €180 million for breaches in relation to its Instagram service.[5]

Most recently, Ireland's Data Protection Commission recently ruled that even Apple is not safe. Their App Store was just slapped with a fine of €8 million over its ad personalisation practises for not properly collecting consent and making the process of opting out too indirect.[6]

With more data privacy regulation and the fear of fines, however paltry some may appear, personalisation will be forced to evolve into something else. It isn't just the cost that will catalyse that evolution, either, but the perceived effort, as alluded to earlier.

Gartner predicted that 65 per cent of the world's population will have personal data that's covered by privacy laws, up from just 10 per cent the year prior.[7] It's a serious matter, and companies should be taking such data privacy seriously. Whether they are or not is a different question. Such fines seem like insignificant slaps on the wrist.

Given the cookie days have been thoroughly milked, there's going to be this rubber band pullback of unfettered access fury to having customer data owned by someone else. Today, 78 per cent of customers expressed fears about the amount of data being collected, let alone sold and resold.[8] It's time for a change, but that requires effort.

Data is due to be owned and held by the customer centrally, as part of the next evolution of the web. Tomorrow, you'll own your identity (as it should be!) within Web 3.0's centralised customer data profiles. It's a stark contrast to Web 2.0's current centralised database architecture where you currently have several accounts with 50 other retailers and 12 other social media accounts where they own your data. Our current state of play is a place where the internet has become like a massive app store dominated by centralised apps from Google, Facebook and Amazon, where everyone is trying to build an audience, collect data and monetise that data through targeted advertising.[9]

With Web 3.0, that data would be centralised and owned by you, and these entities would request access to it, or some of it, in some form. Not the other way around. Technologies like Blockchain facilitate this decentralised approach to storing data.[10]

In my view, this rebalancing of ownership and simultaneous increase in data regulation won't stop personalisation. Instead, it will force those personalising to be more creative and prioritise, which are two of the three methods I discussed on how to kill the Stubborn Dragon.

The proof in the pudding is that despite the responses to increased regulation, only 4 per cent have moved away from personalisation.[11] About a third of survey respondents say their organisations have invested in data management tools, consent tools, or legal or data experts in response to GDPR. Many of the executives interviewed for this paper say the new regulation has had little impact thus far on their data privacy policies or the way they use data to interact with customers.

Brilliant. This is a rebalance. Hopefully, these regulations will force brands to focus on personalising in a way that works for the customer, not for the business. This might be perceived as an increase in effort, and we all know that brands don't like that. Yet, such regulations are a good thing, as they will help the industry move in a direction that works with the customer and their data, not against them. This should, in theory, create a mutual trust between the two, building on what the foundations of personalisation are built upon: a relationship.

Chapter 39

Say Hi to AI: Awesome

"The future of personalisation is absolutely algorithmic. The amount of human-driven personalisation is going to be very low. I think it will be the plaything of the very rich and elite. Massive companies with loads of money. The combination of business characteristics and individual characteristics is too rare and difficult to scale when, on the other hand, algorithms can scale much better."

Anonymous Source, Optimizely[1]

Effortless navigation of data privacy laws will reveal who's truly swimming with their trunks down. While some may be scared of increased effort due to regulations, it means only the bold will venture into personalisation and reap the rewards. However, history has shown that with every regulation that raises the bar, there's often a technological innovation that makes it easier. Enter AI, the game-changer that could streamline the personalisation process and help brands stay ahead of the competition. So, say hi to AI and wave goodbye to the fear of increased effort. The future of personalisation might just be smoother than we think!

According to Gartner, data is the biggest hurdle to personalisation. I disagree. In my research for this book, I have come to the conclusion that the perceived effort-to-value ratio is the real setback. This feeling of trying to run a marathon in high heels. In my interviews on my quest, that response easily surpassed all others. The human resource needed to power personalisation technology is so great that there is a narrative that it renders the value worthless.

What if that effort were to be significantly diminished? Evan Williams, Twitter co-founder[2] spoke about: "Tak[ing] a human desire, preferably one that has been around for a really long time. Identify that desire. And use model technology to take away our steps." We've desired personalisation for a really long time. Us. Over here, Evan. Model technology is therefore surely the answer?

More than one in four marketing leaders cite technology as a major hurdle to personalisation.[3] This feels like a strange statistic given that technology is becoming easier, not harder. Scaling through the use of AI or machine learning (ML) seems to be the only way forward.

Artificial Intelligence has so much sex appeal, although not quite as much as the sausage rolls from Marks & Spencer, that it may be the only thing to get the industry out of its chasm.

Welcome to the "Golden Era" of AI.[4]

It's a technology that is already on track to be the most hyped of 2023, and for good reason. Machine learning, generative design AI, and casual AI are within the current innovation trigger stage of the Gartner Hype Cycle, the first of the five-stage bell curve. One way to prove this hype is to review the investment that's being poured in the category. Over $100 billion has been invested in AI start-ups since 2020, and that funding doubled in 2021.[5] There are now 102 AI unicorns in the US. And it's not just the Yanks hogging the spotlight; Asia's got its fair share of AI unicorns too – 38 of them, prancing around in the Asian tech scene.

And if you can turn the skyline of New York into a painting by Van Gogh with the click of a button, why couldn't you personalise a website experience with that very same click? The big, red AI button.

Personalisation vendors Intellimize, Mutiny and others are exploring this avenue. The former is on the Inc 5000 and raised $52 million and the latter has raised $72 million on a $600 million valuation. Brands are catching up, too, such as a true pioneer of personalisation within the last ten years, StitchFix, which is making fashion recommendations using part-AI and part-human. They claim: "The algorithms provide the science; the stylists provide the art". Their market cap might have been $10 billion in the heights of 2021,[6] when that quote was reported, but now in 2023 it sits at just $500 million. The reason: "StitchFix just arrived at the concept a few years too early, when AI wasn't yet sophisticated enough to take the place of a lengthy questionnaire and a small army of data scientists," Rex Woodbury, Partner, Index Ventures,[7] explained. Now should be their time.

Maybe I'm just getting old and set in my ways, but from all my research and on-the-ground observations, I can't help but feel that AI will follow in the footsteps of commerce and lead brands down the wrong path. Where a focus on the commercials has taken brands down a garden path where personalisation is designed for the business, not the customer, AI will take brands down the one-way street that technology fixes all their problems so they don't have to try. A place where brands may fall for the illusion that technology is the magic bullet that will solve all their problems with a simple click of the big, red AI button.

As I've mentioned before, that's a false belief when slaying one of the Three Dragons. If the goal is to truly connect with customers on a personal level, it's not technology alone that will achieve that. Sure, it can facilitate the process, but relying solely on it will only limit the objective of creating an authentic relationship. A relationship that requires effort. Time. One that requires emotional intelligence, not just artificial intelligence. I ask, "Does an over-reliance on technology create nothing more than an inauthentic, superficial, artificial relationship?"

What AI could facilitate is a power-shift. Alongside new data regulation that puts more control back in the hands of the customer, volitional personalisation[8] could also wage the war against dominant commerce. It is the latest addition to the buzzword bonanza, and perhaps this will finally be the year of personalisation because this actually has metaphorical legs. Volitional personalisation is the process of enabling a person's ability to make their own decision – not just within the experience, but within the product, too. Juan Mendoza, the now father of this newly coined phrase, said that "rather than have personalization based on what a company thinks a customer wants, customers can use their own volition to tell brands what they want".[9] There's no questioning the intent behind Mendoza's own volition.

This shift is facilitated by the move from generative search to generative products. Theoretically, this could open the door to infinite choices, which is semi-exhilarating. Customers can leverage AI and new tools to customise their interactions with brands in a way that suits them. Putting the control back in the customer's hands is something that I am fully on board with. AI could be what the lightsabre is to the Rebellion. Giving the little guy a chance to take control from the Dark Side and a chance to defeat the evil Darth Zuckerberg.

SHEIN, the world's third most-valuable start-up, is an example of a company that could achieve this. It has grown over 100 per cent every year for eight straight years. Its latest private market valuation makes it worth more than Zara and H&M – combined. To compare – 8,000 new items are added to SHEIN every day, while Zara adds 500 every week. SHEIN stays ahead of the fashion game by keeping a close eye on competitors' websites and Google Trends. They swiftly create trendy designs, forecast demand, and make real-time adjustments to their inventory. It's a seamless process that allows them to always stay in style and keep up with the ever-changing fashion landscape. SHEIN does this by anticipating the clothes customers want to buy.

Hereto, we land on the predictive, not the retrospective. The implicit, not the explicit. This is still an example of asking customers to browse for a product, and the available products will show. But Mendoza argues it's only a matter of time until the narrative flips — "Why not ask customers to create what they want?"

As limitless as this might be, it is also semi-terrifying. In theory, this paves the way for infinite choice, which is scary given that the world, especially in social media, is experiencing a rubber band pullback of impersonal, personalised content that's paradoxically so relevant while being myopically irrelevant.

Whilst it can facilitate the impossible, AI requires humans to be there side-by-side. Stitch Fix have it figured out. In fact, all tools, be they personalisation, analytical, or otherwise, require step changes within the organisation. They merely facilitate. But personalisation requires not just a process reorientation, but a mindset one too.

To feed these platforms, brands need quality ingredients. Those ingredients aren't just good data or lots of resources, but the willingness to change. When that change requires a modicum of effort, is when personalisation starts to fall apart.

> "Let's turn on the personalisation tool. Well, sure, but it requires us to fail at scale and actually do some hard work. And we're not willing to do that work. The organisation doesn't allow for creativity or for product teams to work on these problems like they should. They just want the tool to do it for them."
>
> **Ben Labay, Managing Director, Speero**[10]

If the utilisation rate of personalisation platforms is just 48 per cent, as I identified as part of our Three Dragons, we must start to question why that is the case.[11] A recent technology vendor acquisition could help explain this.

In 2020, the role model for the experimentation world, Optimizely, was sold to Episerver, a content management company. This was significant for two reasons. The first is that the chatter within the industry was that Optimizely would always IPO. Being sold to a content management company was surprising. "On March 3, 2018, they added a second market offering to the list of their funding history, which is the last and clear signal they are going IPO soon," wrote Dennis van der Heijden, founder of Convert.com[12] — just a small reflection of the wider belief within the optimisation world.

The second is that the deal was reportedly worth just $600 million.[13] Hardly pocket money. Yet, this is significantly lower than the industry expected, given that this was *the* experimentation platform. The one that started it all and received over $250 million in funding along the way.[14] Sources suggest that Dan Siroker, the founder of Optimizely, spoke to employees and told them that if they didn't believe the company would be bigger than Google, they should just quit.[15] There's certainly something to be said for backing your own horse. The almost cult-like belief was felt throughout their obsessive customers and those within the CRO and A/B testing communities. It was (and is, it is absolutely still around) beloved. So why sell for (reportedly) so little? Especially when compared to Tableau's $1 billion acquisition a few months earlier, an interactive data visualisation software company that raised only one-sixteenth of Optimizely's funding.[16] Or the acquisition of Looker, a data exploration and discovery analytics vendor, in the same year by Google for $2.6 billion?[17]

There are many reasons why this could be the case. The narrative that expectation didn't match reality is one − as we potentially saw with McDonald's. But there is one strong suggestion, seen within underground threads on the likes of Y Combinator, that the "self-serve model at Optimizely was flawed".[18] Tools within the personalisation and experimentation space are similar. They require effort, purpose and process changes in organisations. They require a mindset shift that needs to come along with these tools if they are to be successful. Arguably unlike the analytical platforms of Tableau and Looker.

I therefore believe that the only way to get out of the chasm that personalisation is stuck in is by using technology, but with a word of warning. An acknowledgment and appreciation that it's not solely the weapons or the wizardry that will be the heroes of our story, it'll be people. It's about putting the person back into personalisation.

Chapter 40

2024: The Year of Personalisation

"2024 is the year of personalisation. Maybe. But probably not."
David Mannheim

2024 *probably* won't be the year of personalisation, but that's OK. No single year needs to own that title. As I've mentioned, personalisation just needs more time to work through the cycles, shake off those paradoxes, and make a few right turns to course correct. It will absolutely help if there are a few regulatory or technological shifts along the way; data governance and artificial intelligence are the two that are at the forefront of my mind.

Ultimately, all that really matters is that brands progress with personalisation in the right direction and push/pull it back towards its original purpose: being personal.

Despite my evident cynicism throughout this quest, I remain an optimist about the future of personalisation. This adventure started with me as a frustrated marketing professional (and die-hard Disney brand advocate) waiting in an endless line to experience *Monsters, Inc. Laugh Floor* at Disney World, Orlando. I felt like just another number, not a person.

Across all my interviews, I heard tale after tale of woe and despair, frustration and demotivation about personalisation and heard all sorts of name-calling, experts validating the way I too felt. There's no question that PTSD exists. The Three Dragons have moulded personalisation into a self-serving commodity imbalanced for profit not purpose. And we need to train the dragons to be something else, just like in that animated Dreamworks film whose title I can't remember.

After conducting my interviews, and overwhelming my Google browsing history with personalisation research, I fell to the rockiest of bottoms. I couldn't see the light at the end of the tunnel. Where was personalisation headed?

But, then I started to read about the purposeful personalisation innovations of Marks & Spencer, Gousto and Bloom and Wild, and my spirits soon started to lift me back up. There were brands that wanted to – and could, if they were bothered – defeat those three naughty dragons. All they had to do was have an appreciation for what personalisation was originally designed for and forget what it currently is. Brands can put care back into communicating with their customers through acknowledgement, listening more, understanding customer intent and a desire to establish a genuine customer relationship.

Right now, in 2023, I am beginning to see a shift from the current world of personalisation which is about pure *relevance* to a new world of *resonance*. Daphne Tideman, Growth Advisor & Consultant, spoke of a future world she predicted where customers "don't want to be sold to, they want to be seen".[1] While it may sound unrealistic in this capitalist world of ours, look around — people are crying out for change and to be seen as more than a number. Irrespective of their age, gender, race, or whether they are behind a blue-lit screen or in the queue to see Mike Wazowski crack a few jokes. We are people. When we come together to be seen as more than a number, personalisation will make the giant leaps it has to. Otherwise, brands will die on the vine.

That shift, that sea-change, is what has made me believe personalisation has a future. It's already an integral element of how brands sell products; it just needs a little more time for the penny to drop fully. There's too much history and evidence that tailoring messages toward individuals works. The technology is only getting better. Consumers' expectations are only increasing and becoming savvier. Regulation is giving control back to the user. Competition is getting stronger, and the need to differentiate beyond being just competent at selling something is becoming more. Where brands need to offer their customers more than just a level of convenience when, in reality, it's really just convenient for them.

I believe in people. I believe in personalisation. I believe the best of both is yet to come.

Chapter 41

The Final Word

I wanted to tell the story of personalisation as a personal story. My story of personalisation. I wanted to put the person back into personalisation so I made that person be me. And, rather optimistically, I now expect others to do the same. To put people back into the conversation. Heck, to have a conversation to begin with would be a start.

Currently, that's not the case, clearly.

As a consumer of personalised experiences, I just wanted to be heard, listened to, cared for and cuddled. As a practitioner, I am told to exploit, extract and prey on the vulnerable. These two sides seem misaligned with one another, creating that ever-present personalisation paradox. The hero versus the villain.

When there's so much at stake, brands can't afford to just drag their heels. Relationships take time, sure, but mess it up once and — much like this book — there won't be a sequel. There needs to be a line drawn in the sand. Enough is enough: personalisation must be allowed time and patience to progress properly. To do so, remember its purpose. Remember your purpose. Remember those three little syllables at the front of the verb itself: *pers-on-al.*

If you enjoyed this book, or want to talk, rant or rave more about personalisation, please feel free to get in touch with me at <u>david@madewithintent.ai</u>

Acknowledgements

There's nothing like a bit of self-deprecation within a story to help a reader warm to an author. None of it is contrived, I promise. Despite many years of experience and knowledge in the digital marketing industry, never have I felt more of an imposter than when writing this book. Speaking to the industry leaders who gave up their precious time for my curiosity into personalisation was beyond interesting and lots of genuine fun, it broadened my perspective on what personalisation is and what it could be, all while making new friends and collaborators. The actual sitting down and writing of the damn thing I found cathartic too. I spent hundreds of hours in various cafés and coffee houses, growing a beard and getting fat. I felt like a proper author, even though I felt like an imposter 99 per cent of the time.

This book was never meant to be what it is. All I wanted to do was scratch a tiny itch. But much like anyone else who considers themself slightly more creative than analytical, my curious, obsessive mind got the better of me. And then took over. The ten interviews that turned into twenty, that turned into fifty, that turned into one hundred that turned into one-hundred and fifty-three, was never planned. I simply enjoyed them, and the results, enough to continue making the next call. I can't thank those who spoke with me enough. Some were friends, sure, but most were fellow curious practitioners who I'm proud to say are now friends, too. Like the Fellowship of the Ring, our journey to find our precious personalisation, has bonded us together. I'd like to say the biggest thank you to all my interviewees. You gave me your time, the most precious commodity for anyone in this day and age, and I am highly grateful. Some I interviewed just once, and some more than five times. To all those who gave up their time to speak to me, thank you.

I'd like to also thank my editor, Malcolm Croft. We bonded over both being fathers of two and kept our football teams' fierce rivalry at an unspoken distance. I couldn't have done this without him. Well, I could, but it would not have been anywhere near as tidy.

For emotional support, I'd like to thank Rasmus Houlind, who raced ahead with his own personalisation book, *Hello $FirstName*, for always giving his advice and time when I asked, calming my anxiety.

My magic three – Leon Andrews, Bhavik Patel and Ryan Jordan – were also my emotional rocks throughout. Thanks for everything.

To Laura, Max and Zachary …

You gave me your patience when I needed time, your forgiveness when I wasn't there, and your sympathy when I hit the lows. You also put up with my smelly and scruffy motivational beard, which I look back on in pictures now and realise how ridiculous I looked.* Thanks for being you, and I promise to never write the sequel. Or reboot the original.

---

* I insisted I grow a beard while writing the book, refusing to shave it off until it had been handed into my editor … four months later.

Notes

Foreword
1. Catmull, E. & Wallace, A. (2014) *Creativity, Inc.: Overcoming the Unseen Forces That Stand in the Way of True Inspiration.* United States: Random House Publishing Group.
2. Netcore Cloud (2022) *Ecommerce Personalization Benchmark Report 2021.* Available at: https://netcorecloud.com/ebook/ecommerce-personalization-benchmark-report-2021.
3. *The value of getting personalization right—or wrong—is multiplying* (2021) Available at: https://www.mckinsey.com/capabilities/growth-marketing-and-sales/our-insights/the-value-of-getting-personalization-right-or-wrong-is-multiplying.
4. Emarsys (2021) *Retail – Customer Loyalty Index 2021 [Report].* Available at: https://emarsys.com/learn/white-papers/customer-loyalty-index-2021/.
5. *The value of getting personalization right—or wrong—is multiplying* (2021b) Available at: https://www.mckinsey.com/capabilities/growth-marketing-and-sales/our-insights/the-value-of-getting-personalization-right-or-wrong-is-multiplying.
6. *Predicts 2018: Brand Relevance Under Fire, Automation on the Rise* (no date) Available at: https://www.gartner.com/en/documents/3823237.
7. *Gartner Predicts 80% of Marketers Will Abandon Personalization Efforts* (2019) Available at: https://www.gartner.com/en/newsroom/press-releases/2019-12-02-gartner-predicts-80-of-marketers-will-abandon-person.
8. Nicastro, D. (2018) *Personalized Marketing: Where We Are in 2018.* Available at: https://www.cmswire.com/digital-experience/personalized-marketing-where-we-are-at-2018/.

Part I: The Ordinary World
1. Howarth, J. (2023) *57+ Personalization Statistics* (New 2023 Data). Available at: https://explodingtopics.com/blog/personalization-stats.
2. *Conversion Rate Optimization Software Market. 250 Report* (2022) Available at: https://www.futuremarketinsights.com/reports/conversion-rate-optimization-software-market
3. *360iResearch – Market Research Reports & Consulting Services* (no date). Available at: https://www.360iresearch.com/library/research-report/global-personalization-software-market.

Chapter 1: Hype Versus Reality
1. Axon, T (2022) Interview with David Mannheim, "Personalisation Interview", March 23, 2023
2. Team, A. C. (n.d.) *Personalization at scale has never been more crucial for your business.* https://business.adobe.com/blog/how-to/personalization-at-scale-has-never-been-more-crucial-for-your-business
3. Langston, G. (2020) *How eharmony created the perfect audience-messaging match.* Think With Google. https://www.thinkwithgoogle.com/marketing-strategies/search/eharmony-audience-message-targeting/

4. Bcg (2017) *Personalization Programs Increase Leading Companies' Revenues by 6% to 10%.* Available at: https://www.globenewswire.com/news-release/2017/05/08/979826/0/en/Personalization-Programs-Increase-Leading-Companies-Revenues-by-6-to-10.html.

5. Harvard Business School Publishing (2018) *"The Age of Personalization",* Crafting a Finer Edge [Preprint]. Available at: https://hbr.org/resources/pdfs/comm/mastercard/TheAge OfPersonalization.pdf.

6. Mani, K. & Considine, R. (2020b) *You don't just need personalization — you need the right personalization.* Think With Google. https://www.thinkwithgoogle.com/consumer-insights/consumer-trends/you-dont-just-need-personalization-you-need-the-right-personalization/

7. *M&S scales personalization with Adobe Analytics and Target* (no date). Available at: https://business.adobe.com/uk/customer-success-stories/marks-spencer-case-study.html.

8. Sailthru (2022) Retail Personalization Index | Top Retail Marketing Campaign. Available at: https://www.sailthru.com/personalization-index/.

Chapter 2: Awesome Versus Shit

1. Malki, B. (2022) Interview with David Mannheim, "Personalisation Interview", March 30, 2022

2. Sailthru (2022b) Retail Personalization Index | Top Retail Marketing Campaign. Available at: https://www.sailthru.com/personalization-index/.

3. Sailthru (2022c) Top 100 Omnichannel Marketing Brands | Best Omnichannel Retailers. Available at: https://www.sailthru.com/personalization-index/winners/.

4. Sailthru (2022b) Retail Personalization Index | Top Retail Marketing Campaign. Available at: https://www.sailthru.com/personalization-index/.

5. The Next Level of Personalization in Retail, Google/BCG, U.S., "Business Impact of Personalization in Retail" study, 2019

6. Boudet,J. etal. (2021) *Thefutureofpersonalization—andhowtogetreadyforit.* Availableat: https://www.mckinsey.com/capabilities/growth-marketing-and-sales/our-insights/the-future-of-personalization-and-how-to-get-ready-for-it.

7. Wikipedia contributors (2023) Pete Weber (bowler). Available at: https://en.wikipedia.org/wiki/Pete_Weber_(bowler).

8. Rduch, M. (2022) Interview with David Mannheim, "Personalisation Interview", May 10, 2022

9. Stewart, T. (2022) Interview with David Mannheim, "Personalisation Interview", Mar 23, 2022

10. Survey Manheim, D. "Is Netflix good or bad at personalisation", 2022, https://www.linkedin.com/posts/davidleemannheim_is-netflix-really-that-good-at-personalisation-activity-6922528606975897601-FEZH?utm_source=share&utm_medium=member_desktop

11. Zarum, L. (2018) *Some Viewers Think Netflix Is Targeting Them by Race. Here's What to Know.* The New York Times. https://www.nytimes.com/2018/10/23/arts/television/netflix-race-targeting-personalization.html

12. Carlos A. Gomez-Uribe and Neil Hunt (2016) The Netflix Recommender System: Algorithms, Business Value, and Innovation. ACM Trans. Manage. Inf. Syst. 6, 4, Article 13 (January 2016), 19 pages. https://doi.org/10.1145/2843948

13. Elsworth, S. (2022) Interview with David Mannheim, "Personalisation Interview", Apr 19, 2022

14. Biddle, G. (2022) *A Brief History of Netflix Personalization.* Available at: https://gibsonbiddle.medium.com/a-brief-history-of-netflix-personalization-1f2debf010a1.

15. Team,A.C.(2021c) *IntroducingtheFutureofMarketingResearchSeries|Adobe.* Availableat: https://blog.adobe.com/en/publish/2021/10/04/introducing-the-future-of-marketing-research-series.

Chapter 3: Good Versus Evil
1. Marsden, P (2022) Interview with David Mannheim, "Personalisation Interview", August 4, 2022
2. Jerit, J. & Barabas, J. (2012) Partisan perceptual bias and the information environment. The *Journal of Politics*,74(03), 672–684. doi:10.1017/S0022381612000187
3. Smith, A., Toor, S., Van Kessel, P. & Atske, S. (2020, August 27) *Many Turn to YouTube for Children's Content, News, How-To Lessons.* Pew Research Center: Internet, Science & Tech. http://www.pewinternet.org/2018/11/07/many-turn-to-youtube-for-childrens-content-news-how-to-lessons/
4. Pariser, E. (2011) *The Filter Bubble. How the new personalized web is changing what we read and how we think.* New York, NY, Penguin Books
5. *The Social Dilemma.* Directed by Jeff Orlowski, Exposure Labs. (2020) Netflix, netflix.com/title/81254224.
6. Pasquale, F. (2015) *The Black Box Society: The Secret Algorithms That Control Money and Information.* Harvard: University Press.
7. Pariser, E. Beware online "filter bubbles", 2 May 2011, YouTube, https://www.youtube.com/watch?v=B8ofWFx525s
8. Hodson, J. (2017) *When a squirrel dies: The rapid decline of local news.* Available at: https://theconversation.com/when-a-squirrel-dies-the-rapid-decline-of-local-news-82120.
9. Mani, K. & Considine, R. (2020b) *You don't just need personalization — you need the right personalization.* Think With Google. https://www.thinkwithgoogle.com/consumer-insights/consumer-trends/you-dont-just-need-personalization-you-need-the-right-personalization/
10. Clark, C. J., Liu, B. S., Winegard, B. M. & Ditto, P. H. (2019) Tribalism Is Human Nature. *Current Directions in Psychological Science*, 28(6), 587–592. https://doi.org/10.1177/0963721419862289

Chapter 4: Definition Versus Definition
1. Keown, D. (2022) Interview with David Mannheim, "Personalisation Interview", Feb 23, 2022
2. Jordan, R. (2022) Interview with David Mannheim, "Personalisation Interview", March 30, 2022
3. Laja, P. (2022) Interview with David Mannheim, "Personalisation Interview", Feb 23, 2022
4. Walker, L. (1998) *Amazon Gets Personal With E-Commerce.* Available at: https://www.washingtonpost.com/wp-srv/washtech/daily/nov98/amazon110898.htm.

Part II: The Call to Adventure
1. Manjunath, S. (2022) Interview with David Mannheim, "Personalisation Interview", May 5, 2022
2. Sunikka, A. & Bragge, J. (2012) Applying text-mining to personalization and customization research literature—Who, what and where? *Expert Systems with Applications*, 39(11), pp. 10049–10058. https://onlinelibrary.wiley.com/doi/10.1002/mar.21670#mar21670-bib-0210

Chapter 5: Rubbish Recommendations
1. Jordan, R. (2022) Interview with David Mannheim, "Personalisation Interview", March 30, 2022
2. Smith, B. & Linden, G. (2017) Two decades of recommender systems at Amazon. com. *IEEE internet computing*, 21(3), pp.12–18.

3. Medvedev, I. (2021) *Powered by AI: Instagram's Explore recommender system.* Available at: https://instagram-engineering.com/powered-by-ai-instagrams-explore-recommender-system-7ca901d2a882.
4. Beattie, L., Taber, D. & Cramer, H. (2022) Challenges in Translating Research to Practice for Evaluating Fairness and Bias in Recommendation Systems. In *Proceedings of the 16th ACM Conference on Recommender Systems* (RecSys 2022). Association for Computing Machinery, New York, NY, USA, pp. 528–530. https://doi.org/10.1145/3523227.3547403
5. Marr, B. (2019) The Amazing Ways Retail Giant Zalando Is Using Artificial Intelligence. *Forbes.* https://www.forbes.com/sites/bernardmarr/2019/09/20/the-amazing-ways-retail-giant-zalando-is-using-artificial-intelligence/?sh=62433b2c4d93
6. Patel, B. (2022) Interview with David Mannheim, "Personalisation Interview", March 17, 2022
7. Manjunath, S. (2022) Interview with David Mannheim, "Personalisation Interview", May 5, 2022
8. Barry, T.E. (2012) The development of the hierarchy of effects: an historical perspective, *Journal of Current Issues in Research and Advertising* 10(1)
9. Usmani, F. (2022) *AIDA Model: Definition, Example and Limitations,* Parsadi. https://parsadi.com/aida-model/#:~:text=Elmo%20Lewis%20in%20one%20of,it%2C%20he%20will%20believe%20it.
10. Marsden, P. (2022) Interview with David Mannheim, "Personalisation Interview", August 4, 2022
11. Mani, K., & Considine, R. (2020) *You don't just need personalization — you need the right personalization.* Think With Google. https://www.thinkwithgoogle.com/consumer-insights/consumer-trends/you-dont-just-need-personalization-you-need-the-right-personalization/
12. Mani, K., & Considine, R. (2020) *You don't just need personalization — you need the right personalization.* Think With Google. https://www.thinkwithgoogle.com/consumer-insights/consumer-trends/you-dont-just-need-personalization-you-need-the-right-personalization/
13. Product recommendations. (n.d.). *Cylindo.* https://learn.cylindo.com/hc/en-us/articles/360002090197-Product-recommendations#:~:text=Research%20from%20Salesforce%20shows%20that,didn't%20click%20on%20recommendations.
14. Marsden, P. (2022) Interview with David Mannheim, "Personalisation Interview", August 4, 2022
15. Chen, S.J., Qin, Z., Wilson, Z., Calaci, B., Rose, M., Evans, R., Abraham, S., Metzler, D., Tata, S. & Colagrosso, M. (2020) Improving recommendation quality in google drive. In *Proceedings of the 26th ACM SIGKDD international conference on knowledge discovery & data mining* (pp. 2900-2908).
16. TechCrunch is part of the Yahoo family of brands (2020) Available at: https://techcrunch.com/2020/02/03/alphabet-earnings-show-google-cloud-on-10b-run-rate/.

Chapter 6: Diverse Definitions

1. Nobile, T.H., Kalbaska, N. (2020) An Exploration of Personalization in Digital Communication. Insights in Fashion. In Nah, F.H., Siau, K. (eds) HCI in *Business, Government and Organizations.* HCII 2020. Lecture Notes in Computer Science, vol 12204. Springer, Cham. https://doi.org/10.1007/978-3-030-50341-3_3
2. Chandra, S. *et al.* (2022) Personalization in personalized marketing: Trends and ways forward, *Psychology & Marketing,* 39(8), pp. 1529–1562. Available at: https://doi.org/10.1002/mar.21670
3. Forrester Glossary (no date) Available at: https://www.forrester.com/staticassets/glossary.html.

Chapter 7: Pecking-Order of Personalisation

1. Stjernvall, M. (2022) Interview with David Mannheim, "Personalisation Interview", June 15, 2022
2. Travis, E. (2022) Interview with David Mannheim, "Personalisation Interview", May 27, 2022
3. Wesseling, T. (2022) Interview with David Mannheim, "Personalisation Interview", March 28, 2022
4. This is the difference between personalization and segmentation — and why it matters (2017) Available at: https://www.businessinsider.com/sc/sailthru-personalization-segmentation-revenue-marketing-2017-11?international=true&r=US&IR=T.
5. Personalization in retail: simplifying a complicated relationship (no date) Available at: https://www.thoughtworks.com/en-gb/insights/blog/customer-experience/personalization-retail-simplifying-complicated-relationship.
6. Chandra, S. et al. (2022) Personalization in personalized marketing: Trends and ways forward, *Psychology & Marketing*, 39(8), pp. 1529–1562. Available at : https://doi.org/10.1002/mar.21670
7. Chandra, S. et al. (2022) Personalization in personalized marketing: Trends and ways forward, *Psychology & Marketing*, 39(8), pp. 1529–1562. Available at: https://doi.org/10.1002/mar.21670

Chapter 8: Insisting On Individualism

1. Gibbins, C. (2022) Interview with David Mannheim, "Personalisation Interview", April 12, 2022
2. Chandra, S. et al. (2022) Personalization in personalized marketing: Trends and ways forward, *Psychology & Marketing*, 39(8), pp. 1529–1562. Available at: https://doi.org/10.1002/mar.21670
3. Randall, P. (2022) Interview with David Mannheim, "Personalisation Interview", May 20, 2022
4. Peppers, D., Rogers, M. (1993) *The One-to-One Future: Building Relationships One Customer at a Time*. United Kingdom: Currency Doubleday.
5. Elsworth, S. (2022) Interview with David Mannheim, "Personalisation Interview", April 19, 2022
6. Netflix (NFLX) — Revenue (no date). Available at: https://companiesmarketcap.com/netflix/revenue/.
7. Tideman, D. (2022) Interview with David Mannheim, "Personalisation Interview", September 21, 2022
8. Frank, A. (2015) *The Personification of Digital Marketing*. Available at: https://blogs.gartner.com/andrew_frank/2015/03/20/the-personification-of-digital-marketing/.
9. Scaysbrook, M. (2022) Interview with David Mannheim, "Personalisation Interview", April 11, 2022

Chapter 9: Connection & Conversation

1. Solberg, S. (2022) Interview with David Mannheim, "Personalisation Interview", September 21, 2022
2. Blake, M. B. (2017) *Two Decades of Recommender Systems at Amazon*.
3. This is the difference between personalization and segmentation — and why it matters (2017). Available at: https://www.businessinsider.com/sc/sailthru-personalization-segmentation-revenue-marketing-2017-11?international=true&r=US&IR=T
4. Most Leaders Don't Even Know the Game They're In, 2 Nov (2016, 2 Nov) Video: https://www.youtube.com/watch?v=RyTQ5-SQYTo

5. Howard Schultz Quotes (no date) Available at: https://www.brainyquote.com/quotes/howard_schultz_579198.
6. Howard Schultz Quotes (no date) Available at: https://www.brainyquote.com/quotes/howard_schultz_579198.
7. Bronkhorst AW. (2015) The cocktail-party problem revisited: early processing and selection of multi-talker speech. *Atten Percept Psychophys.* 77(5):1465-87. doi: 10.3758/s13414-015-0882-9. PMID: 25828463; PMCID: PMC4469089.
8. Greenwood, M. (2021) *This is How Best Buy is Bringing Experiential Retail Online.* BrainStation®. https://brainstation.io/magazine/this-is-how-best-buy-is-bringing-experiential-retail-online
9. Rigby, C. (2022) Burberry takes 'social-first' approach to retail and partners with Tencent in China. Available at: https://internetretailing.net/strategy-and-innovation/burberry-takes-social-first-approach-to-retail-and-partners-with-tencent-in-china-20570/.
10. Greenwood, M. (2021) *This is How Best Buy is Bringing Experiential Retail Online.* BrainStation®. https://brainstation.io/magazine/this-is-how-best-buy-is-bringing-experiential-retail-online
11. Rigby, C. (2022) *Burberry takes 'social-first' approach to retail and partners with Tencent in China.* Available at: https://internetretailing.net/strategy-and-innovation/burberry-takes-social-first-approach-to-retail-and-partners-with-tencent-in-china-20570/.
12. An Emotional Connection Matters More than Customer Satisfaction (2017) Available at: https://hbr.org/2016/08/an-emotional-connection-matters-more-than-customer-satisfaction.
13. Waqar N., Teck Ming T., Mina T. & Nick H. (2021) How do experiences enhance brand relationship performance and value co-creation in social commerce? The role of consumer engagement and self-brand-connection, *Technological Forecasting and Social Change*, Volume 171, 120952, ISSN 0040-1625,https://doi.org/10.1016/j.techfore.2021.120952

Part III: Paradise Lost
1. Elsworth, S. (2022) Interview with David Mannheim, "Personalisation Interview", April 19 2022
2. Morys, A. (2022) Interview with David Mannheim, "Personalisation Interview", June 28 2022
3. Morys, A. (2022) Interview with David Mannheim, "Personalisation Interview", June 28 2022

Chapter 10: Don't Believe the Hype
1. Wesseling, T. (2022) Interview with David Mannheim, "Personalisation Interview", March 28, 2022
2. Pilewski, S. (2020) *Personalization: Tomorrow is Now.* Available at: https://www.dynamicyield.com/article/personalization-tomorrow-now/.
3. Fenn, J. (2007) *Understanding Gartner's Hype Cycles*
4. Fenn, J. (2007) *Understanding Gartner's Hype Cycles*
5. Hype Cycle Research Methodology (no date) Available at: https://www.gartner.co.uk/en/methodologies/gartner-hype-cycle.
6. Fenn, J. (2007) *Understanding Gartner's Hype Cycles*

Chapter 11: Origin Story: The History of Personalisation
1. Shah, S. (2022) Interview with David Mannheim, "Personalisation Interview", April 5, 2022
2. Johannes Gutenberg: Father of Mass Communication (no date). Available at: https://www.veranijveld.com/history/johannes-gutenberg-father-of-mass-communication.

3. Greenslade, R. (2020) *Mass media is over, but where does journalism go from here?* Available at: https://www.theguardian.com/media/greenslade/2016/may/31/mass-media-is-over-but-where-does-journalism-go-from-here.

4. Smith, W. R. (1956) Product differentiation and market segmentation as alternative marketing strategies. *Journal of Marketing*, 21(1), pp. 3–8.

5. Wedel, M. & Kamakura, W. (2000) *The Historical Development of the Market Segmentation Concept*. 10.1007/978-1-4615-4651-1_1.

6. Tedlow, R. S. (1996) *New and Improved: The Story of Mass Marketing in America*. United Kingdom: Harvard Business School Press.

7. Petrison, L., Blattberg, R. & Wang, P. (1997) Database marketing – Past, present and future. *Journal of Direct Marketing*, 11(4), pp. 109–125.

8. Houlind, R. & Riemersma, F. (2023) *Hello $FirstName*, Omnichannel Institute

9. Berry, L. (1995) *Relationship marketing of services—growing interest, emerging perspectives*. Available at: https://link.springer.com/article/10.1177/009207039502300402?error=co okies_not_supported&code=43b47f58-1153-4f96-88db-45a415df8ba3.

10. Bezos, J. (1997) *Shareholder letter*. Accessed at: https://media.corporate-ir.net/media_files/irol/97/97664/reports/Shareholderletter97.pdf

11. Grove, S. J. & Fisk, R. P. (1992) Observational data collection methods for services marketing: An overview. *Journal of the Academy of Marketing Science*, 20(3), pp. 217–224.

12. Hornik, J., Zaig, T. & Shadmon, D. (1991) Increasing compliance in costly telephone interviews: A test of four inducement techniques. *International Journal of Research in Marketing*, 8(2), pp. 147–153.

13. Johnston, C.A.T. (2012) *Netflix Never Used Its $1 Million Algorithm Due To Engineering Costs*. Available at: https://www.wired.com/2012/04/netflix-prize-costs/.

14. Thompson, C. (2016) *Texting Isn't the First New Technology Thought to Impair Social Skills*. Available at: https://www.smithsonianmag.com/innovation/texting-isnt-first-new-technology-thought-impair-social-skills-180958091/.

Chapter 12: The Years of Personalisation

1. Richter, N. (2022) Interview with David Mannheim, "Personalisation Interview", May 9, 2022

2. Ross, N. (1992) *A history of direct marketing*. Direct Marketing Association

3. Reed, O. (1949) *Some random thoughts on personalizing*. The reporter of direct mail advertising, April.

4. Ariel, A. (2021) *Announcing our investment in Dynamic Yield – Vertex Ventures IL*. Available at: https://medium.com/vertex-ventures-il/announcing-our-investment-in-dynamic-yield-and-my-new-blog-33f838051cb8.

5. Litmus Software (2022) Blog. Available at: https://www.litmus.com/blog/.

6. Yalif, G. (2022) Interview with David Mannheim, "Personalisation Interview", Jan 9, 2023

7. Intellimize. (n.d.) Crunchbase.com. https://www.crunchbase.com/organization/intellimize

8. Meet the Inc. 5000 Companies: Winning in a Time of Change and Achieving Spectacular Growth. (n.d.). Inc.com. https://www.inc.com/inc5000/2022

9. Smith, B. & Linden, G. (2017) Two decades of recommender systems at Amazon. com. *IEEE internet computing*, 21(3), pp.12–18.

10. Epsilon Marketing (no date) *The power of me: The impact of personalization on marketing performance*. Available at: https://www.slideshare.net/EpsilonMktg/the-power-of-me-the-impact-of-personalization-on-marketing-performance/1.

11. Statista (2021) *Umfrage zum Interesse an Personalisierung im E-Commerce in Deutschland 2018*. Available at: https://de.statista.com/statistik/daten/studie/921812/umfrage/interesse-an-personalisierungsstrategien-im-e-commerce-in-deutschland/.

12. Swant, M. (2021) *Mutiny Raises $18.5 Million From Sequoia, Cowboy Ventures—And Even A Few Chief Marketing Officers.* Available at: https://www.forbes.com/sites/martyswant/2021/09/15/mutiny-raises-185-million-from-sequoia-cowboy-ventures-and-even-a-few-chief-marketing-officers/?sh=19e3de617a17.
13. Mutiny — Crunchbase Company Profile & Funding (no date). Available at: https://www.crunchbase.com/organization/mutinyhq.
14. Personalization: The ANA 2019 Marketing Word of the Year (no date). Available at: https://www.ana.net/blogs/show/id/mm-blog-2019-word-of-the-year.
15. Nâo8, S. (no date) Home. Available at: https://www.storeno8.com/.
16. Dignan, L. (2019) *Nike's purchase of analytics firm Zodiac highlights focus on customer lifetime value.* Available at: https://www.zdnet.com/article/nikes-purchase-of-analytics-firm-zodiac-highlights-focus-on-customer-lifetime-value/.
17. Digital Transformation (no date). Available at: https://www.bcg.com/capabilities/digital-technology-data/digital-transformation/overview.
18. Gartner Says 35% of Digital Marketing Leaders Believe the Biggest Cha (no date). Available at: https://www.gartner.com/en/newsroom/press-releases/gartner-says-35-of-digital-marketing-leaders-believe-the-bigges.
19. Think Blog Editor (2021) *Why your Organization Needs Personalization at Scale.* Available at: https://www.ibm.com/blogs/think/be-en/2021/06/21/why-your-organization-needs-personalization-at-scale/.
20. Chandra, S. et al. (2022) Personalization in personalized marketing: Trends and ways forward, *Psychology & Marketing*, 39(8), pp. 1529—1562. Available at: https://doi.org/10.1002/mar.2167
21. Attraqt (2022) *Crownpeak Finalises Acquisition of Attraqt to Expand its Digital Experience Portfolio with Product Discovery Capabilities.* Available at: https://www.attraqt.com/resources/crownpeak-finalises-acquisition-of-attraqt-to-expand-its-digital-experience-portfolio-with-product-discovery-capabilities/.
22. AB Tasty (2022) *Welcomes Epoq to its Team of Magic Makers.* Available at: https://www.abtasty.com/news/ab-tasty-epoq-acquisition/.
23. Bloomberg Interviews Optimizely CEO on Series A Funding and Personalization (2021). Available at: https://www.optimizely.com/insights/blog/bloomberg-interviews-optimizely-ceo-dan-siroker/.
24. Galloway, S. (2022) *AI.* Available at: https://www.profgalloway.com/ai/.
25. Wiggers, J (2022) *AI content platform Jasper raises $125M at a $1.5B valuation.* Available at: https://techcrunch.com/2022/10/18/ai-content-platform-jasper-raises-125m-at-a-1-7b-valuation/?guccounter=1.
26. Crino, T. (2023) *Why Business Owners Should Focus on Personalization in 2023.* Available at: https://www.inc.com/tim-crino/why-business-owners-should-focus-on-personalization-in-2023.html.
27. Drenik, G. (2021) *Why 2022 Should Be The Year Of Personalization In Retail.* Available at: https://www.forbes.com/sites/garydrenik/2021/11/11/why-2022-should-be-the-year-of-personalization-in-retail/.
28. MacRae, D. (2023) 65% of consumers say personalisation earns loyalty in 2023. *Marketing Tech News.* https://www.marketingtechnews.net/news/2023/jan/26/65-of-consumers-say-personalisation-earns-loyalty-in-2023/
29. Hoogenboom, H. (2022) Interview with David Mannheim, "Personalisation Interview", May 4, 2022

Chapter 13: Vendor-Tinted Glasses
1. Scott, S. (2020) *Personalisation will be 2020's most overhyped marketing practice.* Available at: https://www.thedrum.com/opinion/2020/01/07/personalisation-will-be-2020-s-most-over hyped-marketing-practice.
2. The State of Personalization Maturity – 2021. Available at: https://www.dynamicyield.com/ personalization-maturity/.
3. Epperson, J. (2022) Interview with David Mannheim, "Personalisation Interview", March 8, 2022
4. MacIntyre, J. (2022) Interview with David Mannheim, "Personalisation Interview", May 4, 2022
5. Unlocking the value of personalization at scale for operators (2022). Available at: https:// www.mckinsey.com/industries/technology-media-and-telecommunications/our-insights/ unlocking-the-value-of-personalization-at-scale-for-operators.
6. Benami, Y. (2023) *The ROI of Personalization – Here's How It Pays Off. Idomoo Personalised Video.* https://www.idomoo.com/en-gb/blog/the-roi-of-personalization/
7. Apáthy, S (2022) *History of recommender systems: overview of information filtering solutions.* Available at: https://onespire.net/news/history-of-recommender-systems/.

Chapter 14: The Fear Factor
1. Harvard Business School Publishing (2018) *"The Age of Personalization," Crafting a Finer Edge* [Preprint]. Available at: https://hbr.org/resources/pdfs/comm/mastercard/ TheAgeOfPersonalization.pdf.
2. Scott, S. (2020b) *Personalisation will be 2020's most overhyped marketing practice.* Available at: https://www.thedrum.com/opinion/2020/01/07/personalisation-will-be-2020-s-most-over hyped-marketing-practice.
3. Revieve (no date) *7 Brands Getting Beauty Personalization Right | AI Beauty Tech.* Available at: https://www.revieve.com/resources/7-brands-getting-beauty-personalization-right.
4. Randall, P. (2022) Interview with David Mannheim, "Personalisation Interview", May 20, 2022
5. Burke, P. (2022) *Why I regret inventing the innocent smoothie brand.* Available at: https:// www.spectator.co.uk/article/why-i-regret-inventing-the-innocent-smoothie-brand/.
6. Mansfield, K. (2018) *Internet Computing Magazine 20th Anniversary.* Available at: https:// www.computer.org/press-room/2017-news/ic-20th-anniversary.
7. Popken, B. & Kent, J.L. (2018) *As algorithms take over, YouTube's recommendations highlight a human problem.* Available at: https://www.nbcnews.com/tech/social-media/algorithms-take-over-youtube-s-recommendations-highlight-human-problem-n867596.
8. Smith, A., Toor, S. & van Kessel, P. (2020) *Many Turn to YouTube for Children's Content, News, How-To Lessons.* Available at: https://www.pewresearch.org/internet/2018/11/07/ many-turn-to-youtube-for-childrens-content-news-how-to-lessons/.
9. Solsman, J. E. (2018) YouTube's AI is the puppet master over most of what you watch. *CNET.* https://www.cnet.com/tech/services-and-software/youtube-ces-2018-neal-mohan/
10. YouTube Regrets. (n.d.) Mozilla Foundation. https://foundation.mozilla.org/en/youtube/ findings/
11. 10, H. (2022) *How Much Does Amazon Make a Day?* Available at: https://www.helium10. com/blog/how-much-does-amazon-make-a-day/.
12. Statista (2022) *Total global visitor traffic to Amazon.com 2021–2022.* Available at: https:// www.statista.com/statistics/623566/web-visits-to-amazoncom/.
13. MacKenzie, I., Meyer, C. & Noble, S. (2013) How retailers can keep up with consumers. *McKinsey & Company.* https://www.mckinsey.com/industries/retail/our-insights/how-retailers-can-keep-up-with-consumers

14. Recommendation Engine Markets: Collaborative Filtering, Content-based Filtering, & Hybrid Recommendation Systems – Global Industry Trends, Share, Size, Growth, Opportunity and Forecast to 2027. (2022) https://finance.yahoo.com/news/recommendation-engine-markets-collaborative-filtering-133000581.html#:~:text=The%20global%20recommendation%20 engine%20market,35.61%25%20during%202022-2027.
15. Travis, E. (2022) Interview with David Mannheim, "Personalisation Interview", May 27, 2022
16. Andrews, L. (2022) Interview with David Mannheim, "Personalisation Interview", Apr 20, 2022
17. Swant, M. (2021) Mutiny Raises $18.5 Million From Sequoia, Cowboy Ventures— And Even A Few Chief Marketing Officers. *Forbes.* https://www.forbes.com/sites/ martyswant/2021/09/15/mutiny-raises-185-million-from-sequoia-cowboy-ventures-and-even-a-few-chief-marketing-officers/?sh=4d371f6b7a17
18. Rezaei, J. (n.d.) *Subscribe to MUTINY: Join 12,000+ B2B marketers | Mutiny.* https://www. mutinyhq.com/subscribe
19. Digital ad spend worldwide 2026 | Statista. (2023) *Statista.* https://www.statista.com/ statistics/237974/online-advertising-spending-worldwide/
20. Bond, C. (2022) Conversion Rate Benchmarks: Find Out How YOUR Conversion Rate Compares. *WordStream.* https://www.wordstream.com/blog/ws/2019/08/19/conversion-rate-benchmarks
21. Marshall, R. (2021) How Many Ads Do You See in One Day? *Red Crow Marketing.* https:// www.redcrowmarketing.com/2015/09/10/many-ads-see-one-day/
22. Stewart, T. (2022) Interview with David Mannheim, "Personalisation Interview", March 23, 2022

Part IV: The Three Dragons
1. Morys, A. (2022) Interview with David Mannheim, "Personalisation Interview", Jun 28, 2022

Chapter 15: Know Thy Enemy: The Golden Dragon
1. Tolkien, J.R.R. (2012) *The Hobbit.* United Kingdom: Houghton Mifflin Harcourt.

Chapter 16: Amazon Versus The Golden Dragon
1. Beerthuyzen, M. (2022) Interview with David Mannheim, "Personalisation Interview", May 20, 2022
2. Bezos, J. (2021) *2020 Letter to Shareholders.* US About Amazon. https://www.aboutamazon. com/news/company-news/2020-letter-to-shareholders
3. Schwartz, B. & Schwartz, D. (2004) *The Paradox of Choice: Why More Is Less.* United Kingdom: HarperCollins.
4. Dhar, R. (1997) Consumer preference for a no-choice option. *Journal of Consumer Research,* 24, pp. 215–231.
5. Wikipedia contributors. (2023) *Buridan's ass.* Wikipedia. https://en.wikipedia.org/wiki/ Buridan%27s_ass
6. Walker, L. (1998) *Amazon Gets Personal With E-Commerce.* https://www.washingtonpost. com/wp-srv/washtech/daily/nov98/amazon110898.htm
7. Retta, L. (n.d.) *Amazon: The Chronicles of a Personalization Giant.* United States: Dynamic Yield.
8. MacKenzie, I., Meyer, C. & Noble, S. (2013) How retailers can keep up with consumers. *McKinsey & Company.* https://www.mckinsey.com/industries/retail/our-insights/how-retailers-can-keep-up-with-consumers
9. Blake, M. B. (2017) *Two Decades of Recommender Systems at Amazon.*

10. Stillman, J. (2014) 7 Jeff Bezos Quotes That Outline the Secret to Success. *Inc.com.* https://www.inc.com/jessica-stillman/7-jeff-bezos-quotes-that-will-make-you-rethink-success.html
11. Amazon Startup Story – Fundable. (n.d.). *Fundable.* https://www.fundable.com/learn/startup-stories/amazon
12. Hern, A. (2022) Amazon facing £900m lawsuit for 'pushing customers to pay more.' *The Guardian.* https://www.theguardian.com/technology/2022/oct/20/amazon-facing-900m-lawsuit-claiming-users-manipulated-into-paying-higher-prices

Chapter 17: Victoria's Real Secret

1. Brunner, J. (2021) *Victoria's Secret's Journey with Personalization Capabilities – S721.* Available at: https://business.adobe.com/summit/2022/sessions/victorias-secrets-journey-with-personalization-cap-s721.html.
2. Brunner, J. (2021) *Victoria's Secret's Journey with Personalization Capabilities – S721.* Available at: https://business.adobe.com/summit/2022/sessions/victorias-secrets-journey-with-personalization-cap-s721.html.
3. Bennett, M. (2022) Victoria's Secret gets up close and personal with Adobe. *Diginomica.* https://diginomica.com/victorias-secret-gets-close-and-personal-adobe
4. Brunner, J. (2021) *Victoria's Secret's Journey with Personalization Capabilities – S721.* Available at: https://business.adobe.com/summit/2022/sessions/victorias-secrets-journey-with-personalization-cap-s721.html.
5. Richter, N. (2022) Interview with David Mannheim, "Personalisation Interview", May 9, 2022

Chapter 18: Sexy Sparks & Spencer

1. Devlin, E. (2023) *M&S relaunches Sparks loyalty scheme with updated app.* Available at: https://www.thegrocer.co.uk/marks-and-spencer/mands-relaunches-sparks-loyalty-scheme-with-updated-app/646032.article.
2. Williams, A. & Klein, M. (2021) *M&S Personalised Customer Interactions: A Recipe for Success – E125.* Available at: https://business.adobe.com/summit/2022/sessions/na-ms-personalised-customer-interactions-a-recipe-e125.html.
3. Laja, P. (2022) Interview with David Mannheim, "Personalisation Interview", Feb 23, 2022
4. Abraham, M. et al. (2021) *The $70 Billion Prize in Personalized Offers.* Available at: https://www.bcg.com/publications/2021/personalized-offers-have-a-potential-70-billion-dollar-growth-opportunity.
5. M&S scales personalization with Adobe Analytics and Target (no date). Available at: https://business.adobe.com/uk/customer-success-stories/marks-spencer-case-study.html.
6. Obama, B. (2021) *Barack Obama shares his approach for making tough decisions | Medium.* Available at: https://barackobama.medium.com/how-i-approach-the-toughest-decisions-dc1b165cdf2d.

Chapter 19: Defeating the Golden Dragon

1. Patel, B. (2022) Interview with David Mannheim, "Personalisation Interview", Mar 17, 2022
2. Travis, E. (2022) Interview with David Mannheim, "Personalisation Interview", May 27, 2022
3. Palmer, O. (2022) Interview with David Mannheim, "Personalisation Interview", April 6th, 2023
4. Biddle, G. (2022) #2 From DHM to Product Strategy, *Gibson Biddle.* Available at: https://gibsonbiddle.medium.com/2-from-dhm-to-product-strategy-a3781b2aadca.
5. Andrews, L. (2022) Interview with David Mannheim, "Personalisation Interview", Apr 20, 2022

6. Harvard Business School Publishing (2018) *"The Age of Personalization,"* Crafting a Finer Edge [Preprint]. Available at: https://hbr.org/resources/pdfs/comm/mastercard/TheAgeOfPersonalization.pdf.
7. Pavlovich, S. (2020) Interview with David Mannheim, "Return on Investment in Experimentation Interview", May 21, 2020
8. Williams, A. (2022) Interview with David Mannheim, "Personalisation Interview", Jan 23, 2023
9. Brunner, J. (2021) *Victoria's Secret's Journey with Personalization Capabilities – S721.* Available at: https://business.adobe.com/summit/2022/sessions/victorias-secrets-journey-with-personalization-cap-s721.html.
10. Nameless Source, H. (2022) Interview with David Mannheim, "Personalisation Interview", April 22, 2023
11. Harvard Business School Publishing (2018) "The Age of Personalization," Crafting a Finer Edge [Preprint]. Available at: https://hbr.org/resources/pdfs/comm/mastercard/TheAgeOfPersonalization.pdf.
12. Unlocking the value of personalization at scale for operators (2022). Available at: https://www.mckinsey.com/industries/technology-media-and-telecommunications/our-insights/unlocking-the-value-of-personalization-at-scale-for-operators.
13. Brunner, J. (2021) *Victoria's Secret's Journey with Personalization Capabilities – S721.* Available at: https://business.adobe.com/summit/2022/sessions/victorias-secrets-journey-with-personalization-cap-s721.html.
14. Personalizing the customer experience: Driving differentiation in retail (2020b). Available at: https://www.mckinsey.com/industries/retail/our-insights/personalizing-the-customer-experience-driving-differentiation-in-retail.
15. Jordan, R. (2022) Interview with David Mannheim, "Personalisation Interview", Mar 30, 2022
16. Wu, Q., Wang, H., Hong, L. & Shi, Y. (2017) Returning is Believing: Optimizing Long-term User Engagement in Recommender Systems. In *Proceedings of the 2017 ACM on Conference on Information and Knowledge Management* (CIKM 2017). Association for Computing Machinery, New York, NY, USA, 1927–1936. https://doi.org/10.1145/3132847.3133025
17. Wu, Q., Wang, H., Hong, L. & Shi, Y. (2017) Returning is Believing: Optimizing Long-term User Engagement in Recommender Systems. In *Proceedings of the 2017 ACM on Conference on Information and Knowledge Management* (CIKM 2017). Association for Computing Machinery, New York, NY, USA, 1927–1936. https://doi.org/10.1145/3132847.3133025
18. McDonald, G. (2022) Interview with David Mannheim, "Personalisation Interview", Mar 30, 2022
19. From Red Envelopes to Red Carpets: Netflix's Todd Yellin Talks Innovation and Personalization. (2022) *Bain.* https://www.netpromotersystem.com/insights/from-red-envelopes-to-red-carpets-netflixs-todd-yellin-talks-innovation-and-personalization-podcast/
20. Biddle, G. (2022c) A Brief History of Netflix Personalization, *Medium.* Available at: https://gibsonbiddle.medium.com/a-brief-history-of-netflix-personalization-1f2debf010a1.
21. Richter, N. (2022) Interview with David Mannheim, "Personalisation Interview", May 9, 2022
22. Marsden, P. (2022) Interview with David Mannheim, "Personalisation Interview", Aug 4, 2023

Chapter 20: Money Makes Personalisation Go Round

1. Williams, A. (2022) Interview with David Mannheim, "Personalisation Interview", Jan 23, 2023

2. Mandjuth, S. (2022) Interview with David Mannheim, "Personalisation Interview", May 5, 2022

3. Biddle, G. (2022b) #2 From DHM to Product Strategy, *Medium*. Available at: https://gibsonbiddle.medium.com/2-from-dhm-to-product-strategy-a3781b2aadca.

4. Wikipedia contributors (2023) *Stranger Things*. Available at: https://en.wikipedia.org/wiki/Stranger_Things.

5. Personalizing the customer experience: Driving differentiation in retail (2020). Available at: https://www.mckinsey.com/industries/retail/our-insights/personalizing-the-customer-experience-driving-differentiation-in-retail.

6. Palumbo, S. et al. (2021) *AI Has Launched a $200 Billion Revolution in Content Personalization*. Available at: https://www.bcg.com/publications/2021/ai-content-generation-is-a-2-billion-dollar-revolution-in-content-personalization.

7. Field, D., Patel, S. & Leon, H. (2022) *The Dividends of Digital Marketing Maturity*. Available at: https://www.bcg.com/publications/2019/dividends-digital-marketing-maturity.

8. The biggest celebrity endorsement deals of all time. (n.d.). https://www.lovemoney.com/galleries/110420/the-biggest-celebrity-endorsement-deals-of-all-time?page=1

9. Williams, A. (2022) Interview with David Mannheim, "Personalisation Interview", Jan 23, 2023

Part V: The Stubborn Dragon
1. Shakespeare, W. (1877) *King Lear*. Oxford :Clarendon Press.

Chapter 21: Know Thy Enemy: The Stubborn Dragon
1. Solberg, S (2022) Interview with David Mannheim, "Personalisation Interview", September 21, 2022.

2. Dimri, M. (2022) Personalization in retail: All you need to know in 2022. *Netcore Cloud*. https://netcorecloud.com/blog/retail-personalization/

3. Personalizing the customer experience: Driving differentiation in retail. (2020) McKinsey & Company. https://www.mckinsey.com/industries/retail/our-insights/personalizing-the-customer-experience-driving-differentiation-in-retail

Chapter 22: Data, Data, Data: The Mouse House's MagicBands
1. Doyle, A. (1892) *Adventure 12: "The Adventure of the Copper Beeches". The Adventures of Sherlock Holmes* (Lit2Go Edition). Retrieved April 06, 2023, from https://etc.usf.edu/lit2go/32/the-adventures-of-sherlock-holmes/363/adventure-12-the-adventure-of-the-copper-beeches/

2. Labay, B. (2022) Interview with David Mannheim, "Personalisation Interview", April 27, 2022

3. Zanolla, L. (2016) Disney foot tracking patent to improve guest experience? *The DIS*. https://www.wdwinfo.com/news-stories/disney-foot-tracking-patent-to-improve-guest-experience/

4. How many customers does McDonald's have per day? (n.d.). Zippia. https://www.zippia.com/answers/how-many-customers-does-mcdonalds-have-per-day/

5. Transcripts, S. (2022) McDonald's Corporation (MCD) CEO Chris Kempczinski on Q2 2022 Results — Earnings Call Transcript. *Seeking Alpha*. https://seekingalpha.com/article/4525838-mcdonalds-corporation-mcd-ceo-chris-kempczinski-on-q2-2022-results-earnings-call-transcript

6. Unnamed Source (2022) Interview with David Mannheim, "Personalisation Interview", Spring, 2022

7. Harvard Business Review (2018) The Age of Personalization: Crafting a Finer Edge. *The Age of Personalization*. https://hbr.org/sponsored/2018/09/the-age-of-personalization
8. Nightingale, K. (2022) Interview with David Mannheim, "Personalisation Interview", August 18, 2022
9. Rodenhausen, D., Wiener, L., Rogers, K. & Katerman, M. (2022) Consumers Want Privacy. Marketers Can Deliver. *BCG Global*. https://www.bcg.com/publications/2022/consumers-want-data-privacy-and-marketers-can-deliver
10. BBC News (2018) *Facebook value drops by $37bn amid privacy backlash*. https://www.bbc.co.uk/news/business-43462423
11. TED (2019) *Facebook's role in Brexit — and the threat to democracy | Carole Cadwalladr* [Video]. YouTube. https://www.youtube.com/watch?v=OQSMr-3GGvQ
12. O'Neil, C. (2016) *Weapons of Math Destruction: How Big Data Increases Inequality and Threatens Democracy*. United Kingdom: Crown.
13. Book Review: O'Neil's Weapons of Math Destruction — Present Tense. (n.d.). https://www.presenttensejournal.org/volume-6/book-review-oneils-weapons-of-math-destruction/
14. Pasquale, F. (2015) *The Black Box Society: The Secret Algorithms That Control Money and Information*. United Kingdom: Harvard University Press.
15. Making it personal — One in three consumers wants personalised products. (n.d.). Deloitte United Kingdom. https://www2.deloitte.com/uk/en/pages/press-releases/articles/one-in-three-consumers-wants-personalised-products.html
16. Loyalty, B. B. (n.d.) *Press Release: Gen Z and Millennial Consumers are Changing Loyalty — Open to Behavior Tracking, Paid Loyalty, and Deeper Brand Engagement Through Technology*. https://info.bondbrandloyalty.com/press-release-loyaltyreport2018
17. Rodenhausen, D., Wiener, L., Rogers, K. & Katerman, M. (2022) Consumers Want Privacy. Marketers Can Deliver. *BCG Global*. https://www.bcg.com/publications/2022/consumers-want-data-privacy-and-marketers-can-deliver
18. Data Privacy Survey (2021) KPMG. https://info.kpmg.us/news-perspectives/industry-insights-research/data-privacy-survey-orson-lucas.html
19. Cloarec, J. (2020) The personalization-privacy paradox in the attention economy, *Technological Forecasting and Social Change*, Volume 161, 120299, ISSN 0040-1625, https://doi.org/10.1016/j.techfore.2020.120299.
20. Rodenhausen, D., Wiener, L., Rogers, K. & Katerman, M. (2022) Consumers Want Privacy. Marketers Can Deliver. *BCG Global*. https://www.bcg.com/publications/2022/consumers-want-data-privacy-and-marketers-can-deliver

Chapter 23: Too Much Trouble: AI Engines

1. Nicastro, D. (2018c) *Personalized Marketing: Where We Are in 2018*. Available at: https://www.cmswire.com/digital-experience/personalized-marketing-where-we-are-at-2018/.
2. Gartner Magic Quadrant & Critical Capabilities | Gartner. (n.d.). Gartner. https://www.gartner.com/en/research/magic-quadrant
3. The 2022 Gartner Marketing Technology Survey. (n.d.). Gartner. https://www.gartner.com/en/marketing/research/marketing-technology-survey-2022
4. Unlocking the value of personalization at scale for operators. (2022) McKinsey & Company. https://www.mckinsey.com/industries/technology-media-and-telecommunications/our-insights/unlocking-the-value-of-personalization-at-scale-for-operators?ref=themartechweekly.com
5. Nameless source (2022) Interview with David Mannheim, "Personalisation Interview", April 22, 2022

6. Peter Weinberg on LinkedIn: What is the worst idea in marketing? My vote would be ... (no date). Available at: https://www.linkedin.com/posts/weinbergpeter_what-is-the-worst-idea-in-marketing-my-activity-6607673178544320512-PoeJ/.
7. Weinberg, P. (2022) Forget personalisation, it's impossible and it doesn't work. *Marketing Week*. https://www.marketingweek.com/peter-weinberg-jon-lombardo-personalisation-impersonal isation/
8. AB Tasty (2018) "Perfecting Personalization," How to Hone Your Website Personalization Strategy Using a/B Testing [Preprint]. Available at: https://www.abtasty.com/resources/ perfecting-web-personalization-ab-testing/.
9. Andrews, L. (2022) Interview with David Mannheim, "Personalisation Interview", Apr 20, 2022
10. Mani, K. & Considine, R. (2020b) *You don't just need personalization — you need the right personalization*. Think With Google. https://www.thinkwithgoogle.com/consumer-insights/ consumer-trends/you-dont-just-need-personalization-you-need-the-right-personalization/
11. Nicastro, D. (2018) Personalized Marketing: Where We Are in 2018. *CMSWire.com*. https:// www.cmswire.com/digital-experience/personalized-marketing-where-we-are-at-2018/
12. Swant, M. (2021) *Mutiny Raises $18.5 Million From Sequoia, Cowboy Ventures — And Even A Few Chief Marketing Officers*. Available at: https://www.forbes.com/sites/ martyswant/2021/09/15/mutiny-raises-185-million-from-sequoia-cowboy-ventures-and-even-a-few-chief-marketing-officers/?sh=111fbc1f7a17.
13. PRNewswire. (2023. Intellimize Rewrites the Rules of Personalization and CRO with AI Content Studio. *Benzinga*. https://www.benzinga.com/pressreleases/23/02/n31090102/ intellimize-rewrites-the-rules-of-personalization-and-cro-with-ai-content-studio
14. Gartner. (2021) *Gartner Says 63% of Digital Marketing Leaders Still Struggle with Pers.* https://www.gartner.com/en/newsroom/press-releases/-gartner-says-63--of-digital-marketing-leaders-still-struggle-wi
15. Miller, A. P. (2019) How Targeted Ads and Dynamic Pricing Can Perpetuate Bias. *Harvard Business Review*. https://hbr.org/2019/11/how-targeted-ads-and-dynamic-pricing-can-perpetuate-bias
16. What Consumers Really Think About AI: A Global Study | Pega. (2018) https://www.pega. com/ai-survey
17. Schiffer, Z. & Newton, C. (2023) Microsoft lays off AI ethics and society team. *The Verge*. https://www.theverge.com/2023/3/13/23638823/microsoft-ethics-society-team-responsible-ai-layoffs
18. Kang, C. & Satariano, A. (2023) As A.I. Booms, Lawmakers Struggle to Understand the Technology. *The New York Times*. https://www.nytimes.com/2023/03/03/technology/ artificial-intelligence-regulation-congress.html
19. Sorkin, A. R., Mattu, R., Warner, B., Kessler, S., De La Merced, M. J., Hirsch, L. & Livni, E. (2023) Why the U.S. Government Isn't Rushing to Regulate AI. *The New York Times*. https:// www.nytimes.com/2023/03/03/business/dealbook/lawmakers-ai-regulations.html
20. Singh, M. (2023) *India opts against AI regulation*. https://techcrunch.com/2023/04/05/ india-opts-against-ai-regulation
21. Cordato, A. (2022) *Trivago fined $44.7m for falsely advertising hotel room prices as best price*. Available at: https://www.lexology.com/library/detail.aspx?g=579457c5-2e64-46ae-93b2-2afacd437aeb.
22. Shyne, S. (2022) Interview with David Mannheim, "Personalisation Interview", April 28, 2023
23. Yong, E. (2018) A Popular Algorithm Is No Better at Predicting Crimes Than Random People. *The Atlantic*. https://www.theatlantic.com/technology/archive/2018/01/equivant-compas-algorithm/550646/

24. Mattu, J. L. a. K. (2020, February 29). How We Analyzed the COMPAS Recidivism Algorithm. *ProPublica*. https://www.propublica.org/article/how-we-analyzed-the-compas-recidivism-algorithm
25. Equivant. (2020) FAQ – equivant. *Equivant*. https://www.equivant.com/faq/

Chapter 24: Slaying the Stubborn Dragon
1. Gibbins, C. (2022) Interview with David Mannheim, "Personalisation Interview", April 12, 2022
2. Stjernvall, M. (2022) Interview with David Mannheim, "Personalisation Interview", Jun 15, 2022
3. Hern, A. (2018) Would you trust a stylist with 50,000 clients to get your look right? *The Guardian*. https://www.theguardian.com/technology/2016/jul/19/thread-fashion-stylist-startup-machine-learning-ai
4. Hern, A. (2018) *Would you trust a stylist with 50,000 clients to get your look right?* Available at: https://www.theguardian.com/technology/2016/jul/19/thread-fashion-stylist-startup-machine-learning-ai.
5. Santi, A. (2022) For and against the AI stylist. Available at: https://www.raconteur.net/technology/artificial-intelligence/ai-stylists-for-against/.
6. Santi, A. (2022) *For and against the AI stylist.* Available at: https://www.raconteur.net/technology/artificial-intelligence/ai-stylists-for-against/.
7. Stitch Fix (SFIX) (no date) *Market capitalization.* Available at: https://companiesmarketcap.com/stitch-fix/marketcap.
8. Morys, A. (2022) Interview with David Mannheim, "Personalisation Interview", Jun 28, 2022
9. MacIntyre, J. (2022) Interview with David Mannheim, "Personalisation Interview", May 4, 2022
10. Growjo (no date) *Mutiny: Revenue, Competitors, Alternatives.* Available at: https://growjo.com/company/Mutiny.
11. Wiggers, K. (2022) *Mutiny, which personalizes website copy and headlines using AI, raises $50M.* Available at: https://techcrunch.com/2022/04/20/mutiny-which-personalizes-website-copy-and-headlines-using-ai-raises-50m/.
12. Crunchbase database – Gusto (no date) Available at: https://www.crunchbase.com/organization/gusto.
13. Wiggers, K. (2022) *Mutiny, which personalizes website copy and headlines using AI, raises $50M.* Available at: https://techcrunch.com/2022/04/20/mutiny-which-personalizes-website-copy-and-headlines-using-ai-raises-50m/.
14. Dropbox to Acquire DocSend | Dropbox (no date). Available at: https://dropbox.gcs-web.com/news-releases/news-release-details/dropbox-acquire-docsend.
15. Swant, M. (2021b) *Mutiny Raises $18.5 Million From Sequoia, Cowboy Ventures – And Even A Few Chief Marketing Officers.* Available at: https://www.forbes.com/sites/martyswant/2021/09/15/mutiny-raises-185-million-from-sequoia-cowboy-ventures-and-even-a-few-chief-marketing-officers/?sh=65947b637a17.
16. Woodhead, K. (2022) Interview with David Mannheim, "Personalisation Interview", Mar 11, 2022
17. Rajyaguru, A. (2022) Interview with David Mannheim, "Personalisation Interview", Aug 04, 2022
18. Rajyaguru, A. (2022) Interview with David Mannheim, "Personalisation Interview", Aug 04, 2022
19. Kelso, A. (2022) McDonald's Is Evolving Its Approach To Value To Be More Personalized. *Forbes*. https://www.forbes.com/sites/aliciakelso/2022/07/26/mcdonalds-is-evolving-its-approach-to-value-to-be-more-personalized/?sh=2f7519d7676d

20. Kelso, A. (2022) McDonald's Is Evolving Its Approach To Value To Be More Personalized. *Forbes.* https://www.forbes.com/sites/aliciakelso/2022/07/26/mcdonalds-is-evolving-its-approach-to-value-to-be-more-personalized/?sh=2f7519d7676d
21. Gartner (2016) https://www.instagram.com/p/BJlFMxMBjSR/

Part VI: The Deepfake Dragon
1. A quote by Friedrich Nietzsche (n.d.) https://www.goodreads.com/quotes/359917-he-who-fights-too-long-against-Dragons-becomes-a-Dragon

Chapter 25: Know Thy Enemy: The Deepfake Dragon
1. Denby, P (2022) Interview with David Mannheim, "Personalisation Interview", May 4, 2022
2. Nicastro, D. (2018b) The Challenges of Delivering Personalized Customer Experiences. *CMSWire.com.* https://www.cmswire.com/digital-experience/the-challenges-of-delivering-personalized-customer-experiences/
3. McLaughlin, R. (2022) Interview with David Mannheim, "Personalisation Interview", April 27, 2022

Chapter 26: McPersonalisation
1. Littman, J. (2019) *Deal of the Year: McDonald's acquires Dynamic Yield.* Available at: https://www.restaurantdive.com/news/deal-mcdonalds-acquires-dynamic-yield-restaurant-dive-awards/566467/.
2. Stern, M. (2019) *McDonald's AI Drive-Thrus May Be Too Smart For Their Own Good.* Available at: https://www.forbes.com/sites/retailwire/2019/11/11/mcdonalds-ai-drive-thrus-may-be-too-smart-for-their-own-good/?sh=31c118ab6910.
3. The impact of website personalization on customer lifetime value. (n.d.). https://www.markettailor.io/blog/impact-of-website-personalization-on-customer-lifetime-value
4. Poddar, B. (2022) Maximize Customer Lifetime Value with Personalization. *Annex Cloud.* https://www.annexcloud.com/blog/maximize-customer-lifetime-value-with-personalization/
5. Kelso, A. (2022) *McDonald's Is Evolving Its Approach To Value To Be More Personalized.* Available at: https://www.forbes.com/sites/aliciakelso/2022/07/26/mcdonalds-is-evolving-its-approach-to-value-to-be-more-personalized/?sh=379e8c9f676d.
6. Haddon, H. and Vranica, S. (2021) *McDonald's Considers Partial Sale of Digital Startup Dynamic Yield.* Available at: https://www.wsj.com/articles/mcdonalds-considers-partial-sale-of-digital-startup-dynamic-yield-11614390736.
7. Maze, J. (2020) McDonald's franchisees want more control over technology. Available at: https://www.restaurantbusinessonline.com/financing/mcdonalds-franchisees-want-more-control-over-technology.
8. Maze, J. (2020) *McDonald's franchisees want more control over technology.* Available at: https://www.restaurantbusinessonline.com/financing/mcdonalds-franchisees-want-more-control-over-technology.
9. Rogers, K. (2021) *McDonald's franchisee fight over tech fees could wind up in court.* Available at: https://www.cnbc.com/2021/05/20/mcdonalds-franchisee-fight-over-tech-fees-could-wind-up-in-court.html.
10. Kelso, A. (2022b) *McDonald's Is Evolving Its Approach To Value To Be More Personalized.* Available at: https://www.forbes.com/sites/aliciakelso/2022/07/26/mcdonalds-is-evolving-its-approach-to-value-to-be-more-personalized/?sh=379e8c9f676d.
11. Kaye, K. (2021) *McDonald's sells another tech startup, this time to Mastercard.* Available at: https://www.protocol.com/bulletins/mcdonalds-sold-tech-company-mastercard.

12. Rduch, M. (2022) Interview with David Mannheim, "Personalisation Interview", May 10, 2022
13. Adobe (2022) Digital Trend Report: Experience Index, *Adobe* [Preprint]. Available at: https://business.adobe.com/uk/resources/digital-trends-report.html.
14. Nicastro, D. (2018d) *The Challenges of Delivering Personalized Customer Experiences*. Available at: https://www.cmswire.com/digital-experience/the-challenges-of-delivering-personalized-customer-experiences/.

Chapter 27: Unexpecting the Expected
1. Roy H. Williams Quotes. BrainyQuote.com, BrainyMedia Inc, 2023. https://www.brainy quote.com/quotes/roy_h_williams_357726, accessed April 6, 2023.
2. Haddon, H. and Vranica, S. (2021b) *McDonald's Considers Partial Sale of Digital Startup Dynamic Yield*. Available at: https://www.wsj.com/articles/mcdonalds-considers-partial-sale-of-digital-startup-dynamic-yield-11614390736.
3. Mani, K. and Considine, R. (2020) *You don't just need personalization – you need the right personalization*. Available at: https://www.thinkwithgoogle.com/consumer-insights/consumer-trends/you-dont-just-need-personalization-you-need-the-right-personalization/.
4. Pybus, M. (2022) Interview with David Mannheim, "Personalisation Interview", March 23, 2022
5. Andrews, L. (2022) Interview with David Mannheim, "Personalisation Interview", Apr 20, 2022
6. Nicastro, D. (2018b) *Personalized Marketing: Where We Are in 2018*. Available at: https://www.cmswire.com/digital-experience/personalized-marketing-where-we-are-at-2018/.
7. Crunchbase (n.d.). https://www.crunchbase.com/organization/mutinyhq
8. Crunchbase (n.d.). https://www.crunchbase.com/organization/namogoo
9. Wiggers, K. (2021) Intellimize raises $30M to optimize websites with AI. *VentureBeat*. https://venturebeat.com/marketing/intellimize-raises-30m-to-optimize-websites-with-ai/
10. Crunchbase (n.d.). https://www.crunchbase.com/organization/nosto
11. Longden, S. (2022) Interview with David Mannheim, "Personalisation Interview", Apr 5, 2022

Chapter 28: Vanquishing The Deepfake Dragon
1. Taub, D. (2022) Interview with David Mannheim, "Personalisation Interview", April 28, 2022
2. Boidron, J. (2022) Interview with David Mannheim, "Personalisation Interview", April 15, 2022
3. Crunchbase (n.d.). https://www.crunchbase.com/organization/gousto
4. Barnham, R. (2022) Interview with David Mannheim, "Personalisation Interview", Jan 3, 2023
5. Boldt, T. (2017) Letter to my younger self: one day you'll have to take your hands off the wheel. *The Guardian*. https://www.theguardian.com/small-business-network/2017/sep/02/letter-to-my-younger-self-timo-bolt-gousto
6. Von Oech, R. (1990) *A whack on the side of the head: how you can be more creative*. New York: Warner Books.
7. Elsworth, S. (2022) Interview with David Mannheim, "Personalisation Interview", Apr 19, 2022
8. Jordan, R. (2022) Interview with David Mannheim, "Personalisation Interview", March 30, 2022
9. Hetu, R. (2014) New Research on Personalization Highlights the Challenges. Available at: https://blogs.gartner.com:443/robert-hetu/new-research-on-personalization-highlights-the-challenges/.

10. Peter Weinberg on LinkedIn: What is the worst idea in marketing? My vote would be for (no date). Available at: https://www.linkedin.com/posts/weinbergpeter_what-is-the-worst-idea-in-marketing-my-activity-6607673178544320512-PoeJ/.
11. Netflix Research and Development Expenses 2010–2022 | NFLX (no date). Available at: https://www.macrotrends.net/stocks/charts/NFLX/netflix/research-development-expenses.

Part VII: The Six Spells
1. Colin Powell Quotes (n.d.). BrainyQuote.com. Retrieved April 6, 2023, from BrainyQuote. com Web site: https://www.brainyquote.com/quotes/colin_powell_385927

Chapter 29: The Memory Spell
1. Carreri, L. (2022) Interview with David Mannheim, "Personalisation Interview", April 11, 2022
2. United States Bureau of Chemistry (1917) *Service and Regulatory Announcements*. U.S. Government Printing Office.
3. O'Flaherty, K. (2022) *Facebook Owner Meta Fined $275 Million By Irish Regulator*. Available at: https://www.forbes.com/sites/kateoflahertyuk/2022/11/29/facebook-owner-meta-fined-275-million-by-irish-regulator/?sh=1d87182f1a37.
4. Brontén, G. (2023) A brief history of modern sales methodologies for sales leaders. Available at: https://www.membrain.com/blog/a-brief-history-of-modern-sales-methodologies-for-sales-leaders.
5. Link, H. C. (1932) *The New Psychology of Selling and Advertising*. United States: Macmillan.
6. Carnegie, D. (2016) *How to Win Friends and Influence People*. India: General Press
7. Tracy, B. (2006) *The Psychology of Selling: How to Sell More, Easier, and Faster Than You Ever Thought Possible*. United States: Thomas Nelson Publishers.
8. Rawat, R. (2022) Interview with David Mannheim, "Personalisation Interview", March 28, 2022

Chapter 30: The Acknowledgement Spell
1. Hill, T. (2022) Interview with David Mannheim, "Personalisation Interview", May 4, 2022
2. McLaughlin, R. (2022) Interview with David Mannheim, "Personalisation Interview", April 27, 2022
3. MacIntyre, J. (2022) Interview with David Mannheim, "Personalisation Interview", May 4, 2022
4. Richter, N. (2021) Personalization in financial services – the power and prerequisites. *Dynamic Yield*. https://www.dynamicyield.com/article/personalization-in-financial-services/
5. Adobe (2022) Digital Trend Report: Experience Index, *Adobe* [Preprint]. Available at: https://business.adobe.com/uk/resources/digital-trends-report.html.
6. Houlind, R. & Riemersma, F. (2023) *Hello $FirstName*, Omnichannel Institute
7. Schulz, J. (2017) Using a person's name in conversation. *Michigan State University Extension*. Available at: https://www.canr.msu.edu/news/using_a_persons_name_in_conversation.
8. Carnegie, D. (2016) *How to Win Friends and Influence People*. India: General Press
9. Stewart, T. (2022) Interview with David Mannheim, "Personalisation Interview", March 23, 2022

Chapter 31: The Listening Spell
1. Sudjono, N. (2023) 5 Ways To Lose Your Co-Worker's Respect For You In 5 Minutes (Or Less). *Medium*. https://medium.com/mind-cafe/5-ways-to-lose-your-co-workers-respect-for-you-in-5-minutes-or-less-2a10a1bc1fef

2. Ryen, J. H., White, W., Buscher, G. and Wang, K. (2012) Improving searcher models using mouse cursor activity. In *Proceedings of the 35th international ACM SIGIR conference on Research and development in information retrieval* (SIGIR 2012). Association for Computing Machinery, New York, NY, USA, 195–204. https://doi.org/10.1145/2348283.2348313
3. Davies, D. (2020) *A Complete Guide to the Google RankBrain Algorithm*. Available at: https://www.searchenginejournal.com/google-algorithm-history/rankbrain.
4. Moz (2022) *Understanding Google Rank Brain And How It Impacts SEO*. Available at: https://moz.com/learn/seo/google-rankbrain.
5. Alderson, J. (2022) Interview with David Mannheim, "Personalisation Interview", Jan 18, 2023
6. De Valk, J. (2022) *Google's Medic update, and how to deal with it*. Available at: https://yoast.com/googles-medic-update/.
7. Nayak, P. (2019) *Understanding searches better than ever before*. Available at: https://blog.google/products/search/search-language-understanding-bert/.
8. Alderson, J. (2022) Interview with David Mannheim, "Personalisation Interview", Jan 18, 2023
9. Understanding Buyer Intent and the New Sales Funnel (no date). Available at: https://www.linkedin.com/business/sales/blog/strategy/understanding-buyer-intent-and-the-new-sales-funnel.
10. Carreri, L. (2022) Interview with David Mannheim, "Personalisation Interview", April 11, 2022
11. UXmatters (no date) *Remote UX Research: Advantages and Disadvantages, Part 2: UXmatters.* Available at: https://www.uxmatters.com/mt/archives/2020/10/remote-ux-research-advantages-and-disadvantages-part-2.php.
12. Belludi, N. (2017) Albert Mehrabian's 7-38-55 Rule of Personal Communication. *Right Attitudes.* Available at: https://www.rightattitudes.com/2008/10/04/7-38-55-rule-personal-communication/.

Chapter 32: The Observation Spell

1. Salesforce – Bombora (2021) Available at: https://bombora.com/case-studies/salesforce/.
2. Teradata (2020) *How Disney Plus Personalizes Your Viewing Experience*. Available at: https://www.forbes.com/sites/insights-teradata/2020/04/21/how-disney-plus-personalizes-your-viewing-experience/
3. Guo, Q. & Agichtein, E. (2010) Towards predicting web searcher gaze position from mouse movements. In *Proceedings of CHI*, pp. 3601–3606.
4. Guo, Q. & Agichtein, E. (2010) Towards predicting web searcher gaze position from mouse movements. In *Proceedings of CHI*, pp. 3601–3606.
5. Guo, Q., Jin, H., Lagun, D., Yuan, S. & Agichtein, E. (2013) Mining touch interaction data on mobile devices to predict web search result relevance. In *Proceedings of the 36th international ACM SIGIR conference on Research and development in information retrieval.* ACM, pp. 153–162
6. Guo, Q. & Agichtein, E. (2010) Ready to buy or just browsing?: detecting web searcher goals from interaction data. In *Proceedings of SIGIR*, pp.130–137.
7. Guo, Q. & Agichtein, E. (2010) Ready to buy or just browsing?: detecting web searcher goals from interaction data. In *Proceedings of SIGIR*, pp.130–137.
8. Fox, S., Karnawat, K., Mydland, M., Dumais, S. & White, T. (2005) Evaluating implicit measures to improve web search. *ACM Transactions on Information Systems*, 23(2).
9. Fox, S., Karnawat, K., Mydland, M., Dumais, S. & White, T. (2005) Evaluating implicit measures to improve web search. *ACM Transactions on Information Systems*, 23(2).

10. Sullivan, C. (2022) Interview with David Mannheim, "Personalisation Interview", May 10, 2022

11. Levy, T.W. (2023) *Route to Ready: How 7 agency leaders are evolving their businesses and helping customers do the same*. Available at: https://www.thinkwithgoogle.com/future-of-marketing/digital-transformation/digital-transformation-tips/.

12. Kiseleva, J., Williams, K., Awadallah, A. H., Crook, A. C., Zitouni, I. & Anastasakos, T. (2016) Predicting User Satisfaction with Intelligent Assistants. In *Proceedings of the 39th International ACM SIGIR conference on Research and Development in Information Retrieval* (SIGIR 2016). Association for Computing Machinery, New York, NY, USA, 45–54. https://doi.org/10.1145/2911451.2911521

13. Geher, G. (2021) *Why Actions Speak Louder Than Words In Psychology*. Available at: https://themindsjournal.com/actions-speak-louder-than-words-in-psychology/.

14. Paul, M.S. (2022) *Spotlight: Signet Jewelers' Craig Kistler on why your personalization strategy should be fueled by experimentation insights*. Available at: https://conversion.com/blog/spotlight-signet/.

15. Paul, M.S. (2022) *Spotlight: Signet Jewelers' Craig Kistler on why your personalization strategy should be fueled by experimentation insights*. Available at: https://conversion.com/blog/spotlight-signet/.

16. Fagan, P. (2022) Interview with David Mannheim, "Personalisation Interview", August 9, 2022

17. Esposito, A. (2013) *Farfetch Builds Trust And Drives Sales With Personalized Content*. Available at: https://www.retailtouchpoints.com/topics/customer-experience/farfetch-builds-trust-and-drives-sales-with-personalized-content.

18. Elsworth, S. (2022) Interview with David Mannheim, "Personalisation Interview", Apr 19, 2022

19. Lalmas, M. (2020) Personalising and diversifying the listening experience. In *Proceedings of the 2020 ACM SIGIR on International Conference on Theory of Information Retrieval*.

20. Fishbein, M. & Ajzen, I. (1977) *Belief, attitude, intention, and behavior: An introduction to theory and research*.

Chapter 33: The Appropriate Spell

1. Axon, T. (2022) Interview with David Mannheim, "Personalisation Interview", March 23, 2023

2. Understanding Buyer Intent and the New Sales Funnel (no date). Available at: https://www.linkedin.com/business/sales/blog/strategy/understanding-buyer-intent-and-the-new-sales-funnel.

3. Nahai, N. (2017) *Trust, Persuasion and Manipulation*. Available at: https://www.psychologytoday.com/intl/blog/webs-influence/201309/trust-persuasion-and-manipulation.

4. Company, E.-S. (2022) *Emma reports quarterly revenues of $212 million, the best in company history*. Available at: https://www.prnewswire.com/news-releases/emma-reports-quarterly-revenues-of-212-million-the-best-in-company-history-301678319.html.

5. Qadri, M.J. (2023) *Mattress company Emma investigated by CMA over "pressure-selling" tactics*. Available at: https://www.independent.co.uk/news/business/news/emma-sleep-cma-mattress-which-b2236455.html.

6. Kidd, A. (2022) *Emma Sleep becomes first company investigated as CMA looks at online selling practices*. Available at: https://interiorsmonthly.co.uk/5353-emma-sleep-becomes-first-company-investigated-as-cma-looks-at-online-selling-practices.

7. Monaghan, A. (2019) *Hotel booking sites forced to end misleading sales tactics.* Available at: https://www.theguardian.com/business/2019/feb/06/hotel-booking-sites-forced-to-end-misleading-sales-tactics

8. Gillett, S. (2019) *Expected Goals: The Metric Set to Revolutionise Football.* https://www.playmakerstats.com/news.php?id=271522

9. The Real Story of the Retail Personalization Gap | Bluecore. (2023) Bluecore. https://www.bluecore.com/blog/retail-personalization-gap/

Chapter 34: The Care Spell

1. Tracy, B. (2006) *The Psychology of Selling: How to Sell More, Easier, and Faster Than You Ever Thought Possible.* United States: Thomas Nelson Publishers.

2. Carnegie, D. (2016) *How to Win Friends and Influence People.* India: General Press

3. Corner, L. (2015) *How Etsy became a crafty little earner.* Available at: https://www.independent.co.uk/news/business/analysis-and-features/how-etsy-became-a-crafty-little-earner-the-online-market-has-been-floated-for-ps1-2bn-but-can-craft-and-capitalism-coexist-10199793.html.

4. Engert, B. (2022) *Handmade Millionaire: How Etsy's Founder Struggled to Make Commerce Human.* Available at: https://medium.com/actoncapital/handmade-millionaire-how-etsys-founder-struggled-to-make-commerce-human-fe2033803648.

5. Lepusic, A. (2022) *How was Etsy Developed?* Available at: https://wiredelta.com/how-was-etsy-developed/.

6. Engert, B. (2022) *Handmade Millionaire: How Etsy's Founder Struggled to Make Commerce Human.* Available at: https://medium.com/actoncapital/handmade-millionaire-how-etsys-founder-struggled-to-make-commerce-human-fe2033803648.

7. Etsy, Inc. (no date) *Statistics & Valuation Metrics – Stock Analysis.* Available at: https://stockanalysis.com/stocks/etsy/statistics/.

8. Fiske, S. T. and Malone, C. (2013) *The Human Brand: How We Relate to People, Products, and Companies.* Germany: Wiley.

9. Nolan, C. (dir.) (2014). *Interstellar.* Paramount Pictures.

10. 2022 Edelman Trust Barometer (no date). Available at: https://www.edelman.com/trust/2022-trust-barometer.

11. Walsh, H. (2022) *98% of Black Friday deals weren't worth buying last year.* Available at: https://www.which.co.uk/news/article/98-of-black-friday-deals-werent-worth-buying-last-year-aoIJw3j40Sou.

12. Tims, A. (2023) Poor customer service costs UK firms billions – so why can't they get it right? *The Guardian.* https://www.theguardian.com/money/2023/jan/30/poor-customer-service-costs-uk-firms-billions-so-why-cant-they-get-it-right

13. Birkett, A. (2022) Interview with David Mannheim, "Personalisation Interview", April 27, 2022

14. McDonald, G. (2022) Interview with David Mannheim, "Personalisation Interview", March 30, 2023

15. Yong, E. (2018) A Popular Algorithm Is No Better at Predicting Crimes Than Random People. *The Atlantic.* https://www.theatlantic.com/technology/archive/2018/01/equivant-compas-algorithm/550646/

16. Hern, A. (2022) Amazon facing £900m lawsuit for 'pushing customers to pay more.' *The Guardian.* https://www.theguardian.com/technology/2022/oct/20/amazon-facing-900m-lawsuit-claiming-users-manipulated-into-paying-higher-prices

17. Wu, Q., Wang, H., Hong, L. & Shi, Y. (2017) Returning is Believing: Optimizing Long-term User Engagement in Recommender Systems. In *Proceedings of the 2017 ACM on Conference*

on Information and Knowledge Management (CIKM 2017). Association for Computing Machinery, New York, NY, USA, 1927–1936. https://doi.org/10.1145/3132847.3133025

18. Flavius, S. (2021) *The unbanked: What it's like not to have a bank account.* Available at: https://www.money.co.uk/guides/unbanked-what-its-like-not-to-have-a-bank-account.

19. Statista (2022) *Yearly current bank account switching numbers in the United Kingdom (UK) 2012–2022.* Available at: https://www.statista.com/statistics/417417/number-of-switching-current-bank-accounts-annually-uk/.

20. Syzygy. (2019) *The Future of Digital Banking in the UK.* https://digitalwellbeing.org/wp-content/uploads/2019/10/Trust-Tech-The-Future-of-Digital-Banking-SYZYGY-Digital-Insight-Report-2019-UK-1.pdf

21. Syzygy. (2019) *The Future of Digital Banking in the UK.* https://digitalwellbeing.org/wp-content/uploads/2019/10/Trust-Tech-The-Future-of-Digital-Banking-SYZYGY-Digital-Insight-Report-2019-UK-1.pdf

22. Syzygy. (2019) *The Future of Digital Banking in the UK.* https://digitalwellbeing.org/wp-content/uploads/2019/10/Trust-Tech-The-Future-of-Digital-Banking-SYZYGY-Digital-Insight-Report-2019-UK-1.pdf

23. Fournier, S. (1998) Consumers and Their Brands: Developing Relationship Theory in Consumer Research, *Journal of Consumer Research,* 24(4) pp. 343–373, https://doi.org/10.1086/209515

24. Nightingale, K. (2022) Interview with David Mannheim, "Personalisation Interview", August 18, 2023

25. Kim, W. (2020) *The Intern Who Created Spotify Wrapped's Story Format Never Got Her Due.* Available at: https://www.refinery29.com/en-us/2020/12/10208481/jewel-ham-artist-spotify-wrapped-internship.

26. How ethical is Amazon.com Inc? | Ethical Consumer. (2023) *Ethical Consumer.* https://www.ethicalconsumer.org/company-profile/amazoncom-inc

27. Amazon's tax avoidance could have cost the UK economy around half a billion pounds in 2021 | Ethical Consumer. (2022) *Ethical Consumer.* https://www.ethicalconsumer.org/retailers/amazons-tax-avoidance-could-have-cost-uk-economy-around-half-billion-pounds-2021

28. Kinnell, L. (2022) Give Your Customers What Amazon Can't. *Brooks Bell.* https://www.brooksbell.com/resource/white-paper/give-your-customers-what-amazon-cant/

29. McLaughlin, R. (2022) Interview with David Mannheim, "Personalisation Interview", April 27, 2022

30. Shyne, S. (2022) Interview with David Mannheim, "Personalisation Interview", April 28, 2023

31. Glenday, J. (2020) Bloom and Wild leads 'thoughtfulness' opt-out movement. *The Drum.* https://www.thedrum.com/news/2020/03/02/bloom-and-wild-leads-thoughtfulness-opt-out-movement

Part VIII: The Great Unknown

1. Gartner Predicts 80% of Marketers Will Abandon Personalization Efforts. (2019) *Gartner.* https://www.gartner.com/en/newsroom/press-releases/2019-12-02-gartner-predicts-80-of-marketers-will-abandon-person

Chapter 35: Follow the Money: Advertising

1. Daniels, I. (2022) Interview with David Mannheim, "Personalisation Interview", April 26, 2023

2. Dynamic Yield (2023) *State of Personalisation Maturity Report,* Available at: https://www. dynamicyield.com/personalization-maturity
3. Weinberg, P. (2022b) *Forget personalisation, it's impossible and it doesn't work.* Available at: https://www.marketingweek.com/peter-weinberg-jon-lombardo-personalisation-imperson alisation/.
4. Peterson, T. (2023) *Netflix lets advertisers take their money back after missing viewership targets.* Available at: https://digiday.cmail19.com/t/t-l-fqlitk-jliytdtthk-x/.
5. Fletcher, B. (2022) *Netflix hints at future personalized ad experiences on new lower-priced plan.* Available at: https://www.fiercevideo.com/advertising/netflix-hints-future-personalized-ad-experiences-new-lower-priced-plan.
6. Netflix Net Income 2010-2022 | NFLX (no date). Available at: https://www.macrotrends. net/stocks/charts/NFLX/netflix/net-income.
7. Youyou W. Kosinski M. & Stillwell D. (2015) Computer-based personality judgments are more accurate than those made by humans. *Proceedings of the National Academy of Sciences of the United States of America,* 112(4), pp. 1036–1040. 10.1073/pnas.141868011225583507
8. Lin, Y. (n.d.) *Facebook Ad Revenue (2015–2022) [Feb 2023 Upd] | Oberlo.* oberlo.com. https://www.oberlo.com/statistics/facebook-ad-revenue
9. Nielsen. (2022) *When it Comes to Advertising Effectiveness, What is Key?* https://www. nielsen.com/insights/2017/when-it-comes-to-advertising-effectiveness-what-is-key/
10. John, L. K. (2017) Targeting Ads Without Creeping Out Your Customers. *Harvard Business Review.* https://hbr.org/2018/01/ads-that-dont-overstep

Chapter 36: Spin Cycle: Everything That Goes Around Comes Back Around

1. A quote by Johann Wolfgang von Goethe. (n.d.). https://www.goodreads.com/quotes/ 135983-the-more-one-knows-the-more-one-comprehends-the-more
2. Fenn, J. (2007) *Understanding Gartner's Hype Cycles*
3. Marsden, P. (2022) Interview with David Mannheim, "Personalisation Interview", Aug 4, 2023
4. A Brief History of the QR Code | Real Time Consultants (no date). Available at: https://www. realtimeconsultants.co.uk/a-brief-history-of-the-qr-code.
5. Statista (2021) *QR code usage increase since shelter-in-place in the U.S. and UK 2020.* Available at: https://www.statista.com/statistics/199328/qr-code-scanners-by-age/.
6. Labay, B. (2022) Interview with David Mannheim, "Personalisation Interview", April 27, 2022
7. The State of Personalization Maturity – 2021. Available at: https://www.dynamicyield.com/ personalization-maturity/.
8. Rogers, E. M. (2003) *Diffusion of Innovations, 5th Edition.* United Kingdom: Free Press.
9. Anderson, G. (2022) Interview with David Mannheim, "Personalisation Interview", October 18, 2022
10. Houlind, R. & Riemersma, F. (2023) *Hello $FirstName,* Omnichannel Institute
11. Gladwell, M. (2014) *The Tipping Point: How Little Things Can Make a Big Difference.* United Kingdom: Little, Brown Book Group Limited.
12. Moore, G. A. (2009) *Crossing the Chasm: Marketing and Selling Technology Project.* United States: HarperCollins.

Chapter 37: Acquisition-Cost-a-lot: Accelerating

1. Siluk, S. & Siluk, S. (2022) Craig Davis on: interruption marketing. *Collective Content.* https://collectivecontent.agency/2016/09/27/craig-davis-on-interruption-marketing/

2. Davis, B. (2023). Personalisation in 2023: What do the experts predict? *Econsultancy.* https://econsultancy.com/personalisation-2023-trends/

3. Hasen, J. (2018) *Despite Recognizing the Importance of Personalization, Marketers Are Still Missing the Mark.* Available at: https://www.adweek.com/brand-marketing/despite-recognizing-the-importance-of-personalization-marketers-are-still-missing-the-mark/.

4. Goldman, J. (2022) *Google Ads' cost per lead is going up and conversion rates are falling.* Available at: https://www.insiderintelligence.com/content/google-ads-cost-per-lead-going-up-conversion-rates-falling.

5. Gaubys, J. (no date) *Google Ad Revenue (2019–2024) [Feb 2023 Update] | Oberlo.* Available at: https://www.oberlo.co.uk/statistics/google-ad-revenue.

Chapter 38: Data-Mine-Your-Business: Disciplined

1. Keown, D. (2022) Interview with David Mannheim, "Personalisation Interview", Feb 23, 2022

2. How To Balance Personalization With Data Privacy. (n.d.). *Gartner.* https://www.gartner.com/smarterwithgartner/how-to-balance-personalization-with-data-privacy

3. Nameless Source (2022) Interview with David Mannheim, "Personalisation Interview", April 22, 2022

4. Leswing, K. (2022) Facebook says Apple iOS privacy change will result in $10 billion revenue hit this year. *CNBC.* https://www.cnbc.com/2022/02/02/facebook-says-apple-ios-privacy-change-will-cost-10-billion-this-year.html

5. Data Protection Commission announces conclusion of two inquiries into Meta Ireland | Data Protection Commission. (n.d.). *Data Protection Commission.* https://www.dataprotection.ie/en/news-media/data-protection-commission-announces-conclusion-two-inquiries-meta-ireland

6. Ikeda, S. (2023) Apple Fined €8 Million for App Store Ad Personalization in France, Consent Process Insufficient. *CPO Magazine.* https://www.cpomagazine.com/data-protection/apple-fined-e8-million-for-app-store-ad-personalization-in-france-consent-process-insufficient/

7. Gartner: By 2023, 65% world's personal data under privacy regulations. (2020) *Gartner.* https://www.gartner.com/en/newsroom/press-releases/2020-09-14-gartner-says-by-2023–65–of-the-world-s-population-w

8. Data Privacy Survey (2021b) *KPMG.* https://info.kpmg.us/news-perspectives/industry-insights-research/data-privacy-survey-orson-lucas.html

9. Silver, C. (2020) What Is Web 3.0? *Forbes.* https://www.forbes.com/sites/forbestechcouncil/2020/01/06/what-is-web-3-0/?sh=645c0a5958df

10. Bhattacharyya, S. (n.d.). *Understanding the User Experience in Web 3.0 | Analytics Steps.* https://www.analyticssteps.com/blogs/understanding-user-experience-web-30

11. Lotfi, J. (2021) Fueling Personalisation: Opportunities for Organisations to Advance (Part 1). *Kabbex.* https://kabbex.com/fueling-personalisation-opportunities-for-organisations-to-advance-part-1/

Chapter 39: Say Hi to AI: Awesome

1. Nameless Source (2022) Interview with David Mannheim, "Personalisation Interview", April 22, 2022

2. Evan Williams Quote: "Take a human desire, preferably one that has been around for a really long time Identify that desire and use modern tech. . ." (n.d.). https://quotefancy.com/quote/1491907/Evan-Williams-Take-a-human-desire-preferably-one-that-has-been-around-for-a-really-long

3. Gartner Predicts 80% of Marketers Will Abandon Personalization Efforts (2019). Available at: https://www.gartner.com/en/newsroom/press-releases/2019-12-02-gartner-predicts-80--of-marketers-will-abandon-person.
4. Dean, J. A. (2022) A Golden Decade of Deep Learning: Computing Systems & Applications. *American Academy of Arts & Sciences.* https://www.amacad.org/publication/golden-decade-deep-learning-computing-systems-applications
5. Galloway, S. (2022) *AI | No Mercy / No Malice. No Mercy / No Malice.* https://www.profgalloway.com/ai/
6. Stitch Fix (SFIX) – Market capitalization. (n.d.). https://companiesmarketcap.com/stitch-fix/marketcap/#:~:text=Market%20cap%3A%20%240.51%20Billion,cap%20according%20to%20our%20data
7. Woodbury, R. (2023) *AI in 2023: The Application Layer Has Arrived.* https://digitalnative.substack.com/p/ai-in-2023-the-application-layer
8. Mendoza, J. (2023). TMW #118 | A new frontier for personalization. *The Martech Weekly.* https://www.themartechweekly.com/a-new-frontier-for-personalization/
9. Mendoza, J. (2023). TMW #118 | A new frontier for personalization. *The Martech Weekly.* https://www.themartechweekly.com/a-new-frontier-for-personalization/
10. Labay, B. (2022) Interview with David Mannheim, "Personalisation Interview", April 27, 2022
11. The 2022 Gartner Marketing Technology Survey. (n.d.). Gartner. https://www.gartner.com/en/marketing/research/marketing-technology-survey-2022
12. Van Der Heijden, D. (2022) *What's Changing at Optimizely (Are They Going Public?).* A/B Testing Software. https://www.convert.com/blog/prioritization/whats-changing-at-optimizely-are-they-going-public/
13. Roof, K. & Baker, L. (2020) Goldman-Backed Startup Optimizely to Be Bought by Episerver. *Bloomberg.com.* https://www.bloomberg.comnews/articles/2020-09-03/goldman-backed-startup-optimizely-to-be-acquired-by-episerver
14. Optimizely (n.d.). Crunchbase.com. https://www.crunchbase.com/organization/optimizely
15. I worked at Optimizely from before its series A in 2012 until the end of 2016, so I have a unique perspective on this. | Hacker News. (n.d.). https://news.ycombinator.com/item?id=24366280
16. Salesforce completes acquisition of Tableau (n.d.). *Tableau.* https://www.tableau.com/en-gb/about/press-releases/2019/salesforce-completes-acquisition-tableau
17. Miller, R. (2020) *Google closes $2.6B Looker acquisition.* https://techcrunch.com/2020/02/13/google-closes-2-6b-looker-acquisition/
18. I worked at Optimizely from before its series A in 2012 until the end of 2016, so I have a unique perspective on this. | Hacker News. (n.d.). https://news.ycombinator.com/item?id=24366280

Chapter 40: 2024: The Year of Personalisation
1. Tideman, D. (2022) Interview with David Mannheim, "Personalisation Interview", September 21, 2022